OUTLAWS OF THE LEOPOLDS

ION IDRIESS

ETT IMPRINT
Exile Bay

This 5th edition published by ETT Imprint, Exile Bay 2023

This book is copyright. Apart from any fair dealing for the purposes of private study, research, criticism or review, as permitted under the Copyright Act, no part may be reproduced by any process without written permission. Inquiries should be addressed to the publishers:

ETT IMPRINT
PO Box R1906
Royal Exchange NSW 1225 Australia

First published by Angus & Robertson Publishers 1952
Reprinted 1952, 1955
Published by ETT Imprint in 2021

First electronic edition published by ETT Imprint in 2021

Copyright © Idriess Enterprises Pty Ltd, 2021

ISBN   978-1-922473-74-5   (pbk)
ISBN   978-1-922473-75-2   (ebk)

Cover: Members of the Ngaluma tribe on the Upper Sherlock station, thirty miles east of Roebourne, Western Australia, 1895.

Designed by Tom Thompson

CONTENTS

AUTHOR'S NOTE *5*

1. RICHARDSON'S LAST PATROL *8*
2. FEVERED MEMORIES *13*
3. THE TIGERS PLAY WITH THEIR MOUSE *16*
4. THROUGH THE FEVERED HOURS OF NIGHT *19*
5. THE CAPTURE OF ELLEMARA *23*
6. ELLEMARA ENTERTAINS THE TRACKERS *27*
7. THE WORKING OF BLACK THOUGHTS *33*
8. THE TREACHERY OF PIGEON *40*
9. OLD MOTHER JINNY *46*
10. DEEP INJURY SETS VENGEANCE BROODING *49*
11. THE SUB-INSPECTOR'S FURROWED BROW *53*
12. THE PIONEER OUTFIT TOILS ONWARD *56*
13. DEATH IN WINGINA GORGE *60*
14. SPOILS TO THE VICTORS *64*
15. PIGEON PLANS CLEVERLY, HANDICAPPED BY TIME *69*
16. THE PATROLS RIDE OUT *71*
17. ELLEMARA THE CUNNING *74*
18. RIFLE SHOTS IN THE DAWN *77*
19. THE FIGHT IN WINGINA GORGE *81*
20. RETREAT IN THE CAVES *85*
21. ELLEMARA SCHEMES, FIGHTS FOR LIFE *89*
22. INTRIGUE AND DEATH CAMP WITH CAPTAIN'S GANG *95*
23. CAPTAIN FLIES FROM GALLOPING PATROLS *99*
24. THE FIGHT IN GEIKIE GORGE *104*
25. LONG FRANKEY AND WAGGARRIE DIE FIGHTING *112*
26. TROUBLE AT OOBAGOOMA *116*
27. THE OOBAGOOMA WARRIORS STAND GAMELY *121*
28. THE CAVE OF THE BATS *125*
29. THE "RESURRECTION" OF PIGEON *129*
30. PIGEON MOVES TO ATTACK THE SUPPLY WAGON *134*

CONTENTS

31. ELLEMARA FEELS UNEASY *137*
32. CAUGHT LIKE RATS IN A TRAP *143*
33. THE ESCAPE *149*
34. THE ELUSIVE PIGEON *151*
35. THE OLD SHEARER-PROSPECTOR *155*
36. THE GREYBEARD'S LONE FIGHT *160*
37. THE CHAIN GRIPS COLD UPON THE NECKS OF CAPTAIN AND ELLEMARA *166*
38. VENDETTA DOGS PIGEON *169*
39. MARAWON SEEKS VENGEANCE *176*
40. THE STOCKMAN SLEEPS SOUNDLY *180*
41. THE FIGHT AT THE HOMESTEAD *186*
42. DEMON FIRES HIS LAST SHOT *190*
43. PIGEON'S "MOB" FIGHTS AGAIN *193*
44. THE PATROLS ARE CLOSING IN *196*
45. THEY FIND HIS CAVE OF THE BATS *201*
46. DEATH JOKES WITH JOE BLYTHE *205*
47. DEATH CLAIMS POOR WISEGO *210*
48. PIGEON'S LAST FIGHT *213*

EXPLANATORY NOTES *216*

AUTHOR'S NOTE

I WRITE this story of the well-known native Kimberley outlaws because, when riding "over the Range" with a police patrol some years ago, the country, the settlers, and the aboriginals interested me keenly. It followed naturally then that, as Time dreamed by, I absorbed, among other interesting local facts, the story of Jandamara, "white feller name" Pigeon.

To the best of my knowledge Jandamara, the one-time black-tracker, is the only Australian aboriginal who, though first through force of circumstances, actually planned and tried to carry out a feasible scheme to drive the white people from his country. But for the ceaseless work of the hard-riding police patrols he would have caused a lot of white tragedy in our Australian Kimberleys. This is the story of his own tragedy.

I have avoided using Aboriginal language in this book, and seldom use the far better known "pidgin English". It would not be understood by readers unfamiliar with the "language", and is also unnecessary. The aboriginal, though of course with an ever so much more limited vocabulary than our own, still expresses himself under his conditions and environment as lucidly as we do under our own; a fact which many of us do not realize. Hence, here I write and speak his thoughts and feelings just as we, and he, would do.

The collecting of the material used here took place over considerable distances, and long wandering. And from numerous folk, both white and black, and from official records, letters, and official reports written at the time. So, I acknowledge my indebtedness to the Police Department, Office of the Commissioner, Perth; to the Police Station, Derby, West Kimberley for reports and records and to reports made to Headquarters by Sub-Inspector Overend Drewry, Inspector Lawrence, Inspector C. H. Ord, Corporal Cadden, Corporal J. Pearson, Senior Constable A. H. Buckland, Senior Constable R. H. Pilmer, Constables J. A. McDermott, David Brice, H. R. Anderson, J .. Nicholson, H. Chisholm and Spong.

I am indebted also to the journal of reminiscences of the late Sergeant R. H. Pilmer, to the reports of M. S. Wharton, Resident Magistrate, Derby, W.A., to the reminiscences of "specials" who rode with the patrols, and to old-timers among the station folk and settlers, those tough old pioneers of the West Kimberley who alone knew to the full the anxiety during those near three years when "Pigeon's mob" were "out". Apart from thanks for the first-hand yarns about "Pigeon's mob" that these old die-hards gave me I gladly take this opportunity of sending a Cheerio to folk of both the West and East Kimberleys. For happy days indeed I have spent in that interesting country among the great-hearted folk there.

I must not forget Aboriginal friends, either. For during a particularly long patrol, from the Lennard, the Fitzroy, to right throughout the Leopolds we met, among the tribes and sub-tribes, every here and there, men and women who had been actively associated with Pigeon or his auxiliary bands of cattle-spearers during the "Time of the Big Patrols". And each of these by many a campfire obliged with "big feller talk" of those exciting days, though only when urged by our head tracker "old Larry". For Larry, as a lad with "Pigeon's mob", was wounded soon after the killing of stockman Tom Jasper at Collins's Oscar Range station. Tracker Larry himself by campfire and while riding side by side on patrol gave me many a first-hand story of the daily life of Pigeon, Captain, Ellemara, Lillimarra, Demon and numerous others of "the mob".

Cangamvara, Pigeon's favourite young lubra, known now as "old Rosie" and no longer alas the lively little daredevil who was the life of Pigeon's "lookout women", I heard of in Derby only twelve months ago. But she will not speak of those days of "the Big Patrols" now, except when out in the bush among her own people.

Although, due to lack of space caused mainly by production problems in these difficult times, I have been compelled to leave out a great deal of material collected about those days, still I believe I have faithfully portrayed the story of "Pigeon's mob" from every angle, the patrols, the settlers, the Aboriginals themselves, and the country. It is up to you to decide whether this picture of one small episode in the development of our great continent has been worth while, or not. One further little fact, vast in its practical possibilities for the development of Northern Australia, will surely interest the reader.

Joe Blythe, mentioned frequently in this book, is one of the Kimberley pioneers who have lived through the wild Kimberley days of "spear and gun" and almost impenetrable isolation to see the dawn of probable rapid development of their beloved Kimberleys - which will be almost certainly followed by practical development of the Northern Territory, indeed, of all Northern Australia.

For Blythe's three sons are very successfully active in Air Beef Proprietary Limited, a company of far sighted enthusiasts formed to overcome the paralysing isolation of the Kimberleys and prove that its wealth of stock lands can in the very near future actively take its part in the far more rapid development of all Northern Australia.

The scheme is far too big and interesting and fraught with possibilities to discuss fully in a short note. Suffice to say the germ of the idea was to kill prime cattle in the roadless bush, and air-freight it over the ranges to the port of Wyndham, then ship it to Australian and world markets.

Active operations began only in 1949, barely three years ago.

Results have been remarkably successful. To over one hundred per cent in figures - and practice.

But the really big thing is the proof that a chain of "cattie-abattoir-flying stations" such as Air Beef has established at Blythe's Glenroy station, if placed across the Kimberleys, then across the Northern Territory and North Queensland, would quickly hasten development of the great latent wealth in North Australian lands and quickly place that wealth on the market.

The wonderful work of the AI.M., the bush hospitals with the Flying Doctor Service, started rather similarly, until the A.I.M. had "girdled the North" with its chain of bush hospitals and flying doctors. In these "modern" days, the girdling of the North with commercial "abattoir-flying-stations" could develop ever so much more rapidly than the work of mercy because of swiftly moving events, hastened by the modem machines of today.

The "Flying Beef" scheme started from Blythe's Mount House but particularly Glenroy stations. Certainly it will mark a new and rapid era in the development of our great North.

The scheme is merely mentioned here as a point of interest to this story. For the pioneer father with horse and gun and his own strong will to carve a living out of the wilderness, and from the "wild and woolly" days of the "Pigeon Terror" to live to see his sons pioneers in the "flying beef" development of our great, isolated North, seems an interesting fact to me.

For photos illustrating this book, apart from my own, I am indebted to Inspector C. Treadgold of Perth, W.A., and to Mr E. M. Mitchell, now also of Perth.

And so, farewell to the "Days of the Big Patrols".

March, 1952.
ION IDRIESS

I

RICHARDSON'S LAST PATROL

STARS twinkling high up. A star too, far down on earth. Though but the twinkling of a campfire I believe that to the All Seeing it was more brilliant by far than the stars to us. That He compassionately noted the age-long drama around it, the clash of man against man, of tribe and nation, the fierce little differences by which we Children of the Earth have built up troubles throughout thousands of years.

Mounted Constable Richardson intended to keep that camp-fire bright throughout all the long night. He must. For he was alone, and in charge of a hornets' nest. "Hornets!" he smiled wryly; "more like a mob of tigers-worse, because these tigers possess brains! And cunning. And the patience to bide their time."

The "tigers" squatting around their campfire, seemingly oblivious of the policeman, appeared in high good humour.

For Richardson, having reached this sanctuary after two strenuous months in the wilderness, had given his "tigers" a good "feed", made the station boys kill a bullock for them. And the tigers responded, cracking, gnawing the juicy beef bones with teeth as serviceable as those of any tiger, eyes as fierce but anon veiled with cunning, chuckling a guttural joke now and then with a sneer at the sulky "tame" natives squatting morosely by their own campfire a short distance away.

It was a scene familiar in the year 1894 in the Australian Kimberleys, as indeed it is today "way over the Range".

The dull iron roof of Lillamaloora homestead reflected starlight. But it was a station homestead no longer. It had been. Had been a cattle station belonging to James Munro, about this time the Honourable James Munro, Agent-General for distant Victoria. But the station had been abandoned, as had Mundooma, due to marketing difficulties and because of the depredations of the cattle-spearers. As Oobagooma station away west on the coast was again being threatened. This one-time homestead was now an isolated police outpost, near where the Lennard River flows through the castellated Napier Range at the Wingina Gorge.

This homestead on what but recently had been a million-acre cattle run was built ambitiously. A four-roomed cottage of rough stone with a passageway separating the rooms, a veranda all around. Then a large stone storeroom and a large, detached kitchen. All enclosed by a ten-foot-high wire-netting fence as protection against the natives. This palatial homestead now made an ideal Kimberley police outpost.

Yes, starlight on the iron roof, but walls of buildings in black shadow. The little front veranda, bright in reflected firelight, was littered in orderly confusion with pack and riding-saddles, hobbles and bells and pack bags, all the gear of a hard riding police patrol. The sick constable, sitting with his back to the wall, was smoking while thankfully resting, rifle to hand, revolver at belt, his ears listening for suspicious murmur from the station blacks away to the right, his eyes never leaving his "tigers" squatting out there in the firelight.

Primitive men yes, but cunningly resourceful. Twelve of the fifteen blessed also with perfect physique, obvious in their naked strength. Six footers among them, though all were broad-chested, heavily shoulder-muscled, sinewed for extreme endurance. Gleam of eyes in the firelight, eyes quickly shadowed under deep-set, protruding brows, teeth flashing to some guttural joke, a chesty growl in reply. Black-bearded some, others clean-shaven - the razor a jagged flake from quartz or flint. Sinewy hands with the grip of an ape. Savage, heavy-browed faces that yet could break into rollicking laughter. Yes, a tough bunch of primitives these, though heroes to numerous tribesmen and women. All notorious horse-and cattle-spearers, each had killed natives, three had speared a white man. Laid by the heels at last, bound now for the "white man" town of Derby and-prison.

With just behind them walls of blackness that were their mountain fastnesses and-freedom. Run to earth-at last, to feel the cold brake of the chain; marched down to the edge of the plains, and now squatting in the firelight before an abandoned frontier homestead.

A grunt, a guttural sentence that carried distinctly in the quietness. A roar as the Stone Age prisoners threw back their heads and laughed with abandon. The stockboys squatted sullenly away by their own campfire; the young lubras barely restrained their giggles.

For the cattle-spearers were "poking borak" at the "tame" natives so gutless as to work for the white man. And the contemptuous bitterness in their sneers brought fury to the hearts of the stockboys, sparkle to the eyes and eager smiles to the faces of the young lubras to whom these wild men were heroes.

The young constable, listening for every sound, every low inflection of voice, sharply ordered the fire to be livened up. He must hear, and guess at everything. See everything, even in the outer darkness of night. No slinky lubra must be given chance to snake her way close to throw a horseshoe nail or clip of wire towards those unresponsive backs around the firelight.

"How devilishly cunning they are," thought Richardson, "with a nail, a bit of wire, a few strands of horsehair. Some can unlock a handcuff with a nail, while given a piece of wire a padlock is but play to them. And yet they are supposed to be, and they are, Stone Age men!"

He pulled himself together. He must not dream, must not waver in attention, must keep alert all through the night. He reached out for the fever mixture. Thank heaven he was feeling a lot better since they had arrived at the station. He drank deeply of the blessed fever mixture that was kept in every homestead and police outpost. Mixed up in a kerosene tin, generally brought slowly to the simmer, then poured into rum bottles, it was a recipe according to the experience of some old-timer. Bitter experience of malaria had made those old-timers as canny as their bitter mixtures.

Iron and quinine! Sometimes other stuff. Ugh! The young constable shuddered as he swallowed the bitterness on tongue and in throat. But how good the mixture was-how unbelievably better he felt after these last forty-eight hours.

Corking the bottle, he put it carefully beside him. How unlucky he was to have developed the fever the very day after old Daisy had slipped over into the Isdell Gorge and broken her neck and the patrol's fever mixture bottle. During the long chase for these prisoners he would have been done again and again had it not been for Pigeon and Captain. What grand boys they were! How often had Pigeon held him to his horse, his strong black arm around him as the horse half slid down some precipitous ravine, floundered across some mountain stream. And at nights, when he was "bad", he had awakened to find Captain watching beside him while Pigeon slept, rifle in hand, with "one eye" on the prisoners.

What a patrol it had been! But apart from the fever what an unbelievably successful patrol! To catch these particular fifteen, fifteen of the most notorious native killers and trouble makers in all the West Kimberley! What a triumph when he should get them all safely to Derby. These beauties had been making trouble these last three years and more, had sworn they were out to spear every white man they could, had boasted to station natives that no white man born was man enough to shoot them, let alone catch them. And yet he on his own, while handicapped by fever, had had the unbelievable luck to run each of the fifteen to earth! With Pigeon and Captain to help him, of course; without those two grand boys he could have accomplished. nothing, would not even be here now. What wonderful trackers they were! And staunch as the staunchest white man.

He filled his pipe; he must not lose caution for an instant.

Long hours would pass before daylight; neither drowsiness nor fever must dull his watchfulness-he must fight this urge to lie back and sleep. . . .

With a start he gazed out at his "tigers" squatting there around the prisoners' fire, unconsciously frowning at Lillimarra's clean-shaven, intelligent face, chocolate bronze in the firelight. For Lillimarra was the most dangerous of natives, an ex-police boy who had taken to the bush. Yes, Police Tracker Lillimarra, alias Jackey, had deserted from his patrol and taken to the bush some two years ago. He had been a ringleader amongst the trouble makers ever since.

Lillimarra glanced up, read the thoughts of the constable watching from the veranda and clouding his eyes muttered something with a grin. A chuckle acknowledged delight at the police man's difficulties.

The prisoners were connected by a long, light chain looped around each man's neck. The loop not so large that he could squirm his head through, nor yet so tight as to chafe. Each loop padlocked. Length of chain between man and man was about five feet, allowing plenty of room when on the march. How many hundreds of miles had he marched them thus! Limbs and hands were perfectly free, as of necessity they must be when trailing across this wildest of bush country. And now, at night, one end of the chain was padlocked around a tree butt. A tree was safer than a log for, unless a monster log, these fifteen powerful "tigers" would silently pick it up and vanish away should policeman and trackers fall asleep.

This had happened to other patrols. Then, when out of hearing, the "tigers" would lay down the log, place a link of the chain upon a hard rock and, with a stone, pound the link until they flattened and smashed it, in a surprisingly short time. Then, with incredible swiftness, they would jog-trot back into cover of the hills. Then crouch down among the rocks, each man pounding the chain midway between himself and his mate. Man after man would thus be freed, then they would separate and vanish away. If there was not time for this they would travel on into the hills until meeting fellow tribesmen who would soon pick the padlocks with a precious nail.

That was what Richardson was afraid of now, would be all through this long night. That some sympathetic station native, especially some young girl, would crawl close enough unobserved to throw them a nail, or wire.

He peered towards each man's neck in turn, trying to distinguish the padlock through the light haze of smoke. From up here on this low veranda he could look over and a little down upon each of those squatting black bodies. All seemed in order. But Byerbell and Tyemering and Fouringer were now lying down, dozing. That was when they did their cunning work best, when some were sitting up, gossiping and joking, others curled up in pretended sleep. Coiled up with head pillowed on arms, but agile fingers working a nail in the padlock. Ah well, he'd make as sure as possible, once every hour throughout the night.

He stood up, gazing down at his "tigers". Then, making sure his revolver was loose in its holster, he stepped from the veranda and strolled towards them. Standing a little distance away, sharply he ordered the fire to be livened up. He waited until the firelight threw every man into sharp relief. Then ordered the three sleepers to sit up. Yawningly they obeyed, shamming sleep to perfection to the silent amusement of their mates. Richardson ordered each man in turn to jerk his portion of the chain, jerk against the padlock.

Grinning, they obeyed.

Apparently chain and padlocks were quite in order.

He stood there awhile, gazing at each man in turn. The fifteen, each in his own way, gazed quietly, challengingly, amusedly, sullenly up at him. Fitting countenances for the rugged Leopolds that bore these Stone Age sons, but the lone white man well knew that not one of these primitives was a fool. He frowned at the questioning innocence of Lillimarra and Wongamarra and Bundermen, the blank masks of Tumanurumberry and Mererimer, the scowl of Muckerawarra and Talburner, the cheeky insolence of Teebuck and Byerbell, the sham fear of Luter and Tyemering, the disinterest of shaggy Laweraway and the others. Each was laughing deep inside. All were silently laughing, knowing perfectly well the worry in the mind of the policeman, knowing he was weak from fever, knowing how he must fight through this night to hold them.

Ah well, they could laugh. But they would not escape.

He strolled back to. the veranda and sat down again, facing them. He had not gone too near those beauties of his-not on your life. Had he gone within reach then suddenly a black body would have hurtled out, claws would have snatched his ankles and jerked him in amongst them, while a horror of hands would have wrestled for his throat and he would have been choked to death under a chuckling again at his expense.

2

FEVERED MEMORIES

YES, he mused, that last patrol had been a very near thing. It had happened a few months previously when riding down the Barker. For days the Range natives had threateningly dogged the patrol, yelling to the prisoners to break away and fight, yelling encouragement that they would kill the policeman and roast the trackers before they could ride clear of the Barker.

After which, there followed several days of bushland quietness; not a native within sight or hearing, not even a hunting or smoke signal.

Then came that early dawn. Tracker Pigeon had gone for the horses, Captain down to the river for water. Richardson was bending over the fire, preparing breakfast for all. Some uneasy intuition had made him glance up. The sleepy prisoners, crouched around their smouldering fire, were doing nothing in particular. But there was a "something" about their hunched-up bodies, almost as if they were sheltering something; he could not distinctly see two of them - he noticed a furtive glance.

He had walked straight to them, bent down to examine the chain. Instantly he was dragged down amongst them as clawing hands snatched at his throat and his hair, bestial breaths were panting in his face as his arms and legs were twisted and wrenched by twenty hands and legs kicking, tearing and gouging. Thank God the writhing mass was entangled within its own self. He was losing consciousness to animal snarls, bestial grunts as bumping heads, struggling bodies and limbs were twisted in the tautened chain, choking victim and prisoners alike. Then Pigeon was amongst them with a waddy striking right and left; he laid out four before they upended him too, then their claws were at his throat, biting into his body, wrenching apart his limbs. Richardson's last feelings were the sickening upheavals, his last thoughts, "What a great fight good old Pigeon is putting up!

It was Captain who saved both policemen and fellow tracker, running up from the creek and bashing into the prisoners with a waddy. Even so Captain had his cheek laid open by a bite, an eye half gouged from its socket.

"Great boys, Pigeon and Captain," thought Richardson warmly.

He would not swap them for any half-dozen trackers in all the Kimberleys.

Memory of that recent struggle stirred Richardson uneasily.

He'd better have another look at the chain, though he'd just glanced at it. Vividly now he remembered "waking up" after that fight. Captain slowly pouring ice-cold water over his body from the billy-can. Pigeon, covered in blood, kneeling, still panting beside him, rifle threatening the snarling prisoners. Richardson had painfully sat up, feeling as if every bone in his body was broken, his gashed throat felt torn to shreds as he glared towards the prisoners. Two were sprawled there, still out to it. The others crouched like snarling animals, bloodstained, their eyes rolling, teeth grinding in impotent rage.

But what alarmed him now was that the huddled group were yards away from the tree-the chain must have snapped.

It had - and it had not!

They examined the chain to find that a link had been almost pounded through. A link well behind the last man's neck, midway in the chain between the last man and the end that nightly was padlocked around tree or log.

They must have been working on that link night after night, day after day when a halt was called for tucker, or through some delay caused by the pack animals, or in slow tracking over difficult country. Pounding that one link at every opportunity if only for a moment, the nine squatting around the pounder, sheltering him, laughing and gossiping by day to deaden the muffled blows, groaning, wheezing, snoring by night, whenever certain the trackers slept. The blows would be greatly softened of course, the chain link buried down in a hole scooped in the earth between the pounder's legs, a wad of shredded bark over the link to further deaden the sound. Thus the soft iron link would be gradually Battened, pounded, Battened thinner, thinner, until ... They must have been on the job for three hundred miles; they could only work of course at odd moments, and in silent hours now and then when the trackers, dead beat, slept heavily after some long and arduous chase.

By day, the rear man always carried the rear length of chain.

Natural for him to hold the battered link in his hand. And to still further disguise the bright iron it was rubbed with clay, then a film of red dust, so that the link, brightened by the hammering appeared exactly like the brick-red of iron exposed to air and weather.

That morning, the link had at last been all but severed. It had only needed a few more patient, well directed blows, a sudden wrench and it would have parted.

How lucky it was that Pigeon had awakened a little earlier that morning, decided to go for the horses straight away.

They had planned to have the link broken by that morning.

Then, when Pigeon went for the horses and Captain for water they had planned to make some suspicious movement. The policeman would come straight to them of course. They would up-end and swiftly throttle him. Take his revolver and rifle and the tomahawk, any other weapons handy also, then hurry away with the chain.

The black-trackers, on returning to camp and finding the policeman dead, would probably saddle up and ride for their lives for the nearest police outpost, knowing the prisoners' hillmen friends would soon be stalking them.

But, even should the trackers have been game enough to pursue, then the prisoners though still chained, would possess arms, they would have turned and ambushed the trackers.

Yes, thought Constable Richardson, he had been fortunate indeed on that last patrol. The prisoners had not escaped, he had not been throttled. Though so very, very nearly. Yes, he owed his life to the devotion and bravery of his trackers Pigeon and Captain.

The two best trackers in all the Kimberleys.

Aboriginal tracker with West Australian policemen, 1890s.

3

THE "TIGERS" PLAY WITH THEIR "MOUSE"

CONSTABLE RICHARDSON, forcing himself to keep alert by keeping his mind active, stood up, staring into the night.

"A file!" At the thought his blood ran cold - He knew what Stone Age men could do with even the rusted, broken fragment of a file.

There was a shed called the "blacksmith's shop" at the back of the homestead. There would be a file or two there.

Should the station natives slip the prisoners a file ...

He stared out over the prisoners towards the station natives' fire, listening. From out there came softly a native lullaby, tinkling of kylies beating to some age-old chant. Just a Dream Time song heard at every native campfire on peaceful nights, before they coil up for sleep.

But the young policeman knew that that chant was directed at the apparently unresponsive prisoners; it was not a chant at all, it was the aboriginal method of telling them the news as plainly as if the singers were squatting beside them talking. Telling them the whereabouts of the nearest white men, of happenings on the nearest stations long miles to the east and south-west. Telling of local native happenings, of the whereabouts or believed where-abouts of friend or enemy. Telling of ...

His mind now obsessed by a file, he stepped down from the veranda to again examine the chain, grimly conscious that his "tigers" knew more of local conditions and happenings than he did, now that he was alone and Pigeon and Captain were away.

Stone Age men! but cunning as a bagful of monkeys. Warily he approached his "tigers", hand tingling against his revolver butt, mindful of a happening to another patrol in almost similar circumstances. A station native, crawling over the grass, from an unbelievable distance away back in the dark had softly thrown an ironstone pebble fair in among the prisoners. To the stone was tied a native fishing line. Quietly, deftly, one prisoner had pulled on the string while the others kept joking and gossiping. On the end of the string was tied a spear.

When the patrol officer had come from his fire to have a last look at his prisoners the spear had been hurled straight at his chest.

Slowly the night wore on.

Constable Richardson was tensely anxious to get his prisoners safely into Derby. By far the worst was now over. He was almost out from the hills, down by the Lennard plains which spread south to the valley of the

Fitzroy along which at widely scattered intervals the few pioneer stations led to Derby west on the coast, only a few days' travel now. Should these notorious fifteen escape at this last moment they would scatter amongst the hillmen in boastful disdain of the police and the "white man's law". They would cause endless trouble. It might be years before they could be rounded up again.

They simply must *not* escape.

Carefully again he inspected the prisoners. Some just stared solemnly at the fire. Others gazed up innocently, questioningly. Sarcastic grins behind the rugged expressions of the others.

Enjoying themselves immensely, they had him on tenterhooks. He strolled back to the veranda. Chill night was upon all the bush. The lullaby had ceased. Presently, the night was asleep. Or seemed to be. The "tigers" were sprawling out too, coiling up half around the fire, a comfortable distance apart, the chain slack on the ground between each man. Richardson stared at each slack, he could barely see portions of the chain just here and there. Slowly filling his pipe again he wondered how Pigeon and Captain were getting on.

The two trackers were getting along quite well. Miles away behind the homestead, striding noiselessly through the night, practically invisible, heading straight for the pindan soak. Black bloodhounds on the scent, seeking Ellemara!

"What wonderful luck!" thought Richardson, receiving news of Ellemara here when the patrol was practically over, when they thought the elusive devil was laughing a hundred, two hundred miles back in his mountain hideouts to their rear.

But right here, after they had unpacked and made the prisoners secure, a station boy had whispered to Pigeon that Ellemara at this very moment was camped away down the plain at the pindan soak. Only twenty miles away!

Thus Pigeon had received the news, bitter words of hatred furtively whispered by Danmarra the stockboy. Telling that Ellemara the Cunning had actually stalked the patrol for three hundred miles. (Tracker Pigeon had grinned at that news!) The patrol seeking Ellemara everywhere, Ellemara calmly stalking the patrol but a few miles behind, making a great joke of it to the admiring tribesmen he had met, boasting too that he would stalk the patrol right to the "white man" town of Derby and attempt a rescue, right to the very jail itself before he would turn back to his beloved hills. Already, Ellemara's tribal song maker was busy composing a corroboree in which the star act was to be Ellemara stalking the police patrol that was stalking him.

And the information was quite correct. The day before the patrol had arrived at the homestead Ellemara had made a swift detour and come down to the plain ahead of the horsemen. He was afraid of no plainsman, let alone any station native. He who had already speared a dozen men.

Yes, far and wide they knew and feared him, he who was known as Ellemara the Cunning, Ellemara the Killer.

Aboriginal warrior, Carnavon, Western Australia, 1906.

4

THROUGH THE FEVERED HOURS OF NIGHT

THUS, Ellemara had followed on to conquer. But, like many a far greater man, he had made his mistake. With appraising eye he had noted the attractive young lubra Wondaria, so well becoming her name, Laughing Waters. She had smiled fleetingly with gleam of teeth as she walked past, daring in her bright black eyes.

Ellemara the warrior had simply taken her, caring nothing that she was the new wife, jealously prized because so young and active, of the native stockboy Danmarra. Danmarra the stock boy had dared not protest, dared not challenge Ellemara the Killer.

Ellemara after a few hours' rest had moved on, down to the pin dan soak twenty miles away. Simply he told the station natives just what he intended to do. Camp at the soak with his new bride for a few days until the patrol should arrive at Lillamaloora then move away down the track towards Derby. The policeman and his two trackers would think all was safe, all trouble would be over once they arrived at the station, with the last easy stage the road to Derby. When they moved off along the Derby track he would follow. They would become careless in guarding the prisoners. He would rescue them during the night, probably on the very last night before they should reach Derby.

Calmly then he had purloined the only tomahawk at the station. Efficiently used, a sharp tomahawk can sever a link in a chain at one blow. He had also taken horseshoe nails, some fine wire, and horsehair, and three keys that he thought might unlock padlocks.

As he was leaving, he had turned around with a grin and threateningly shaken his war spears, spears that had killed men. In that harsh, sneering voice of his he told them he knew the white policeman could never find him, while the trackers would never dream he was so near, they thought him far back in the Leopolds.

"But," he snarled, "should the wallaby' be harried from its hideout I'll return here and cut some dingo's kidney fat out and eat it before his shivering eyes!" And he had grinned mockingly at the outraged young husband Danmarra.

The powerful killer had then turned and strode complacently away, followed by the obedient little Wondaria carrying her dilly-bag and her new lord's spare spears. Most of the young lubras envied her, whispering that now Wondaria had a real man for a husband, a warrior who would kill any man who dared attempt to take her from him.

Which added to the raging fires within the husband, "burning him all up inside". Trembling in a misery of fear and hatred he had watched them go until the bush swallowed them up, saying not a word.

But, when the patrol came riding in he had whispered to Pigeon the black-tracker, whispered in bitter words black as the night. That first night, after the patrol had arrived, when opportunity occurred and nobody to notice. Just a few words, hoarse with hatred.

Such words have set in motion the slow wheels that have brought about the downfall of empires in the history of our past. Such words can carry slow poison whether uttered by great king or humble tribesman.

Having spoken, Danmarra the stockboy had stolen back to the native camp. He knew these two dreaded trackers Pigeon and Captain. He knew Ellemara. Ellemara would put up a fight they would shoot him!

It is seldom that a young aboriginal can win a young girl - invariably the older men claim them by tribal right. Danmarra had been so envied in his cherished possession, so lucky - and now so unlucky.

In quiet excitement tracker Pigeon had retailed this unexpected information to the delighted Richardson. If only he could crown this wonderfully successful patrol by the capture of Ellemara, this most notorious leader of all native killers and cattle-spearers, Trouble-maker and jail-breaker too. Wanted on a dozen charges from Derby south to Broome, even right down through the nor'-west and farther south to Cossack, six hundred miles as the crow would By from here. An astounding record for an aboriginal "bad man".

And now he was camped down at the pindan soak!

So Pigeon and Captain slipped away from the rear of the homestead by night, bound for the pindan soak. Which was why the sick policeman was all alone, alternately shivering, alternately sweating from malaria, sitting up all night watching his "tigers", apparently asleep now, huddled around the fire. A still, peaceful night; frantic trumpeting of a brolga away out on the plain, startled by some prowling dingo.

Constable Richardson knocked out his pipe bowl on the heel of his boot, thoughtfully commenced to cut a fill of plug tobacco, rubbing it fine in the palm of his hand. With a wary eye on the sleeping prisoners, fervently he was wishing Pigeon and Captain God speed. Those fellows out there by the fire had been difficult enough to catch, heaven knows. But Ellemara!

Ellemara was that really dangerous native, a wild man who had learned so much that he defied most tribal laws, sneered at the Councils of the Old Men. A wild man who was familiar with the white man's ways, yet sneeringly refused to be tamed, who moreover stored up what he learned to add cunning to his native bushcraft when again and again he returned to his own wild hills.

Thoughtfully filling his pipe, Richardson pondered over Ellemara's record so far as he knew it. Convicted as a particularly ruthless native killer, for attempts at killing white men and incitement to attack lonely stations, a notorious horse-, cattle- and sheep-spearer, at least twice a jail-breaker. Powerfully built and ferociously active on the least provocation and, worse than that, resourceful and cunning to an unprecedented degree. Richardson frowned and abruptly stood up to step from the veranda he must have another close look at the prisoners. They appeared to be snoring and sleeping soundly. He stirred the fire, stared questioningly down at each slumbering form as the firelight blazed up, carefully examined the chain locked around the tree butt, then walked back to the veranda, sat down and took another swig of the fever mixture. Yet again he blessed that mixture and the old-timer whose cunning experience had mixed it. His mind drifted again to Ellemara; it was helping keep him awake, helping pass this slow, anxious night away.

What was this other thing so often mentioned when Ellemara was discussed among the police, the settlers, and around the campfires? Ah! some uncanny power of his of drastically influencing the native mind. Not only of his own particular tribesmen, but something much more extraordinary, practically unheard of-influencing the minds of even hostile tribesmen! What was this strange influence?

In every tribe there were a few men who could and did sway their fellows. But Ellemara seemingly could deeply influence any tribesmen, anywhere. Had done so from the Oscar Range to the Lennard, from the Barrier to the King Leopolds, Far more. Had influenced nor-west natives far to the south when as an escapee he was working his way up amongst them back to the King Leopolds. Almost any other native doing so would inevitably have been tracked down and killed.

But Ellemara seemingly could travel forbidden country with impunity. And influence not only otherwise hostile tribesmen but the scattered, cunning, aggressive bands of cattle-spearers,

What was this remarkable influence Ellemara held over all the savage tribesmen of this wild country?

Since his last escape Ellemara had stirred up serious trouble over a wide area, had proved as elusive as a will-o-the-wisp, He had boasted far and wide that he never would be caught by the white man's ways.

A night owl hooted hoarsely down by the river. Richardson listened a while, then his mind drifted again to Ellemara.

If only he could catch him! And so near to Derby too! The cunning devil, trailing them all that distance! While day by day they had been straining every nerve to run him to earth. And now the cheek of him! - to leave his hills; to camp right here; to steal another man's lubra from the very police outpost where the patrol would camp; to walk calmly away and let all know he intended to camp away down by the pindan soak!

How were Pigeon and Captain getting on?

Aboriginal tracker, two policemen with their camels, and a chained Aboriginal prisoner, near Kalgoorlie 1895.

5

THE CAPTURE OF ELLEMARA

PIGEON and Captain were getting along very well on a job they loved-a man hunt.

They were equipped as efficiently as their quarry even though they carried revolvers, he his trusty spears, and were girdled in their naked pelts. For this would be a test of skill and cunning, of invisibility and intuition, of patience and silent movement. Neither clothes nor boots should betray them by sound whether walking across open country, or creeping through dense pindan. The only civilized articles each wore were belt and revolver. And Pigeon had a pair of handcuffs tucked around his belt.

Noiselessly, their lithe black bodies practically invisible in the night, they strode effortlessly on, straight for their distant objective. Came an approaching "thud!" "thud!" "thud!" They halted but there was neither stone nor throwing stick within reach. The wallaby coming hopping across their path, stopped abruptly before them, sitting back with upraised eyes, inquiringly gazing at the two motionless shadows of the night. Ears twitching, nostrils quivering it inhaled the scent of naked aboriginal and swayed aside in a flying bound, the "thud!" "thud!" "thud!" of its going pronouncing urgent haste.

Pigeon and Captain grinned from "ear to ear", eyes shining with laughter. They walked on, hands still itching with the wish that they could have snatched up a stick. For though the wallaby was useless to them the inborn lust was to kill.

Fine types of men, these two human bloodhounds, Captain was the taller, but both were of powerful physique, deep-chested, long legs built for endurance. Fierce-eyed both but with keen faces, expressive of intelligence, Pigeon's especially, Aggressively confident of themselves and game as they make them, as they had proved on dangerous occasions. Effortlessly they walked on over flat country amongst shadow timber, crossed a creek dark as pitch within its banks of thick scrub. A twenty-mile walk was nothing to them. Neither would they notice the twenty miles back. What made these two yet more efficient and dangerous also was that to a considerable degree they could defy that age-old dread of the aboriginal, fear of the spirits of the night. To an extent - though uneasily they shrugged at such beliefs, particularly Pigeon. Close contact for some years with the police and the whites had partly rid them of such fears, particularly caused them to scorn the tribal laws of the Old Men that are so irksome to aboriginal youth. As trackers too they were beings apart, held in awe by both wild tribes and "tame abos", Such men can become dangerous to white and black alike. Silently they strode on.

Came a silken "swish" as two golden eyes glided by. The owl could see immeasurably better than the wallaby but the trackers' eyes were sufficiently attuned to the night light to note that clenched in the talons of the owl was a squirming marsupial mouse. A low grunt from each acknowledged that the owl had made a kill.

A darkness before them darker than the night was the dense edge of the pindan scrub-small trees densely growing together, interlaced by creeper and vine. Once a hunted animal or native reaches the sheltering pindan he is safe.

But not from trackers such as these - should the hunted man be unaware of their coming.

Pigeon and Captain turned away around the pindan though no one could hear them, no one could see. But an expectant one, granted position and atmospheric conditions, could know of their coming though he neither hear nor see.

Smell! An aboriginal's sense of smell is very keen. Granted a carrying breeze, a suspicious wild man will smell natives an unbelievable distance away.

Pigeon's and Captain's bodies were washed clean of the rancid fats that overpoweringly add to smell but they took no risks. They walked on around the pindan edge until the cool breath of the night bathed their own faces. Then squatted down in shadow to await the hour before dawn, that hour in which the aboriginal sleeps as if there were no awakening.

Chilly the earth, but they sat with the silent stoicism of the primitive prepared to wait. Invisible in the black shadow in which they sat, they could see clearly across the starlit, open country before them to the dense black line of the pindan, their eyes but a few feet above ground. Though it was but dull nightlight not even a shadow could enter or leave the pindan opposite but they must see. A rustle nearby was but a snake viciously slithering over dry grass after having narrowly missed its prey. Time dreamed on with chill wisps of breeze. And presently came the distant, melancholy howl of a dingo slinking down from the hills.

Wordlessly they arose, stepped forward towards the pindan.

Its edge was an almost solid wall of small trees. Pigeon vanished and Captain was gone too. They knew exactly the direction of the soak, the little native well hidden in the heart of the pindan.

Darkness within that tangled scrub meant little, the sense of touch everything. Pigeon's body slowly, surely squirmed forward, Captain following directly behind. Feel of leaf and vine and branch on naked body, hands and arms noiselessly warding them off as the stealthy twisting bodies seemed to slide forward. Halt! as an upraised foot touched twig or vine that might snap or rustle; the foot slid over, gently groped for solid ground, the body slid forward, then half twisted to allow a bunch of leaves to slide noiselessly back.

Those wonderful feet, it almost seemed they might "see".

Poking down upon that dense undergrowth, at faintest touch instantly sending warning to the body of anything below that might cause noise. Never making a mistake as to when the foot could be pressed safely down.

Dense timber, dense undergrowth, black as the pit. Yet any small animal of the pindan would make more noise in its coming than these invisible men.

It was in the first cold grey of dawn that they peered from the pindan out into a tiny clearing. A little circular, open space like a natural air vent in the heart of the pindan. From the grey sky above the first dawnlight came stealing down. There seemed to be nothing in that clearing except the earth and grass. But the trackers' eyes saw the rim of the little well, the ashes of a small, almost dead fire, gnawed wallaby bones, the black patch that was the long, coiled up body of Ellemara the Killer, the little lubra Wondaria cuddled like a possum beside him, his two hunting dogs huddled against the sleepers for warmth.

Those dogs did not sleep with one eye open. Nor did any instinct warn them of danger glaring from the fringe of the pindan.

Calculating eyes sought Ellemara's spears, his wrists. He slept, his head pillowed upon one arm, the spears between his arms, claw-like hands out-thrust.

Noiselessly Pigeon slipped the handcuffs from his belt, stepped out into the clearing, Captain beside him with drawn revolver. In deathly silence . . . just the creeping forward, gleam of triumphant eyes, grim twist to each ruthless mouth.

Pigeon knelt over Ellemara and his hands reached in stealthy caress over Ellemara's gnarled claws. A swift "click!" "click!" and the sleeper was handcuffed. He did not even awake; he slumbered on in the drugged sleep of one who is certain of safety.

Pigeon rose upright; they laughed noiselessly across the blissful captive. For hilarious minutes they gloated in the humour of their triumph.

Then a sneer wiped the grin from Pigeon's face as he kicked the captive in the ribs.

Ellemara sat up with a protesting grunt, amazement frozen on his rugged face as he blinked uncomprehendingly at his leering captors. Understanding painfully dawned as he gaped at Captain's revolver. He gazed down at his wrists with his primitive features an amazing study as his dogs slunk away. Unwillingly then he looked up, grinned from ear to ear to hide the hate in his eyes.

"You got me!" he growled simply.

The trackers chuckled, tension eased by that grin of Ellemara - his black-bearded, savage face could grin with surprising good humour. From the edge of the pindan the eyes of the snarling dogs were blazing green. Little Wondaria had not even awakened.

Craftily Ellemara noted Pigeon's expression as he gazed down upon her, her firm young limbs huddled up in happy abandonment of sleep. Then Pigeon stretched out his leg and placed his foot over her mouth and nose, slowly pressing, grinning as her chest began to heave for breath in sleep. She awoke, lay as if frozen while Pigeon grinned down to the terror in her eyes. Then she sprang away from the suffocating foot and stood trembling in every limb, her eyes almost starting from her head. She glanced down at the handcuffs upon Ellemara's wrists and in an instant had wheeled around into the pindan, followed by laughter from the trackers in which Ellemara hilariously joined.

Captain quickly kindled the fire while Pigeon picked up Ellemara's spears, balancing each at the throw, examining each with the love the aboriginal gives to good weapons. And these were good. Three wicked, beautifully made war spears, four hunting spears, a fish spear, a war wommera and a hunting wommera.

Captain then took his turn; in light conversation they admired each weapon. Then one by one Pigeon put his foot on each and deliberately broke them into pieces, throwing the pieces on the Iire, Ellemara gazed silently on. As the last broken haft was thrown on to the fire he murmured simply, "A pity. Good spears too!"

The trackers said nothing. But each thought regretfully, not of the act of wanton destruction, but of the weapons.

Yes, they had been good spears. Both Pigeon and Captain would have been proud to possess those weapons had they been out in the bush.

6

ELLEMARA ENTERTAINS THE TRACKERS

MORNING grew warm before they strolled out from the pindan, their good humour enhanced by Ellemara who was proving a most engaging captive. There was not a tribesman between the Fitzroy and the Leopolds he did not seem to know, not one about whom he could not tell some interesting story or joke. Knew all the good camping-places too, the lagoons where the lubras swam for the lily roots, all the favourite hunting-grounds. In no time he had Pigeon's and Captain's mouths watering with descriptions of wild turkeys, teal, duck and magpie, geese in whistling, honking thousands, roast duck, roast eggs of duck and geese, brolga and emu and turkey, roast fish, eel, turkey ....

"Pity we burned those spears," he murmured regretfully. "You boys could have knocked a 'roo as we walked along."

The trackers said nothing, now feeling regret that they had destroyed those spears. Yes, it would have been good this sunny morning to have enjoyed a little hunting. Pigeon licked reminiscent lips - he could almost smell a hind leg of a 'roo roasting on the coals. So could Captain. Both had been eating "white man tucker" a long time now-the longing for native food cooked in the native manner was almost overpowering.

"Ah but," chuckled Ellemara, "fat roast bullock is the feast for real men." Noisily he sucked reminiscent lips.

"Especially after a long chase when at last he drops to the spears-the good spears." Noisily he licked thick lips.

"Ah!" he laughed, "I can smell it roasting now! The blue smoke coiling up from the cadjuput fire. The boys hungrily squatting around, some mending broken spears, all yarning happily over the chase, the good fat beef sizzling on the coals. Ah! that fat!" and his mouth was a-gurgle as he gulped.

Pigeon frowned, striding out a little faster. He was now really hungry, hungry for fresh raw fat and beef thrown on the coals to sizzle.

The three walked on, Pigeon in the lead, Ellemara handcuffed striding effortlessly behind him, Captain coming behind Ellemara. Across flat country now lightly timbered, a line of blue-grey brolgas trumpeting and dancing by a waterhole, sunlight bathing their quaintly leaping bodies, their long, outspread wings.

Quietly the three walked on. Ellemara, good humouredly reconciled to his fate, had given not the slightest trouble since seeing the cuffs upon his wrists, Pigeon and Captain, busy with half-awakened longings, gave no thought to their docile captive, unaware of the craft in his eyes as his chuckling, murmurous voice seemed "talking" into the back of Pigeon's head, his ears "hearing" what Captain was "thinking" from the occasional grunt, the "sense" of him walking just behind.

Imperceptibly Pigeon's pace was slackening as he gazed across the grassy plain, seeing a 'roo with his family emerging from the cadjuput to browse away across there, a wild dog slinking down the bank of that creek to the left. After all, there was plenty of time, he had got his man now. Constable Richardson would be anxiously waiting. "Let him wait!" frowned Pigeon. He and Captain had done a good job, Ellemara would be soon on the chain. He was a *munjon*, but sensible to talk to in that he also understood the ways of the whites. After all, what great times the cattle-spearers must enjoy raiding the cattle, living to the law of the spear, defiant of whites and blacks alike. Ah well, he had proved himself a better man than Ellemara for he had laid Ellemara by the heels. He would have shot Ellemara with pleasure had he resisted. Now, he was pleased he had not shot Ellemara, a good man Ellemara, a spearman and a warrior even though a cattle-spearer. What odds - the whites had plenty of cattle!

Yes, beef freshly slaughtered and cooked in the hot earth oven *was* good.

Pigeon, slackening pace in the lead, his nostrils breathing scented timber from the free bush air, was thinking less and less of the anxiously awaiting constable at Lillamaloora police outpost, now but fifteen miles away.

Ellemara, contemplatively silent, jerked his head towards a small ridge crowned by a clump of prettily foliaged bushes, the ridge cap littered with small, rounded stones.

"I had thought my little Wondaria would have been walking that way soon," he chuckled suggestively, "but she can rest easy now that I must go to Derby jail."

Pigeon and Captain chuckled understandingly for that daintily crowned ridge was the delight and fear of all women of the local tribe. It was amongst those bushes and wild flowers and pretty rounded stones that the spirit babies played, eagerly awaiting the near enough approach of a young wife for their turn to be born again.

"The women sham to keep well away from the Spirit Ridge," laughed Ellemara, "but not *all* of them. It's funny to watch a young girl, when she doesn't *know* you're watching. She dawdles closer and closer to the ridge, meaning of course to skirt around it at a safe distance. She edges closer and closer, fearfully glancing up at the bushes where the spirit children play; you know perfectly well she's going to get caught."

They laughed uproariously.

"Your Wondaria of the Laughing Waters would soon have been visiting those bushes," chuckled Captain.

"Yes," mused Ellemara, "but not now. 'Tis a pity. She would have brought home a warrior son - now having a *man* for a father, not a dingo like Danmarra."

"But after all, she may be visiting the Spirit Stones sooner than you think," growled Pigeon. "You may get off light."

"No chance," replied Ellemara sombrely. "They'll make sure of me *this* time!"

And they knew that a stiff jail sentence, if not worse, was certainly awaiting Ellemara the Killer.

They walked a little way in silence. Then Ellemara laughed. "Ah well, it's all in the game," he chuckled. "But the police couldn't do it - it took the two best trackers in all the Kimberleys to catch me. By the way," he added curiously, "who was it put me away'?"

"Danmarra the stockboy," growled Pigeon.

"Ah!" The expression was almost a sigh, soft, bitterly vindicative.

They knew it meant that the wings of death were hovering for Danmarra the stockboy.

They dawdled along now, Ellemara the most entertaining of companions, filling every hundred yards with anecdote or joke and incident, interspersed with ancestral tribal lore such as stirs the heart of every aboriginal.

For across this area, as in every tribal country, every waterhole, lagoon and creek, every tree-shaded hollow, every rise, every hill, every clump of trees or rocks, distinctive outcrop or peak or tree was a book recording the tribal lore and history, even apart from the sacred and initiation grounds. Every natural feature held its story of tribal fight, disaster or victory, flood or drought or plenty, raid or corroboree, love story or chase, vendetta or hero worship, or recalled the stories and heroes of the Dream Time when the tribe was "made". Ellemara thrilled Pigeon and Captain with these stories, both remembering that their own beloved tribal country was rich in similar stories of their own and their fathers' and fathers' fathers' day.

It was midday; they had only come twelve miles. They could have been at the homestead by now. Pigeon frowned at thought of the anxious constable waiting there. Let him wait!

"It's getting hot," suggested Ellemara. "How about a spell?"

He jerked his chin towards a bloodwood ridge. "We enjoyed a great feast of beef there two seasons back. Come and I'll show you the bones." And they turned towards the shade of the ridge.

The bones were there, bones of seven beasts. Ellemara grinned as he pointed to several broken spearheads.

"That one belonged to Lillimarra," he laughed. "You've got him on the chain now back at the white man's police homestead. A good man Lillimarra, you couldn't ask for a better mate. By the way, he was a police tracker at one time just like you two boys, but I think he enjoys spearing the white man's cattle a lot more than working for him." And Ellemara laughed suggestively as he pointed to another broken spear haft. "And that one belonged to Fouringer, and that one to Teebuck; you've got them on the chain too." Ellemara sighed. "There were twenty of us on that bright day, all good men. We drove a little mob here and speared seven, one by one, herding them along the side of this ridge. The others broke away - in a hurry, two with spear hafts sticking out of them to carry the news away to the white men. We enjoyed a great feast," he chuckled, "and all within one little hour's ride of the white men's house, where the boys are on the chain now! For then Lillamaloora was a cattle station. We often enjoyed those Lillamaloora cattle," chuckled Ellemara, "many men and lubras and piccaninnies and our dogs too enjoyed many and many a feast of them. But the white man became tired of growing good fat beef for us, so he rode away. And now Lillamaloora is your police house. That afternoon when we speared these seven beasts we sent up a smoke to signal the men and women and children so they too could come and enjoy the feast. We ate all through the afternoon. And all through the night. We'd just wake up and eat, and fall to sleep, and wake up and eat again. The children's bellies swelled so much they could hardly move. But next morning stockmen came riding along - black stockmen!" Ellemara laughed derisively. "Sitting their horses out of spear throw they shouted us away. We jumped up and fitted spears to wommeras and leaped out to meet them, shouting to them to come on and fight, calling them dingo-livered curs for working for the white man. But they wheeled their horses away. Of course they weren't game to come and fight."

He looked full at the two listening men. "It's a pity," he said soberly, "that the river men have fallen for the white man. What do the river men and the plainsmen get out of it? Nothing! Nothing but work! They work like women to help the white men take their country. The white man takes the big waterholes with the sweet grassy flats, that's the first thing. He chops down our sacred trees to build his house on our own corroboree grounds. He takes the water and grass for his cattle and horses and sheep. He drives away the kangaroos, the wallabies that come to the water to drink, to grow fat on the sweet grass on the river flats - *our* river flats. He shoots the ducks and geese and waterfowl and turkeys, scaring them from their breeding grounds where once they laid so many eggs the tribes could gorge in plenty, *without* work. He shoots the kangaroos and emus and wallabies and anything that eats grass - yet he won't let us kill *his* beasts that eat *our* beasts' grass! He kills or drives away the food that has fed our people since the Dream Time, just because he wants all the water and grass for his cattle and horses and sheep. Then, when he grows strong, he drives us away, he only wants to keep around his station enough young men to help him with his cattle. Do I not speak true?"

He paused, intently reading the faces of the trackers staring out over the tribal flats. Their frowning expressions gave answer.

"The plainsmen have no guts," he hissed, "giving their fathers' lands away to the white man. The white man will never take the hillmen's country; our good spears and our hills will beat their guns and horses too! For the big hills shelter us, there are plenty of us too and we have the guts to fight."

There came a brooding silence. Then Ellemara laughed good humouredly. "'Tis well for the plainsmen, and the cattle, and the whites too, that the cunning police use trackers."

"Why?" snarled Pigeon.

"Because without trackers to help them chase us away and track us down the white men would soon lose *all* their cattle - and their lives too!" he answered suavely.

Pigeon and Captain frowned, without reply.

"Why!" exclaimed Ellemara brightly, "see how it is now!

Muckerawarra, Tilbomer, Teebuck, Talburner, Tumanurumberry, Luter, Mererimer, Byerbell, Lillimarra, Wongamarra, Bundermen, Laweraway, Fouringer, Putter, Tyemering, all on the chain, the best fighters, best gang of cattle-spearers in all the Kimberleys. The whites have never been able to catch them despite all the help from the dingo-gutted river boys - bah! And now you've got me, Ellemara their leader." He held up his manacled wrists, laughing quizzically at the cuffs. "The best among all the Kimberley hillmen are caught now," he chuckled, "but it took the two best trackers in the Kimberleys to catch us," he added proudly.

Pigeon and Captain frowned at the handcuffs. Ellemara's expressive face was all one good-humoured grin, his kindly eyes telling the trackers he was proud of their prowess. Thoughtfully then he gripped his knees, gazing dreamily up at the sky. Musingly he raised his knees, then lowered his chin upon them and burst into hilarious laughter. They stared silently. Presently, he laughed directly at them, his eyes twinkling merrily, overcome by laughter.

"Wouldn't it be funny," he rumbled, "wouldn't the whites be surprised if you two, Pigeon and Captain, the best trackers in all the Kimberleys, joined us, joined Ellemara's gang, the best cattle-spearers in all the Kimberleys. Why, they'd never catch us!" He burst into rollicking laughter.

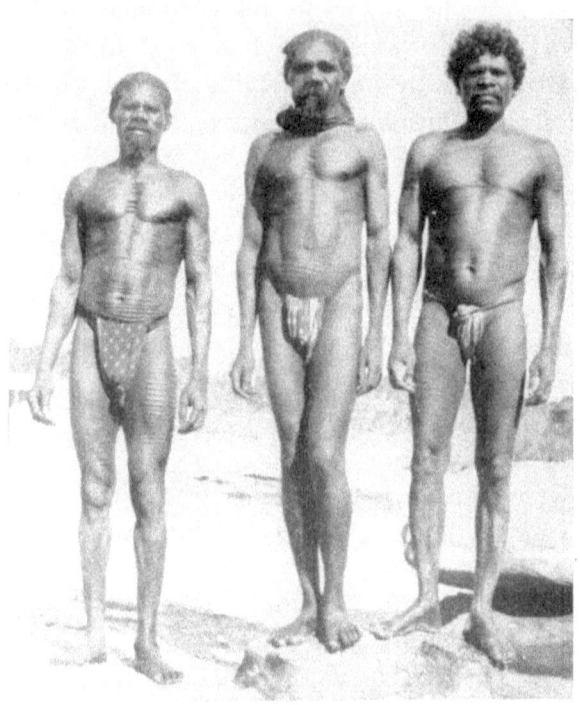

Fine types of West Kimberley coastal Aboriginals.

7

THE WORKING OF BLACK THOUGHTS

PRESENTLY, Ellemara sobered. "Of course, it was only a joke;" he grinned, "but what a joke. Every man in the hills, along the rivers, on the plains; every woman would joy in it, if it came true. Why, every play maker in every tribe would hasten to put it into corroboree."

He gazed out over the grassland, chuckling, his face plainly showing he was seeing in eager reality just what his words meant. The great deed. And then - proud indeed are the warriors whose deeds are sung in "corroboree".

A few head of stray cattle had wandered from a clump of timber to browse quietly on the Mitchell and bundle-bundle grass.

"A fine fat beast," Ellemara murmured with an uplift of the chin, "he'd sizzle well on the cooking stones. What a pity you didn't bring your rifle!"

And Pigeon, his trigger finger itching, knew that if he had had his rifle then there soon would have been juicy beef sizzling on the coals. Captain licked hungry lips.

"That was a beauty," nodded Ellemara toward the clean picked bones of a beast. "Lillimarra speared it. Good spearman Lillimarra; give him a shovel-bladed spear and no beast alive could get away from him."

Reminiscently he began to tell stories of Lillimarra, the run-away police tracker, and of all his good friends languishing back there on the chain at Lillamaloora police outpost. And of others, too, for there were lots more "good men" defying police and whites. "Langooradale for instance," said Ellemara; "he was a police tracker too, and Long Frankey, and Big Paddy. There are plenty good men free in the hills doing what they like. There's Waggarrie, he's already speared a white man. There's Rowally whom white men call Demon, and Goiro and Murramin, Boll and Morinda and Woinmarra, Pyabarra and Wingelly." And Ellemara drawled on with names of native killers and heroes who were "sung" in seasonal corroboree and nightly around the campfires throughout the Leopolds. No, much farther. From the hideouts of Oobagooma on the coast all up along the Fitzroy and far beyond into the East Kimberley. Warriors who had even twenty and more notches in their spear hafts - each a fat beast; who could display six and more notches on their wommeras - each notch the life of a man.

Of Waggarrie he enthused, Waggarrie who all alone had speared the white stockman on the Margaret River but six moons ago - and was still laughing at the police. Waggarrie who would continue to live and laugh.

Of course, admitted Ellemara with an ingratiating grin, it was not Pigeon's and Captain's patrol that had been trying unsuccessfully to lay Waggarrie by the heels. It was the thankless job of the new Fitzroy patrol, for the killing had been done in their district. If Pigeon and Captain had been the trackers, well then it would have been a different matter; Waggarrie would long since have been a hunted man flying from hill and gorge with tongue hanging out like a perishing dingo. But of course, all trackers were not experts like Pigeon and Captain. "Good job too," laughed Ellemara, "else we'd all be on the chain." And he sighed.

In the quiet, noonday warmth, through the dreamy hum of the insects, you could feel what a shame it was, that his best desperado mates, such jolly good fellows, were now on the chain. Absent-mindedly he gazed at an eagle circling in the sky.

Then he laughed, and began to tell them of Long Frankey.

He knew they would be very interested in Frankey. Of course they knew that he too was a police tracker who had taken to the bush and become a great hero. For long he had been the terror of Geikie Gorge. Hard to say how many cattle had fallen to Long Frankey's rifle and spears. Ellemara knew that nine men had fallen, four of them warriors, all silly enough to stand in his way simply because he took some attractive young lubra, or something that was theirs. Unfortunately, Franky's ammunition was finished, except for a few cartridges that he kept just in case some particularly crafty warrior should corner him. But Frankey was an excellent spearman too, everything he wanted was his for the taking. He could travel much farther afield than any other man in the Geikie, could even defy many of the tribal laws. Yes, a great warrior, a great hero was Long Frankey. And he had once been a police tracker! That had taught him a lot! That was why he could live such a wonderful life now, all the women admiring him, feared by every man.

Yes, the tensely listening expressions of Captain and Pigeon showed they certainly were interested in the exploits of Long Frankey, the Geikie Gorge hero, Frankey the one-time police tracker.

In slumbrous tones Ellemara went on to tell them of Demon.

His name, of course, was Rowally but white men called him Demon, Ellemara did not know why, except that white men both hated and dreaded him. Demon was a hero too, a hero of the Margaret and Louisa. He had killed his men, and plenty of cattle, and sheep too when prowling in the sheep country. Very shaggy was Demon, with eyes like a dingo when it crouches back and snarls. When Demon killed his man he snarled like a dingo, snarled with deep growls deep down in his throat while he struck and struck; just the low snarl, no other sound, no other expression from him at all. Yes, Demon was. a feared man. The whites had tried to shoot him but he was far too cunning for them. Many tribesmen would like to kill him. But of the few who had dared lift their hand against him it was Demon who had done the killing.

Yes, Demon led many a foray that filled the bellies of the Margaret and Louisa River tribes with good roast beef. Demon was not afraid of the white men. Demon was sung by many a campfire at night.

He told them, too, stories of Langooradale, who also could use a rifle and knew the white man's ways and defied him. Langooradale had also killed his men, as well as cattle. He had threatened to fire the huts of white settlers, and roast their horses for meat.

The afternoon grew still and drowsy as Ellemara's voice seemed to quieten and just drawl on, merging with the whisperings of the dozing bush. Stories of prowess in war, in hunting, in vendetta and tribal intrigue, in love affairs; of foray against white and black alike. Until, as cool sunset came, Pigeon and Captain had a totally different idea of their "prisoners on the chain". No longer were they native killers, horse-and cattle-spearers to be hunted until at last they would be laid by the heels for the time being. Now each man was human, each a warrior and hunter and lover, each were jolly good fellows. Pity such fine men were now on the chain, bound for prison. But of course, it was the luck of the game.

Shadows were merging into the first breath of night when Pigeon arose. And his brow was sombre.

"We'd better be going," he said quietly.

Silently they moved off. Ellemara seemed to stumble, came a soft tinkle of handcuffs. Pigeon frowned.

Steadily, quietly they moved through the evening. It was when they were only about two miles from the homestead that Ellemara seemed to listen towards the rear. They stopped. The trackers understood.

"Bring her up," said Pigeon soberly.

Disappointedly Ellemara shook his head. "She would not come," he murmured. "She is a girl of the hills; she is afraid of trackers. She knows you'll put me on the chain," he sighed.

They knew well Wondaria would have been following them, keeping just out of sight with Ellemara's two hunting dogs.

"She will hurry on around us now," said Pigeon quietly. "She will warn Danmarra."

"What can I do about it!" replied Ellemara simply. "Soon, I will be on the chain." And again the handcuffs tinkled.

Pigeon stood frowning.

"Let us talk a moment," suggested Ellemara softly. "We will be there soon. Hark! the bark of a dog!"

They squatted down. Ellemara leaned slightly towards Pigeon and his eyes now were agleam in the night.

"You noticed Wondaria," he whispered. "She is good. But you have not seen Cangamvara!"

"Cangamvara?"

"Yes, young daughter of Cadwarry. He comes from Barellam Springs with Cangamvara; she is to marry Marawon at the rise of the moon. With Mother they are camped down at the far end of the waterhole. They are shy people, not liking the plainsmen overmuch. Marawon has come here to marry her, as arranged by their fathers long ago."

"And Cangamvara?"

"Wild as the hills. Quick as the night hawk - and as silent! Young and strong, would die for her man. The wife of a warrior. Wondaria is good as you have seen. But Cangamvara!"

And Ellemara held up expressive hands with gleam of eyes steel-bright as the handcuffs.

"Why did you not take her?" demanded Pigeon.

"I meant to," answered Ellemara simply, "but now I have more than enough troubles on my hands." And with a grin he held up the handcuffs:

"Well then, what means she to me?" demanded Pigeon. "Take her!"

"But we are trackers," frowned Pigeon. "I ride with the police!"

"Are you two not going to join us?" hissed Ellemara.

Black as thunder was Pigeon's brow. "If I joined *you*," he snarled, "then the police would hunt me!"

"Shoot them!" hissed Ellemara.

They stared at him - then at one another.

"Where would I get guns to shoot the police!" sneered Pigeon. "You have your rifle!"

"That belongs to the police," snarled Pigeon. "Do you think my policeman would allow me to take the police rifle to shoot the police!"

"Shoot him!" suggested Ellemara; "then he can't shoot you!

Then Captain can take his rifle and you both have rifles. And the little guns too! And all the bullets! And everything else in the packbags of the patrol! And everything in the police house!"

For fateful moments they sat staring at Ellemara, his such an insistent, such an expressive face, a face from which all humour had gone. Staring doubtfully at one another, drawn back to Ellemara's compelling eyes, each was aware that his thoughts had been turning on this thing for hours past.

A lost breeze came sighing among the trees, carrying the faint odour of decaying leaves. The night seemed listening.

"Join us!" hissed Ellemara.

"And when all my bullets are gone?" answered Pigeon, "and the police close around us! What then? Fight them with spears?" and he sneered again.

"No," snarled Ellemara, "fight them with *more* bullets."

"From where do *they* come?" leered Pigeon.

"From *other* white men! Kill white men! Raid homesteads! Shoot the men driving the teams! We will take all the guns we want, and more!"

A pregnant silence.

"Join us," urged Ellemara insistently, "all the best men in every tribe in the hills will be with you. And," he added cunningly, "you know the white man's ways so well that you will know how to beat their every move. Above all, you know the police and their ways! And you can laugh at the laws of the Old Men of the tribes too! You will be able to come and go as you please among any tribe and none dare say you nay. You who can use the white man's guns so well! The white men are so few - we so many. All tribesmen who will not be with us will be terrified of us dare not lift a hand against us. What you both want you can take, from tribesmen and white man alike. Why work for the white police when all the hills are yours!"

Came the distinct yap of dogs. They knew that Wondaria had reached the native camp barely two miles ahead.

She had. And the first man to see her was the anxiously waiting Danmarra, her stockboy husband.

"Ellemara?" he hissed.

"Coming," she answered sullenly, "they have him."

"Then . . . they did not kill him?"

"No," she replied spitefully.

Danmarra looked for his spears, then stepped out into the night. Disappointed, yet in fierce-eyed delight. For though Ellemara lived he would now be taken away for a long time to come. If he ever came back, ah!

then he Danmarra would have to act. But now he had Wondaria back again. Meanwhile he had best hover on the outskirts until he saw Ellemara the Killer safely on the chain, trudging down the road to Derby and the white man's jail.

Young Constable Richardson, desperately tired now, desperately anxious, eyes aching from need of sleep, stood by the prisoners while listening out into. the new night. All the night before, all that day he had been alone watching, watching, ceaselessly vigilant. He still felt a touch of fever but now he dared not even sit down on. that veranda. Should he fall asleep ...

Anxiously he continued walking up and down. What had happened to Pigeon and Captain? Had they surprised and caught Ellemara they would have been back long before now! Had they found that the bird had flown they would have returned hours ago. They must be hot on his tracks. Probably he had just got away and they were following him up. But could they have been ambushed? Had Ellemara met any of his friends in that pindan? Could the trackers have been noticed, expected, waited for, riddled with spears from the pindan?

Up and down the constable trudged, up and down just out of reach of those grinning prisoners on the chain around the new night's fire.

From the native camp came the plaintive chant of a lullaby, the click of kylies. Again Richardson knew they were talking to the prisoners, and wished he knew what they were "saying". A silence urged him to peer towards the prisoners, sitting in tensely listening attitudes. Then quick expressions, urgent whispers, gleam of excited eyes.

News of definite import had come through.

A little later, movement from a shadow attracted Richardson's attention down the side of the house, out of sight of the prisoners. The constable strolled to the corner, stood filling his pipe. A station black came sidling along the wall.

"Ellemara!" Danmarra whispered excitedly. "Pigeon catch 'im!"

"Where is he now?" whispered Richardson, intent on his pipe.

"Close up; soon feller him come!"

"Good boy," whispered Constable Richardson. "Me give him you plenty feller 'bacca longa morning time!" and strolling back towards the fire, he lit his pipe.

Expressionless his face as he gazed at the prisoners, glad indeed his heart.

It was not until several hours later that Pigeon and Captain with their captive came strolling in from the night.

"Good Pigeon," exclaimed Richardson thankfully as he welcomed them, "good Captain. Good work. Put him on the chain, make certain of him. Then better eat - you must be hungry."

He stood by while they padlocked the chain around Ellemara's unprotesting neck, gazing in grim satisfaction at this dangerous, most elusive, most desired of all prisoners. Ellemara squatted down in place with a quizzical grin as the handcuffs were unlocked. Then murmured greeting to his silent fellow prisoners.

Richardson put the quart pots on himself for the trackers. "Go and take what tobacco you want," he said cheerfully, "then come and tell me all about it." And he set to preparing them a mighty meal.

It was an hour later that with a great thankfulness Constable Richardson spread his blankets just within the little hallway of the rough-built homestead. It was just a little cooler there, and he was feeling feverish again, perhaps from very relief. With a sigh he sat down on the blankets, the homestead lantern on the floor beside him. What a heaven-sent relief it was at last to take off his boots. Pigeon and Captain would watch the prisoners; Pigeon would take the first watch followed by Captain who would wake him for the dawn watch. Meanwhile, he would sleep.

He took a swig at the fever mixture bottle, unloosened his revolver belt, turned down the lantern, lay down and pulled the blankets over him.

How good it felt, to lie down, stretch out and rest at last, with mind at ease.

He just lay there, half listening, did not fall asleep for some time. He felt so very weary, his mind had been too actively anxious.

Presently the lullaby seemed drifting away, the click of the kylies growing softer and fainter.

He fell into deep sleep.

8

THE TREACHERY OF PIGEON

PIGEON and Captain, unusually sombre of brow, were sitting smoking by their own fire midway between the veranda and the prisoners. On the chain by the prisoners' fire Ellemara was urgently, murmurously whispering, the prisoners attentively listening. The night was deathly quiet.

An hour after the policeman fell asleep Captain arose and casually walked away towards the station blacks' camp. Presently he returned and squatted down again beside Pigeon.

A messenger was hurrying to Cadwarry's camp with a message from Ellemara that must be obeyed - it was tribal. Cadwarry. was to come straight to the homestead and bring his young daughter Cangamvara.

Sometime later Pigeon rolled up in his blankets. Captain stood up yawning, about to go on watch. On bare feet he walked to the veranda, stepped up, peered at the sleeper within the open doorway. Then looked around and nodded. Pigeon was instantly on his feet hurrying to the prisoners while two naked tribesmen arose as if from the earth. Both were carrying spears as they hurried to Pigeon who was stooping over Ellemara, unlocking the padlock of the loop of chain around his neck. As Ellemara stood up with a fiendish grin a man handed him spears, his comrade did likewise to Lillimarra when he also stood up free. Ellemara and Lillimarra, grasping their weapons, followed Pigeon who, picking up his rifle, was already on the veranda beside Captain.

Constable Richardson, the dim lantern light vaguely showing his tired face, was deep in sleep, so deep it might have been his *last* sleep.

Pigeon stepped into the hallway, stooped over the sleeping man, held his rifle muzzle to within an inch of the forehead and pulled the trigger.

To the flame and startling report Captain leaped forward and was emptying his revolver into the convulsive body while beside him snarling as they stabbed were Ellemara and Lillimarra, In that smoke-filled hallway it was bestial blood lust quite needless, for Pigeon's first shot had instantly killed the sleeper.

They stood there panting, faces twitching in maniacal triumph as slowly the smoke drifted away. Pigeon reached down, took the keys from the dead constable's pocket, and handed them to Captain who ran out to free all the prisoners, shouting the news. Clinking of chain, a howl of joy, but silence from the awed station natives. Captain came running in with the prisoners at his heels, seized Richardson's rifle and tipped out the police haversack, laughing as he clawed at the cartridges.

But Pigeon, for some queer reason, took Richardson's rifle from Captain and handed Captain his own Winchester.

Thereafter Pigeon was to care for that rifle as he cared for his own life. When inevitably his time would come he was to die with it in his hands, firing his last shot.

But now, through the excitement they stood listening, questioning alarm in their eyes, to the urgent drumming of a horse's hooves - galloping away.

They struggled out to the veranda. A group of station natives were standing outside.

"Who's that?" shouted Pigeon. "Whose horse is that?"

"Danmarral" shrilled a girlish voice, and Wondaria stood there. "Danmarra jumped on a police horse and rode away soon as he knew the policeman was killed."

Ellemara rattled his bloodstained spears, leaping and howling in maddened rage, chewing his beard as the aboriginal does when seized by passion beyond control.

But Ellemara must await his revenge. Danmarra the stockboy was galloping for his life for Lukin's station, knowing his only chance of life was that the police should catch Ellemara before Ellemara caught him.

And now Pigeon took command. "Take all guns and bullets from the packs and house too," he ordered, "and plenty tucker. Bring all outside. Make up the fire so we can see and watch these yellow-livered station boys lest others ride with news to the police."

In boisterous glee they obeyed while Pigeon stepped beside Ellemara, who was raving mad at having been outwitted from a cruel revenge. Ellemara the Cunning, always the leader, now instinctively sensed Pigeon's leadership. From under lidded eyes he glared at Pigeon's grim face, Pigeon who now stood before him, waiting, rifle in hand.

Swiftly Ellemara calculated the chances. Pigeon had the guns!

Pigeon knew how to use guns. Pigeon was used to giving orders and having them obeyed by tracker and tribesman alike. And now Captain stood grinning beside Pigeon with hand loosely on revolver. Ellemara grinned in in friendly fashion. After all, Pigeon would be handy to lead him, Ellemara, and all of them, back to the safety of the hills.

After which ...!

Ellemara was greatly mistaken. Pigeon was always to be the leader.

Alertly, rifle in hand, Pigeon watched the station natives while Captain attended to the sacking of the homestead. Pigeon knew there was plenty of time, even with Danmarra's warning. Derby and the police were a long way away. He smiled grimly, thinking deeply.

When all was sorted out, Pigeon turned to Ellemara. "Cangamvara, the girl," he growled.

Ellemara called out and a tall greybeard, his face rugged as a corrugated rock of his own sunburned hills, came hesitantly forward. Following him came a little lubra barely more than a girl, with a shock of hair, eyes alight with animal caution, lithe little body deceptive of its amazing endurance. A sense of the utterly primitive was about her, as if she could be there and yet vanish on the instant-as indeed she could have. An untamed little savage from the wilds, she stared up at the cold, calculating eyes of Pigeon.

"Plenty of endurance," he was thinking, "eyes of the eagle - eyes that will see for me!"

He stepped forward, laid a hand upon her shoulder. "I take her," he growled to Cadwarry the father, "this lubra, your daughter, now belongs to me!"

Startled alarm showed in the old man's eyes, but he was silent.

Then a tall, middle-aged warrior stepped forward and a spear was twitching in his hand. Marawon's rugged visage showed no trace of fear.

"The girl belongs to *me*," he declared in deep voice, "to be my lubra by tribal law."

Slowly Pigeon's rifle rose until the muzzle covered the tribesman's heart, and death gazed from Pigeon's eyes.

Marawon was no coward. He stood glaring at Pigeon with hate dawning in his face. Pigeon enjoyed it; a grin twisted his lips. He took the girl, not caring that he had made a bitter enemy.

Then Captain took a young girl. With a cynical grin upon his big, wrinkled face, Ellemara took back Wondaria.

The policeman was dead. The prisoners were freed. But Ellemara, Pigeon, and Captain had already each made several bitter enemies for life. They were to make more, many more, before their course was run.

Freed of their chains, gleefully Pigeon's men obeyed his orders, first taking weapons from the station natives, then ordering them to light fires, flourishing their own spears at them. The women obeyed in admiration for of these warriors who were game to kill all the white men, who had actually killed that most feared by far of all men - a policeman! Soon the women were mixing the raided station flour into dampers, cooking beef. Right joyfully Pigeon's men tried out the balance of their stolen spears in the hook of the wommeras to the dancing and war grunts of Lillimarra and Towerdine. But it was Ellemara's hoarse, menacing voice that was loudest in threats against the white men, in jibes at yellow-livered black curs so tame as to work for white men. His the crafty eyes that noted the fleeting expressions, saw all that was going on. Captain stood toying with his revolver, his roving eyes reflecting the firelight as he glared at the bashful young lubras, But Pigeon sat apart, silent throughout, squatting there in the outer firelight carefully cleaning his rifle, Richardson's rifle, the weapon which through thick and thin he was going to keep in perfect trim to the last gasp of his fighting life.

Dawn was breaking as the mob squatted around the fires and gorged, wolfish eyes gloating over their stolen food, now and then howling with exultant laughter at one another. They, who had suffered the indignity of capture, who had trudged for hundreds of miles on the chain, were now free, with weapons to hand again. While the policeman lay dead, just in there within his own police house.

"We will kill every policeman in our land," roared Ellemara, "and every white man until not one is left. We will rouse up all the hill tribes to fight with us, and all the river tribes that are game. We will eat up all the white men. And then ... " he paused with a boisterous laugh that ended in a chuckling snarl, "we will kill all the yellow curs not game to fight with us."

The plainsmen shivered.

As Ellemara talked and boasted and swayed all with voice and words, gesture and gleaming eyes, those same eyes were watching Pigeon sitting out there. Pigeon did not seem to be listening, his sullen lips, lowering brows, shadowed eyes seemed intent only on carefully examining each cartridge with which he was now filling Richardson's cartridge belt.

Ellemara suddenly leaped up rattling his spears. "We'll all go down the river!" he shouted. 'We'll kill bloody old Lukin and raid and burn his house! We'll go and kill bloody old Lukin now!" And they leapt up with a howl to stamp with Ellemara in the war dance.

Minutes later Pigeon casually stood up, buckled on his cartridge belt and stood there, methodically filling his rifle magazine. Caressingly he fingered the trigger. Then his eyes coldly surveyed the dancing braves. Uncertainly, their stamping ceased. They stood, their eyes glaring, chests heaving. Pigeon strolled casually towards them, his face a sullen mask. One at Ellemara, then he spoke coldly to all.

"We leave old Lukin alone. He come second. We want more guns. And men who can use guns. Soon, the police will come. We cannot fight the police without guns."

He paused, and the bush seemed listening in the chill dawn.

"Soon," he growled, "we move down the Lennard. Kill the white men Burke and Gibbs and Edgar. Kill their cattle. Loot their teams."

He paused, watching this master stroke sink in. As slowly it did, comprehension dawned upon deep-chiselled, savage faces expressing surprised delight. Ellemara's sinister countenance mingled chagrin and jealous admiration as he glared at Pigeon, bitter that he had not thought of this breath-taking idea himself. Every native, the length of the Fitzroy, knew that for weeks past three white men with four blackboys had been toiling towards the King Leopold foothills. Stockmen Burke and Gibbs with Fred Edgar's stockboys Georgie and Nigger were slowly droving ahead a mob of cattle, Fred Edgar toiling behind with his teamster blackboy Sambo driving a bullock wagon loaded with station supplies. They were making for wild country amongst the Leopold foothills to form a new station near the Black Hills, north of Fitzroy Crossing, with their cattle and spare horses and blackboys, and bullock wagon loaded with twelve months' supplies.

What loot! So easy to ambush. For now that the Lillamaloora police outpost was wiped out these land-seekers passing through the rough Lennard country were far from help.

"We kill the three white men," growled Pigeon, "take their guns. On the wagon will be rifles too, and plenty of ammunition, axes, knives, iron, and stores. We take the horses - those who ride can use them later on. We kill what beasts we want. Then those that are not fighters who join us will drive the mob back into the hills to feed our people. We take all the rifles and guns and revolvers and ammunition and give them to those amongst us who can use them. Then..."

"We go down river and kill bloody old Lukin!" shouted Ellemara.

"No!" Pigeon's cold voice sounded more distinct than Ellemara's shout.

Pigeon turned to the silent mob with a half sneer. "By the time we have killed the three white men and looted the wagon and driven the cattle back into the hills, a police patrol will be riding fast from the white feller town Derby. A strong patrol," he added impressively, "for we have killed a policeman! That patrol will come riding. By the time we have killed the three white men and looted the wagon and are ready, that patrol will be nearing here. They will have passed old Lukin's place - he will join them with his boys."

Pigeon paused. He could see by the tense faces that they were following his word pictures nearly as plainly as he himself could see what would happen.

"Before they come," he resumed, "we will have killed the three men and their blackboys. The cattle must be driven well into the hills. But we fighting men will remain hidden around the wagon - and the dead men. When the patrol comes, they will see the wagon. They will ride to it and then - they will see the dead men!"

Pigeon paused. They stood there, listening in breathless silence.

"When the patrol men ride up to the wagon and the dead men," resumed Pigeon quietly, "we will kill them!"

Pigeon paused, leaving his astounding idea to sink in. Which it did, to deeply rumbled growls of "Yu-ail", 'Wah!", 'Wah!"

"When we have killed all the patrol," resumed Pigeon impressively, "we will have guns and ammunition enough for so many of our people that we need never be afraid of the white man and his guns again. Every tribe in all the country will join us then. We will. wipe out every river station and the few that are forming in the hills. We will take the guns from all. Then we will go to the sea and kill every man and woman in the white feller town Derby. Until there will not be one white man left alive in all our country."

9

OLD MOTHER JINNY

SUCH was the plan of Sandamara, aboriginal of the Australian Kimberleys, Pigeon the black-tracker. Whether he believed he could carry it out no one will ever know. But his plan was excellent. Given but a little more time at this early stage to organize, arm and train those scattered tribesmen available and he might quite possibly have wiped out the few isolated settlers in the West Kimberleys. To attack Derby would have proved a very different matter, even though the white folk there numbered barely sixty or seventy. But he certainly could have delayed settlement in the rugged interior.

Full dawn had come, birds were singing among the trees, as Pigeon gave his next few orders which when carried into action were to make life for the settlers a nightmare for nearly three years to come.

"Send up the smokes," he ordered, "call the fighters in every tribe to come help us drive out the white men. And," he frowned, "tell them we only want to kill the white men-not the blackmen. The only blackmen we will shoot will be those who help the white men against us."

Many were listening there now, for even within hours "aboriginal telegraph" had travelled fast, with the dawn bringing nearby natives to the scene. Warriors black-bearded, some painted, all with their long, cruel spears; lubras and children in naked, wild-eyed excitement, small groups appeared silently amongst the timber to join the now big circle listening wide-eyed to Pigeon.

"Where is Long Frankey?" inquired Pigeon of a greybeard.

"By his hideout in the Geikie Gorge."

"Good. Frankey can use a rifle. Like Captain and me, he once was a tracker who rode with the police. Send up the smokes for him to come and join us. Where is Waggarrie?"

"Hunting along the Margaret River, maybe now in the Margaret Gorge."

"Good," grinned Pigeon appreciatively, "where no patrol would expect to find him. For he killed a white man on the Margaret not twelve moons ago. Send up a smoke, for he too can use a gun. Where's Langooradale?"

"In the Oscar Range, spearing cattle on white man Collins's station."

"Good. He, too, was once a police tracker. He has killed five men and can use a gun. Send up a smoke for him. Where's Mullenbuddin?"

"Near by. In the Wingina Gorge."

"Good. Send a swift lubra to tell him to come quickly. Where is Rowally, whom white men call Demon?"

"Camped in the Isdell Gorge."

"Ah! he will come when he knows it means the killing of cattle - and men! Send up a smoke for him. And a smoke for Pyabarra and Canada too. Send up a smoke for any tracker who has left the police, for any warrior who knows the white man's ways and can use a gun, to come and join us."

Clever Pigeon, calculating the movements of white and black alike in time and distance, considering conditions of country to be traversed, tribal animosities, the reactions of the Old Men of the tribes, and of the whites. Time was foremost in his mind. All the while he had seemed to be doing nothing but cleaning his rifle he had been thinking. He had killed a policeman! He was in for it now. But - given reasonable time he felt almost sure he could seize sufficient firearms and precious ammunition to defy the whites. But he must collect men who could use firearms and there were few indeed amongst the natives. Given time, he could strike and strike again. After each strike, yet more waverers would join him. Again, a little time was needed for the distances over which most must come. A lot more time was needed though, to overcome tribal animosities on a big scale. Only quick successes against the white men could do that.

He must succeed, but he was afraid of time. The news would soon reach Derby. Then a running around for the men, the horses, the shoeing, the preparations for patrol before they could start out. And then - they would have to catch him! He knew the routine so well, he had been through it all so many times himself.

He frowned deeply. With time, but only with time, he felt sure he could organize a gang capable of wiping out patrol after patrol of the bare half-dozen in the West Kimberley. Soon, the wet season would be here to bog down any patrols and thus help him; he would gain time in the 'Wet'.

And yet ...

Slowly he gave his final order for the morning. "Send up a smoke for Jinny, my mother."

For this happened to be within Pigeon's own country, the beloved country in which he, Sandamara, was born. Yes, he knew every square yard of all this country far away around, the very country itself would shelter him. But should it come to the worst he knew whom he could trust to the last.

So he sent up a smoke call for Jinny, his mother. In the desperate times soon to come it was in women only that Pigeon put his deepest trust. And in Mother Jinny most of all.

Rock walls of the Kimberleys - and Richardson, Pidgeon's first victim.

10

DEEP INJURY SETS VENGEANCE BROODING

WHEN Richardson was killed Danmarra, the outraged stockboy who had so nervously been watching events from the night, had run to saddle a police horse, knowing that soon blood vengeance would bring Ellemara seeking his life. His agitation and fear communicated itself to the horses and only after feverish difficulty did he catch one. He flung on the saddle and was away like the wind, his heart shrieking native curses for the death of Ellemara, Ellemara who had again taken from him Wondaria, his dream girl of the Laughing Waters, his prized young wife. Crouching over the sweating horse's neck, his heels kicking a tattoo on its sides, he shrieked his curses until the maddened horse bolted with its mad black rider and galloped through the night, straight for Lukin's Lennard River station, long miles away.

Within a mile of the station the frothing horse lunged frantically, to crash down, roll over and kick out its life with a broken neck. Danmarra was thrown yards away, to lie still in a crumpled heap.

He lay stunned for a long time, well into the blazing heat of day. Dazedly then he raised his bloodstained head. The roaring was a thunder as the disturbed mass of flies took wing, only to settle hungrily again. Presently Danmarra struggled groaning to his knees, then began to crawl along the track, his head a roaring of pain and flies through which an insistent voice faintly urged "Lukin!", "Ellemara!", "Lukin!", "Ellemara!" Painfully he rose to his feet and began to stagger along.

Lukin was working in the stockyard with his stockboys, busy with the branding iron. A pioneer homesteader Lukin, in shirt and corduroys, his sunburned face caked with sweated dust in the turmoil and heat of the branding job amongst these bellowing calves. He was just about to rope a struggling young micky when at a grunt he glanced up to follow his blackboy's gaze. Back along the track was staggering a blackboy, his bloody head and chest a cloud of flies, his eyes staring from their sockets as he staggered towards Lukin to croak out his story.

Lukin listened with frowning concern. Two efficient, well-known trackers Pigeon and Captain shoot their own constable, seize firearms, liberate a gang of killers and cattle-spearers, threaten to rouse the tribes, burn homesteads, and kill the whites. Lukin knew that, if such a threat were organized and attempted by well-trained trackers used to the ways of the police the result might well prove serious to the widely scattered settlers. The sooner Pigeon and Captain were laid by the heels the better.

"Saddle Prince!" he ordered the head stockboy. "Me write 'em letter longa police belonga Derby. You ride longa Derby, take him letter. Quick feller now!"

Lukin turned towards the homestead to scribble a note to the police at Derby. When the stockboy departed at the gallop Lukin turned to prepare his own blackboys and homestead for probable attack.

Already Danmarra had been busy, pouring into the ears of the goggle-eyed station natives every imaginable lurid threat that he alleged Ellemara, especially Ellemara, and Pigeon and Captain and Lillimarra had uttered against *all* station natives. How they threatened to come with the hillmen and kill every man, woman and child who worked for or was friendly to the whites.

Tomorrow Danmarra would ride to Derby, his mind seething with revenge. He would try to join the avenging police patrol as a horseboy. Then within the safety of the patrol he would poison the mind of every native he met against Ellemara. Until Ellemara was dead.

Other outraged tribesmen were similarly brooding upon revenge against others of the gang. Cadwarry, father of Cangamvara, the girl Pigeon had taken, and Marawon, to whom she had been promised as wife, had walked quietly away back into the foothills when the signal smokes were being lit, their faces grim with hate and making plans for revenge. Captain and Lillimarra had also taken a young lubra each, and here too the father and husband-to-be planned a bitter revenge.

So at the very outset the stirring of vengeance began to work against Pigeon and his band. As time went on they made more vengeance-seeking enemies. These vendettas were to tell heavily against Pigeon's gang individually, while against all was always working the age-old animosity of tribe against tribe.

But this was quiescent in Time and Fate as the morning after the killing of Richardson the signal smokes rose up. Pigeon and his band immediately became heroes, very soon were to be great heroes amongst warrior sections of numerous tribes.

It was a sweltering day in the tiny port of Derby down by the mouth of the Fitzroy. It was low tide, the topmasts of a schooner showing just above the jetty which ran far out among the mangroves.

For the rise and fall of tide here is as great as 40 feet and the schooner was sitting upon her bottom on the mud. The waters of King Sound reflected brilliant sunlight. Seldom are the turbulent waters of the great sound so quiet; more often they are a fury of tide rips, cross currents, whirlpools and tortured waters.

It was November - the breathless pause before the thunderous storms of the coming wet season. There was a constant flickering of lightning far out to sea.

Behind the mangroves fringing the sound shores the wee township was sweltering. Fascinating mirages formed on the great grey, now dry marsh three parts enclosing the township. Back from the wharf at "the Point", with its little hotel, the Adcock Brothers' store, Quan Sing's store and the goods shed, ran the little wooden tramway into the tiny town with its other store, blacksmith's shop, small cottage hospital, police station, telegraph office and jail. There was a handful of little wood and iron cottages bolted together for security against the hurricanes and "Cock-eye Bobs" of the wet seasons, and the Residency. At this period the genial and capable Dr House was "Jack of all Professions", District Medical Officer, Chairman of Quarter Sessions, Governor of the jail, and any other official job that happened along. Some sixty or seventy folk comprised the population of the only port and town in all the West Kimberley. (There are only three times as many today.)

Here in the eighties (for settlement in the Kimberleys came very much later than elsewhere in Australia) had landed from tiny craft the explorer pioneers who pushed westward inland up along the Fitzroy River plains with their little flocks of sheep, their precious horses and cattle and dogs. And right here, at the main camp, had gradually been built up the wee port and town.

There was no overland road communication with the south.

All communication was by sea, by schooner and later by infrequent little steamer. There was none at all during the wet season of course. During the Wet, the West Kimberley was isolated from all southern civilization except for the Overland Telegraph Line, so long as "the niggers" did not cut it to use the wire as iron-pointed spearheads.

That line had been built only some three years before "Pigeon broke out". By degrees it had been extended into the East Kimberley, to Hall's Creek 200 miles farther east, thence north to Wyndham on the Cambridge Gulf; thus linking the southern coast with the far northern. It was a big job among bigger jobs accomplished by the tiny, courageous population of the vast State.

So here, in the wilderness at The Crossing, two thousand miles north by line from Perth and two hundred and ten miles east from Derby, Jack Scott the operator and Abe Harris the linesman in their barricaded little telegraph office greeted with the liveliest satisfaction the slow building of a real police station across the river; not only for safety's sake but for company in their isolation.

Young Constable Pilmer, Constable McDermott and their trackers, hewing the timber and man-handling the logs, toiled from daylight to dark. Pilmer worked with mixed feelings - pride in the building of a frontier police outpost that was to be his very own command; anxiety because his young wife was coming to join him.

A Tenterfield girl, from three thousand miles east in New South Wales, she was coming all the way around by sea, with their baby, to join him here in this wilderness, two hundred miles inland from the few white women in Derby. Here, where armed, naked savages carne daily prowling around the camp. But she had not only insisted-she was corning, was really on her way.

No wonder the young constable's thoughts were tinged with anxiety. Only a week before tribesmen had attempted his life not a mile from the station.

Old Derby Goal.

11

THE SUB-INSPECTOR'S FURROWED BROW

BACK west on the coast at Derby, within the pioneer Police Station Headquarters, Sub-Inspector Overend Drewry sat before a rough table sweltering in his shirt sleeves, frowning as he bent over "requisitions", "supplies", "deficiencies", and reports. Every expense down to a horseshoe had to be accounted for to the authorities "down south", including every horse, saddle and packsaddle, all police and trackers' equipment and the hundred and ten expenses constantly needed in maintaining this station and the four or five isolated police posts strategically placed inland along the Fitzroy, and several northward along the fringe of the King Leopold foothills in the wild lands. The most ambitious one was to be at The Crossing, two hundred and ten miles inland on the border of the East and West Kimberleys. Young Pilmer and McDermott and the trackers were out there now building that station, cutting the timber with the axe from the bush. The authorities down south had promised the iron for the roof, and any ironware needed; and Drewry meant to jolly well keep them up to that promise.

The sub-inspector's mind strayed back from this ambitious project of the new Fitzroy Crossing police station, to "this year's horse wastage".

"Heavens!" Drewry frowned, "it will raise the hair on the heads of the Departmental Big Bugs away down south. 'Lamed!', 'Killed in accidents!', 'Killed by spear!', 'Drowned!', 'Died of walkabout disease!', Heavens!" The Heads did not realize what a hard country this was on horses. They must do many hundreds of miles of patrol each year in roadless country and the wildest area in Australia today, with unknown numbers of wild aboriginals to bluff into subjection - and barely half a dozen scattered patrols to do it with. And all this in an untamed, unmapped, utterly isolated, pioneer country where horses were very scarce in the first place.

The sub-inspector clasped hands behind his head and leaned back with a sigh. The worst was over, thank heaven, for this year anyway. Only one more patrol to report back this season, young Richardson's patrol. The last patrol.

Then the wet season would come, three months anyway in which the horses could be spelled and the patrols built up again. There would be time for repairs to saddlery and equipment and the hundred and one things that must be put in apple-pie order ready for the coming of another year.

Of short build, thick-set, swarthy, keen of face was Sub-Inspector Drewry. He frowned again, this time at a bundle of letters stuck through with a wire. He reached out and began to read through them again.

From Gus Rose of Oobagooma. Typical of the settler-explorers, thought Drewry. Mt Rose was named after Gus Rose. He had pioneered Leopold Downs station with P. D. Hutton, buying their first little mob of cattle from G. C. Rose of Mt Anderson. "G.C." had bought Mt Anderson station from the Daly brothers who came from Dunolly in Victoria with 500 sheep only nine years before. Gus Rose was managing a wild and woolly area of country named Oobagooma, battling to turn it into a station for the McLarty brothers. His letter to the Derby police was an urgent request for assistance to combat the depredations of the natives who had become dangerously out of hand. If not checked, these native troubles could mean the eventual abandonment of the station, if not worse. For he believed that his own life and the life of his white stockman, Tom Jasper, hung upon but a slender thread.

Sub-Inspector Drewry frowned. He had so few men, so few horses to guard these lonely stations and settlers, some could only be visited by a patrol once in a year. He picked out another letter from Felix Edgar, thoughtfully musing about him. Another dependable man, Felix.

Felix Edgar had landed with Tony Cornish from the four-masted barque Tamar with a small mob of horses, sheep and cattle for the Kimberley Pastoral Company. Drewry frowned. Their best blackboy, Willie, and then Tony Cornish were soon speared by the blacks along the Fitzroy. Felix was now developing Meda into a station for W. E. Marchmont. Meda was only a few miles away on the track north to the Lennard. Yet Felix Edgar was experiencing exactly similar trouble to Rose, as was his brother Fred. And also Lukin at his Lennard River station farther north. A note from Collins of Beefacre station on the Oscar Range, though this station was two hundred miles inland, brought the same complaint. Letters from Joe Blythe, developing Brooking Creek station with son Charlie, and Charlie and Willie MacDonald, two hundred-odd miles east on the Margaret, and other letters too, all told the same story. The hillmen spearing the cattle-how many hundreds had they speared that year? - spearing the much more valuable horses, driving away sheep in little mobs on the three or four struggling sheep stations, spearing stockboys, occasionally spearing a white man.

Oh well, it would have to go on, year by year, until the authorities down below gave him more patrols - a lot more patrols. Or until the whites grew numerous enough to stop it all themselves. Which did not seem like happening for many years to come.

The sub-inspector thrust the letters back upon the wire spike, wondering how many natives there were within and over those impenetrable fastnesses of the Leopolds. Just as well many of the Fitzroy

River and plains natives liked working for the whites. Wonderful stockmen they were, both with sheep and cattle. especially with cattle.

Oh well, there was nothing he could do now about the cattle-spearers until after the Wet. When young Richardson's patrol came in that would be the last active patrol work until the beginning of the Dry.

The sound of galloping hooves rapidly approaching caused the sub-inspector to sit back, listening with questioning face. Instinctively he recognized the sound of hooves that come galloping with news.

These hooves brought the news that Constable Richardson had ridden on his last patrol.

A typical police camp post in Western Australia around 1900, this one at Mount Morgan.

12

THE PIONEER OUTFIT TOILS ONWARD

A QUIET Kimberley dawn. Birds chattering sleepily, and, way up along the Fitzroy road over the Barrier Range, trees taking shape in shadowy gullies.

A cheery fire was burning near the wagon with the blackboys crouching over it. Good boys were these, Georgie and Nigger and Sambo "belonga Fred Edgar". The good-humoured Sambo who was Edgar's bullock driver put the billy on as the three white men, Fred Edgar, Francis Burke, and Oswald Gibbs, walked up from the waterhole, hungry after the dawn swim. They had seven hundred head of Oobagooma cattle, five hundred belonging to Edgar and his brother Felix, who was now managing Meda station away back near Derby, for Marchmont. Fred Edgar, Burke and Gibbs were droving the cattle to the wild Black Hills country towards the heads of the Fitzroy, north of Fossil Downs station on the Margaret, to form a new station for the Edgar brothers.

The three white men sat unusually quietly around the breakfast fire, the blackboys hunched over their billy-can muttering in low, uneasy tones. They had only just heard of the killing of Constable Richardson, of the threats of Pigeon and Captain and Ellemara and Lillimarra, of the bloodthirsty boastings of the escaped prisoners. And it had all happened but a few miles away.

But it was not only because of this alarming news that Fred Edgar sat with uneasy brow, munching his breakfast, while Burke ate with determined obstinacy upon his face, Gibbs silently morose.

It was not until Burke nodded to the boys to bring along the saddle horses that Edgar spoke.

"Surely now," he urged, "you will ride armed from today!" "You know our sentiments," replied Burke coldly. "We argued it all out again last night. And that is final!"

"You are fools!" protested Edgar. "You are the only two white men in all the West Kimberley who persist in riding and working unarmed, with the country swarming with armed natives constantly awaiting their chance."

Young Billy Gibbs drained his final pannikin of tea.

"Why not drop the subject," he said; "You should know us by now."

"But young fellow, you are mad!" declared Edgar heatedly.

"You *both* are. I cannot blame *you* so much for you have not been long in the country, though long enough to know that the old hands must know what they are talking about-apart from Burke. You both heard last night that barely twenty miles away two police trackers, Pigeon and Captain whom you both know, killed their own constable only five days ago! liberated a gang of killers and have taken to the bush, threatening to kill every white man in the Kimberleys. And yet you still refuse to carry arms for your own protection!"

"Plenty of natives make threats like that," growled Burke, "but don't mean it."

"Then what if Pigeon and Captain attacked us, this very day," persisted Edgar, "and you two were unarmed?"

"Neither Pigeon nor Captain, nor any other natives would harm me," replied Burke confidently. "Besides, I know Pigeon very well. A good, quiet boy he is. He worked for me at Oobagooma, before becoming a police tracker. I'd trust Pigeon anywhere."

"And yet he has murdered his own police constable," persisted Edgar. "And now - what if he should attack us today?"

"Pigeon and Captain have taken to the hills days ago," snapped Burke. "Who better than they would know that a police patrol will soon be hunting them! And even if they did come, they would not harm us. I know Pigeon and Captain very well." And he stood up with a confident smile.

"For heaven's sake, man," protested Edgar. "Did not Pigeon and Captain know Richardson! Why, you both have heard Richardson boasting that Pigeon and Captain would give their very lives for him if necessary! You have heard him tell of how they very nearly did so! How they rushed to his aid when that mob on the Barker were tearing him to pieces but a few months ago! And yet now, in the dead of night when he was sound asleep, they cold-bloodedly murdered that very Richardson!"

"An armed policeman," replied Burke obstinately, "who must constantly be doing his duty in hunting and arresting natives who have broken the law, is thought of by the natives in a very different way to two unarmed white men who have never lifted a hand to a native in their lives." And he and Gibbs walked towards the horses and the waiting blackboys.

"How about at least carrying a revolver at your belt then?" called Edgar as a last resort.

But the two men mounted and without answer rode away towards the quietly feeding cattle.

Edgar urgently beckoned to the two stockboys. They came to him, leading their horses. "Now you two feller boy, Nigger, Georgie," he ordered impressively, "watch out *all* a time! *all* a day! Watch *out* longa Pigeon,

Captain, Ellemara, he no come! Suppose he come, he killem us altogether! shoot 'im! Spear 'im they two feller dam' fool white men! Shoot 'im me! Shoot 'im Sambo! Shoot 'im you two feller boy! You watch out now Pigeon he no come!"

"U-ai boss!" they nodded and their uneasy eyes told they understood the danger immeasurably better than Burke and Gibbs. As they rode away Edgar nodded to Sambo. "Bring up bullicks!" he muttered. "You watch out too, Sambo! Maybe Pigeon he come!" He turned to his work of packing the camp things back into the wagon and yolking up the team.

Frank Burke was a grizzled old-timer, a quiet type of man, Billy Gibbs a cheery young Englishman seeking "colonial" experience with the Oobagooma Pastoral Company. Both were well liked. They had chummed up, the young fellow modelling his work upon the experience of Gibbs who already had taught him a lot about stock work and the bush. Burke was set against treating natives roughly. He believed in kindness always and believed he had any natives he met thoroughly under control. And young Gibbs now believed the same. Both men resolutely refused to carry arms, no matter how wild the country or the natives.

In practically every area in Australia where the natives have been really dangerous, pioneering history tells us of similar cases. Alas! at times bringing similar results.

Slowly the cattle moved off, driven by Burke and Gibbs with stockboys Georgie and Nigger. The wagon would toil along later, driven by Edgar and Sambo, Fred Edgar wishing that big brother Felix was with him.

He was very uneasy as he helped Sambo yoke up the bullocks. This day they would enter the gorge country, drawing farther and farther northeast into the wild country towards where the new station was to be formed. What fat pickings there would be in this mob of cattle if the cattle-spearers really got busy amongst them, as they might well do when they learned that two of the fool white men droving them refused to carry firearms. Now that Pigeon and Captain and Ellemara had threatened to rouse the country this prize might well prove irresistible.

Fred Edgar shuddered. He objected strenuously to being shot, but above all he had long felt a horror of ever being transfixed by one of those long, cruel, torturously barbed spears. He had seen a stockboy writhing like that for a long, long hour, clawing up the grass-roots with bloody fingers. Instinctively Edgar's hand gripped his revolver butt, his eyes roamed to his favourite horse Pat, a big, powerful old grey. Fred Edgar thought a great deal of that sturdy animal, always kept it in good condition and above all fresh for an emergency; always kept his arms and personal saddlery in apple-pie order.

The morning was well advanced when the wagon slowly moved off in brilliant Kimberley sunlight. Edgar was riding ahead to pick the way, the chuckling voiced Sambo walking beside the toiling team. It was a world of fresh air and clear blue sky, whistling and carking and chattering of birds, slow creaking of the wagon, chuckling encouragement of Sambo talking to each patient bullock in turn, tall grasses and trees and shrubbery, hum of insects. And the wild ranges were now close beside them.

Wingina Gorge.

13

DEATH IN WINGINA GORGE

MIDDAY was hot and sultry when the thirsty cattle reached Wingina waterhole. It was a wild and lovely scene. Walled by limestone cliffs the waterhole stretched down river some four miles amongst tangled groves of trees and riotous grass and creeper life. The crystal clear water tinkled over rocks, or was quiescent in deep, sandy bottomed pools. Trees here and there clung to the cliffs, capped the summit in grey and green clumps of bush. Wildfowl rose with whirring wings and protesting squawks as the vanguard of thirsty beasts came lowing along the banks to splash heavily into the water, still drinking while pushed belly-deep farther out into the pool by their following comrades.

Burke and Gibbs rode slowly around the cattle, then farther on along the bank where the water would not be stirred up by the hooves of the cattle. Burke rode his horse down the bank on to a clean sand-mound and dismounted to allow the horse to drink and to drink himself. Gibbs rode a little farther along then he too rode down the bank on to a nice cleared space and knelt to drink beside his horse.

Burke, bridle rein over arm, sat back on the sand and began to cut a pipeful of tobacco, empty pipe gripped between his teeth, rolling the tobacco between his palms, quietly admiring the beauty of cliff and mirroring water and listening to the splash of contented beasts farther back among the trees along the water-hole. Something urged him to turn his head.

A rifle was pointing down at him from the bank. Behind the muzzle he gazed up into the eyes of Pigeon.

Blank astonishment dawned on Burke's face. Pipe in mouth, knife in hand with palms cupped over the tobacco, he sat there and gaped. Then...

Perhaps it was the black, tautening trigger finger, perhaps the fiendish light in Pigeon's eye .... The pipe dropped from Burke's mouth and in a strange voice he murmured: "You wouldn't shoot me, Pigeon!"

"Wouldn't I!" snarled Pigeon, "you old white h-!"

To the shock of the bullet Burke sprang up and his bridle was over his horse's head, his foot in the stirrup. Except for that startling report smacking back from cliff and water deathly silence instantly reigned, heads of beasts jerked up into big-eyed, alarmed inquiry, every bird call was silenced. Burke's horse plunged up the bank as the sorely wounded man struggled desperately to throw his leg over the saddle. But the well-bred mare was terrified and Burke was still clinging desperately to her neck when Ellemara leapt out from the rocks and shot him. in the back with Richardson's double-barrelled gun, while Mullenbuddin hurled a spear at his back, the blade piercing straight through his chest. Though the dying man was now blown and cut to pieces his fingers still clawed the horse's mane and still clung as he slid from the saddle, until the maddened animal reared in a galloping plunge and shook loose his death grip.

To the thunder of the heavy double-barrelled gun arose another sound, the howl of a war cry as the cliffs above were lined with dancing warriors. Down below natives had seemed to spring up from every rock, every shrub and came pouring up from the river to the screams of a thrashing horse transfixed by spears. Into this bedlam the ashen-faced Gibbs came galloping up from the river into a mightier sound, the roar of seven hundred stampeding cattle now fear - mad from the gunshots and the blood smell and that most terrifying smell- wild men howling and stabbing amongst them. Pigeon fired at Gibbs who lurched convulsively over the saddle as his terrified horse plunged straight amongst the howling natives. Gibbs actually managed to get two hundred yards away though blocked again and again by the stampeding cattle that also blocked the natives running to cut him off. From a sand-mound Pigeon aimed and fired again and yet again and the stricken man almost fell from the saddle. But he still clung on with Pigeon and Lillimarra now running close beside him. But for the stampeding cattle he might have galloped away to die. But Lillimarra snatched at the bridle and Captain clawed him from the saddle and throttled the life out of him.

As the last of the cattle crashed away through the bush howls of exultation were ringing amongst the timber accompanied by frantic bellowings where natives were stabbing crippled beasts. Pigeon and Captain, Ellemara and Lillimarra and Mullenbuddin and all the gang had hung close together. In frenzied exultation they howled their triumph. This second killing of white men had been excitingly strenuous and successful. They began the Triumph Dance, flourishing guns and bloodstained spears as excited lubras came running to admire them; they boasted that now they could kill all the white men.

Suddenly a howl from the river attracted them. Tribesmen had discovered the terror-stricken stockboy Georgie hiding in the river.

When the cattle had begun to drink at the waterhole and Burke and Gibbs had ridden around past the lead, Nigger and Georgie had brought up the tail. They rode warily. There was no sign of natives, but they were frightened. While Georgie had ridden down to the river for his drink Nigger remained behind on horseback, keeping watch. Georgie had dismounted and knelt down to drink, his thirsty horse drinking beside him. It was then that the first shot thundered down the gorge. The horse had jerked up its head, jerking the bridle reins from Georgie's hand. As Georgie leaped up to seize it, the horse plunged around and up the bank. As Georgie scrambled up after it he saw natives leaping up from behind trees and rocks. He slid back down the bank and took refuge in the water while the horse galloped away with the stampede.

But they had found Georgie now. They waited for Pigeon's gang to stroll leisurely along. There would be sport in killing this foreign blackskin who rode with the whites.

From the bank, Pigeon grinned down with cold, derisive eyes.

Standing neck-deep in water, Georgie was staring up, trembling. He was staring not at all those savage faces leering down at him, but only at Pigeon's eyes.

"You work for the white men!" spoke Pigeon coldly. Georgie nodded, he could not speak.

"You work no more for the white man," said Pigeon. "You join us?"

Georgie only stared. His teeth began to chatter.

Slowly Pigeon raised the rifle. "You work no more for the white men?" he inquired.

Georgie's eyes were big from fear. "Me like work for white men," he stuttered bravely.

Pigeon levelled the rifle. "Will you join us?" he demanded deliberately.

Georgie's face turned a sickly greyish-green, his knees were trembling. He tried to plead for his life but his tongue had swollen and was lolling out; he could only shake his head in a helpless way.

Pigeon slowly lowered the rifle.

"Why play with him any more!" snarled Ellemara. "Shoot the dingo and be done with it. We have fat cattle to roast and eat."

It may have been antagonism to Ellemara that decided Pigeon.

Or else he was holding himself in check to carry out what his cunning mind had planned.

"No," he replied harshly, "leave him alone. When you return to the white men," he snarled down at Georgie, "tell all the black stockmen that we do not wish to kill them—only to kill the white men. Advise all your friends to turn against the white men, and join us."

They glowered down at Georgie and the lubras jeered at him until a call drew their attention to Nigger sitting his horse away back among the trees.

Pigeon and Captain began to walk towards him, but the horseman turned his horse. Pigeon stopped, beckoned Nigger ride to them. But Nigger wasn't having any. Then Nigger saw natives at a stooping run racing to get around him. He leaned over his horse's neck and was away at the gallop with bullets from Pigeon and Captain whistling past his ears.

Kimberley tribesmen.

14

SPOILS TO THE VICTORS

FRED EDGAR, following the mob several miles behind with the wagon, heard with the greatest alarm the gunshots Tolling amongst the hills. Some little time later he halted the wagon as Nigger came galloping up to gabble out his story.

"Unyolk the bullocks! Quick!" shouted Edgar and hurried to the wagon for weapons while Samba and Nigger quickly freed the team.

"Here!" said Edgar urgently, "you take this rifle, Nigger! And revolver for you Samba, and this one for Georgie should he turn up. Take plenty bullet. You two feller boy stay longa wagon. Shoot 'im blackfeller 'spose 'im blackfeller try take wagon! Savvy!" They nodded. "Now 'sposem!" said Edgar impressively, "'sposem Pigeon, Captain, Ellemara *he* come then you two feller boy ride for your life! Savvy!"

Their nod was expressive answer.

"Me ride longa Lukin's station," went on Edgar, "bring him help! Send word longa police. Savvy!"

"U-ai!" they nodded.

Edgar swung himself into the saddle and was away at the gallop. He could visualize Pigeon catching Burke's racing mare in pursuit. Edgar leant over his horse's neck, urging and encouraging the old grey.

Way back at the waterhole to Pigeon came running his young lubra Cangamvara with a shrill cry that the wagon had stopped and the white man was galloping away.

Pigeon had long since posted the women as lookouts along the hilltops. He glared around with rage in his eyes. The ambush had been perfectly planned, but he had not thought of the reverberating reports of the gunshots warning the oncoming wagon, nor had he foreseen Nigger's caution and escape.

The bridle of Burke's thoroughbred had been entangled in a thicket, otherwise the mare would almost certainly have been killed or maimed in the stampede. Pigeon ran towards it but the already maddened animal reared and broke the bridle. It took them quite a time to catch it. As Pigeon mounted and dug in his heels he gritted his teeth towards Georgie and shouted:

"But for this horse playing up I would have cut your boss's throat by now! I'll catch him yet!" and he galloped off like the demon he was.

Old hands in the Kimberleys still yarn of that ride, twenty miles through bush with death a certainty for Edgar should he lose. Pigeon came to within sight of him, almost within rifle shot, when only two miles from Lukin's horse paddock. Pigeon thrashed his horse for a last effort and was gaining when the horse suddenly floundered and went down. Burke's pet horse would never race again.

Back at the Wingina waterhole crazy excitement still reigned as nearby natives came running to witness the kill, greeted in shrieking pantomime by those who had been eye-witnesses to the deed. All along the waterhole fires were burning where a beast had fallen to stampede or spears. Men, women, children and dogs were already gorging themselves on the choicest of barely singed beef.

Suddenly a lubra jumped up and screamed to them to loot the wagon. In the excitement and the cutting up of beasts they had forgotten it.

With one accord they sprang up, but Captain and Ellemara leapt up flourishing weapons, shouting threats, halting a stampede to loot the prize. With trigger fingers itching Captain's men warned the mob that first choice of loot was to those warriors who had stood beside them in the ambush. What was discarded by the fighting men the mob could have.

"Strike with us in our next fight," shouted Captain, "then you claim your share of loot with us."

"There'll be plenty of fights," yelled Ellemara, "plenty of loot.

We're going to kill every white man in the land."

And the gang flourished weapons to the admiration of young warriors and the shrieking acclaim of the lubras. But some of the tribesmen frowned their perplexity, tried to hide their sullen distrust. It was not all who believed they could, or who wished to, kill the whites.

With the gang in the lead, in one chattering mob they started back for the wagon.

Nigger and Sambo, who had taken to the bush when Pigeon came galloping past in pursuit of Edgar, were cautiously riding back to guard the wagon. Sambo, with his broad grin remarked in aboriginal lingo to his fellow blackboy: 'Well Nigger, my brave warrior stockman! If this bad boy Pigeon comes riding back he won't see my heels for dust."

"If he's on horseback we'd better stand and fight," replied Nigger sombrely.

"Why?" demanded the not too heroic Sambo.

"Because if he's on horseback he'll ride us down in turn and shoot us from the saddle," replied Nigger.

"We'd better be going now then," suggested Sambo urgently. "The others are corning now," replied Nigger, "but I see no horses - yet!"

As Captain saw the two distant stockboys, almost imperceptibly he thrust up his chin and warriors slipped down into gullies and commenced racing to outflank the two motionless horsemen.

"We'll cut their gizzards out," chuckled Ellemara, "we'll roast their kidney fat and eat it. Pigeon is too easy with them!"

"We'll make them a lesson to the white-livered dingoes who stand by the whites!" threatened Lillimarra grimly.

"Sambo is mine!" declared Captain. "I'll soon cut that grin from his face!" His finger itched on his trigger. Captain, like Pigeon and Ellemara, liked shooting people.

Nigger and Sambo slowly began to walk their horses away from the wagon. Captain and the mob slackened pace. But still Nigger and Sambo rode slowly back along the wagon track. Captain yelled and waved in friendly fashion. But Nigger and Sambo bent over their horses' necks and were away at full gallop. Captain, Ellemara and Lillimarra raised their weapons and fired but the range was too far. Still it was good to hear the howl of delight from the mob at the expense of the fleeing horsemen.

That wagon contained wealth untold. Naturally so, for it was loaded with supplies to stock a new station. The gang supervised the unloading. Then put aside the firearms, ammunition, tobacco, and all except a good many bags of flour. This they distributed for cooking with the beef. All the rest was to remain until Pigeon returned; above all, three full, unopened cases of "firewater" - one of whisky, one of rum, one of "squareface" gin.

Eyes fairly gloated on those cases of firewater, tongues licked thirsty lips, there were guttural growls of unsuppressed anticipation, fingers itched to open a case. But no man yet dared take a tomahawk to it, which was proof of the hold Pigeon already had over his gang. For these men now numbered thirty-odd and they feared no man, except now Sandamara, called Pigeon. And they were fairly trembling in their eagerness to loot this treasure wagon to its dregs.

A sullen Pigeon returned late that night. Not until next morning did he fully distribute the loot. All the firearms were given to those members of the gang who could use them. There were three Winchesters, two double-barrelled guns, a single barrel, a Schneider rifle, and half a dozen revolvers in a case in the wagon, also four thousand rounds of ammunition, ample reloading materials, canisters of shot and powder, lead for the making of bullets, bullet moulds, and cartridge caps. Pigeon's and Captain's eyes gleamed. How shrewd Pigeon had been, admired the gang, to ambush the wagon and seize these added firearms before spreading out to attack the whites. Ellemara frowned. It was he who should have thought of this obvious and certain triumph that at one blow had made Pigeon the most popular tribesman in all the country.

Captain took a great fancy to the heavy Schneider rifle. He handed his Winchester to Carolan and took the Schneider. Thereafter, during the dangerous months to come, its heavy report rolling through the hills was to be dreaded by lukewarm tribesmen within hearing.

Pigeon divided the tobacco and other luxuries amongst his own gang, and a goodly supply of the food. Then he gave the wagon and everything else it contained to the eagerly awaiting mob of men, women and children growing hourly larger as the breathless news spread through the hills. And there was plenty for all, especially of that priceless treasure, iron. Iron that for the making of spearheads was infinitely more efficient than stone or wood or bone.

When that evening a message stick arrived from the Margaret saying that Long Frankey was willing to join them, Pigeon grinned with delight. For Frankey the ex-police boy could use a rifle. Soon another message stick arrived from Langooradale, who was coming from the Geikie Gorge. And Demon was coming from the Oscar Range as soon as he could complete a killing that vengeance demanded. And both these two could use firearms.

As news of this latest victory spread, more and more men would wish to join Pigeon and just an occasional one amongst them would know more or less how to handle a gun.

Pigeon was so pleased to hear so soon that renegade boys used to firearms were prepared to join him that he allowed the case of whisky to be opened. He had meant to keep it for his own gang but under the influence of the unaccustomed firewater he went crazy himself and presently the cases of gin and rum were opened and handed around. Quickly then there developed a Stone Age bacchanalia that would have enlivened a Dante's imaginings. The black gorge was lit by flame after flame of bonfires, the cliff walls reflecting the fires where down below laughing, shrieking groups of men, women and children roasted and gorged on bullocks with their snarling dogs. Black figures sprang frenzied into the war dance to the clash of kylies and the drumming of women. There were fiendish yells as fights broke out and warriors leaped in berserk fury chewing their beards, spears flew, men, women and children ran screaming to snatch weapons and take sides, or fall upon one another, clawing, biting and kicking in maniacal lust to maim and kill.

A rifle shot was swallowed by the thunder of Ellemara's double-barrelled gun. Revolver bullets were whizzing indiscriminately and spears were hurled at any target. Men chased screaming women, while women snatched clubs and struck at any head within reach, trampled upon women biting at the writhing legs of fighters above them.

A man howled in mad terror as a dozen chased him, threw him to earth, spreadeagled him and held the writhing wretch down while one sprawled upon his back and hacked out his kidney fat with a stone knife. Long afterwards, tribesmen admitted that eleven men and some women were killed that night, by bullet, spear and club.

For years afterward that great feast and bloody fight were commemorated in many a tribal corroboree.

A Kimberley corroboree, photographed by Roy Phillipps, c 1910.

15

PIGEON PLANS CLEVERLY, HANDICAPPED BY TIME

PIGEON worked swiftly during the next few days. The mob were eager to go down river and "kill old Lukin" and loot his station. But Pigeon and Captain were much more concerned about the police patrol which inevitably would come riding to avenge Constable Richardson's death.

By day, Pigeon placed chosen women in well-spaced groups in strategic positions along the precipitous range edge whence they could see over this particular area of the Fitzroy and Lennard plains, could see a patrol miles away when it should come riding up along the track. For his lookout work Pigeon always put his greatest trust in women. Cangamvara immediately proved to be his keenest of eye and swiftest of foot, as Wondaria was soon to be for Captain's gang, particularly for Ellemara. But over them all Pigeon put his big old mother Jinny.

Soon after the killing of Burke and Gibbs Pigeon growled out his plan to the startled gang. It was no less than to ambush and wipe out the expected police patrol.

Carefully then he chose a position by the wagon track, and there sprawled the corpses of Burke and Gibbs before a crowd of goggle-eyed tribesmen. Gibbs's body Pigeon placed near a steeply banked creek that ran along down into the nearby, densely tree-lined river. The exact placing of that body and the steep, scrub-lined creek bank was to be the key to the ambush. The whole position, wheel track and looted wagon, dead horse and several dead bullocks, the bodies of the two white men lying out in the open so clear of cover, appeared innocent of ambush.

When all was prepared Pigeon, in hoarse, guttural voice, his gleaming eyes claiming the attentive mob, explained that the avenging patrol would cautiously ride up to this unexpected scene, and from horseback could oversee everything around the dead men. There would be no fresh tracks, no sign of natives; just the hot silence of the bush, the looted wagon, the signs of slaughter, the stiff bodies, and the flies. Just that and every indication that the deed had been done a week and more ago and the natives long since taken to the hills.

Believing this to be so, explained Pigeon, the patrol would ride right up to the wagon. They would then come and group around the dead men, would dismount to examine the bodies. Only when they did so would the women lookouts signal from the heights.

All this time Pigeon's men would be hidden away back down in the river, where the creek mouth emptied into it. At the signal they would pour noiselessly up along the bottom of the steeply banked creek until opposite the body of Gibbs. Swiftly they would congregate there, then swarm up the bank and open fire and hurl spears at close range upon the startled patrol. Men would fall, the horses would break away leaving any survivors at their mercy. And that would be the end of the patrol.

And probably it would have been so, had not Fred Edgar won that race against Pigeon. For had he been killed then Authority in Derby would have been unaware of the killing of Burke and Gibbs. The patrol then outfitting to ride out along the track to investigate the murder of Constable Richardson would have ridden upon unexpected tragedy and into an utterly unexpected, expertly arranged and overwhelming ambush.

Few folk would expect such clever tactics from the Australian aboriginal. But the Kimberley natives were probably the pick of the aboriginal tribes, while Pigeon on many an occasion was to prove that he had brains and could use them.

When Fred Edgar escaped to Lukin's station horseflesh was not spared in relaying the news to Derby. Just as the patrol ordered to investigate the killing of Constable Richardson was ready to ride out Sub-Inspector Drewry heard to his dismay of the killing of Burke and Gibbs. It would require more than an ordinary patrol to cope with this situation. Drewry got busy.

Meanwhile, Pigeon set Captain training his few riflemen to shoot. Both Pigeon and Captain knew that a good rifle shot amongst natives was a rarity, especially at long range. They expected most of the shooting to be at close quarters but even so a man must know how to shoot straight. For the next few days the cliffs echoed to steady, methodical rifle practice.

Yes, indeed, as Superintendents of Police, the Resident Magistrate, and settlers grimly admitted in the months to come, if Pigeon had had only a little more time to organize and train the willing material available, then the position of the few scattered settlers throughout the Kimberleys would have been serious indeed.

More than a week later a police posse with mixed feelings examined a tree almost cut in half by bullets. Examined jam tin targets looted from Edgar's wagon, bullet-pierced targets on rocks and trees. Yes, Pigeon, and all the gang under direction, were earnestly busy. And with the wiping out of the police patrol they would gain yet more rifles, revolvers, and ammunition. At least six to eight more of the gang could be given firearms, while yet more warriors who could handle guns would hurry to join them. Growing stronger and stronger they would be able to attack station after station. Which was perfectly logical tactics, clearly thought out by an aboriginal. The one thing missing for success was sufficient time.

16

THE PATROLS RIDE OUT

THE killing of Constable Richardson, followed so soon by the killing of Burke and Gibbs, and Pigeon's threats of wiping out the stations, then attacking Derby itself, were all startling news in the Kimberleys.

The threat alarmed authority in the distant south also. In reply to W. G. Wharton, the Resident Magistrate, Premier Forrest wired: "Hope you will use every means to deal with the murderers. Expense must not be considered. It is the desire of the Government to act with promptness and decision."

Big John Forrest, now Premier of the great but scantily populated State, knew well what trouble armed police boys on the warpath could bring to the scattered settlers of the distant, dangerously isolated Kimberleys. It was his own brother Alexander who in his exploring expedition in 1879 had tried for six weeks to penetrate through the King Leopold Ranges, and failed. While Big John himself only ten years before had partly surveyed the Fitzroy inland from Derby. So he well understood the difficulties of the country and the plight of the isolated settlers if the numerous natives, well led, really attempted serious trouble.

Drewry in Derby enrolled Felix Edgar (brother of Fred), James Price, Alf Barnett, Jimmy Black, Felisse, and other settlers as special constables. (More were later needed.) He wired to Constable Pilrner at the Fitzroy Crossing Telegraph Station to ride west and join him at Lillamaloora. Then he started from Derby with the main patrol, soon joined by Corporal Cadden's Lennard River patrol. Cadden's patrol comprised four whites and six trackers, the latter very much on edge at the imminent chance of a clash with the now dreaded Pigeon and his growing gang.

Meanwhile, two hundred and ten miles inland at Fitzroy Crossing, Constables Pilmer, McDermott and their trackers, busy at the framework of the new police station, looked up as a black runner came racing towards them from the wee telegraph station across the river. In a cleft stick the runner held was gripped a telegram.

"Milli-milli, boss!" he gasped and held out the stick. Pilmer opened the telegram.

"Richardson, Burke and Gibbs murdered by natives at Lillamaloora. Bring firearms, ammunition .and all trackers you can spare from Fitzroy. Main party leaving for scene of murder. Drewry."

Pilmer was in the saddle within a few hours with tracker Big Ned.

Through bush of good grass and mulga country they rode straight for Lillamaloora.

Drewry rode out of Derby travelling roughly east, passing Kimberley Downs station en route for Lukin's Lennard River station about twenty miles above Kimberley Downs, in the foothills country parallel to the Lennard and Fitzroy plains. At Lennard River homestead he was greeted by a very relieved Lukin.

"I thought you were never coming," he growled. "It's a wonder you didn't find me and the station gone up in smoke."

"You're quite all right," answered Drewry shortly.

"Yes, I know. But I *don't* know who or what I've got to thank for *that*. I've been expecting Pigeon's gang to attack any hour of the day and night. What's' held them back, beats me."

"They've cleared out back into the Leopolds long ago," said Drewry confidently.

"Not on your life they haven't," declared Lukin, "or my boys. would have heard of it. They're scared stiff."

"We'll soon know anyway," replied Drewry.

"Just as well," grumbled Lukin. "I'm a sitting shot for every cattle-spearer along the Lennard as it is. And now that your own police boys have gone bush and taught them how to use rifles my life and the station isn't worth half a carcass of salt beef."

"You'd make pretty tough salt beef," laughed Jack Hamilton. "Even Pigeon couldn't get his teeth through your hide," grinned Jimmy Spong.

"Laugh," growled Lukin, "but you wouldn't laugh if you felt Pigeon's knife cutting out your kidney fat and be forced to watch him wolf it before your eyes. Anyway I'm joining you with two of my best boys - your crowd would never catch Pigeon without me."

There was the bustle then of horses and packs being unloaded and unsaddled, excited station boys lending a hand with the grim faced trackers, the station lubras and piccaninnies all eyes, stamping of heavy boots on the roughly timbered veranda and kitchen, laughter and jokes, thumping of swags and packs and saddles with tinkle of hobble chains and bells thrown on the rough-hewn boards. Never had Lennard River station expected to see a "mob" like this as guests.

It was after the evening meal when, pipes alight, they were lounging on the veranda that Drewry began to muse on the probable whereabouts of Pigeon, and the chances of capturing him and Captain and their mob. Which gave Lukin his chance to be humorous again.

"We're the devil's number!" he remarked and puffed his pipe.

They glanced around meditatively. There were thirteen white men present in the combined patrols.

"What the blazes are you hinting at now?" demanded Drewry.

"Nothing," grinned Lukin, "only we're the devil's number. And Pigeon is up to devilish work. And you're going to have a devilish job catching him."

Which led to an exasperated reply from Drewry and to jokes and laughter until they rolled in their blankets and turned in for the night.

Next morning the patrol rode east through bush among a line of short, particularly rugged little ranges running from the coast eastwards right to The Crossing two hundred and ten miles inland - the Napier, Lennard, Barker, Oscar and Geikie ranges.

Drewry cautiously neared his objective on the evening of the fourth day out from Derby, arriving at Lillamaloora at dawn only to find that the hard riding Pilmer had arrived by moonlight the evening before.

They buried poor Richardson, then sat down for conference - Sub-Inspector Drewry, Corporal Cadden, Constables Buckland, Pilmer, Jimmy Spong, Jack Hamilton, with specials Will Lukin, Felix Edgar, Billy Chalmers, Alf Barnett and several others.

An especially welcome recruit was Alf Barnett. Not only did he bring important news that Pigeon's gang was still believed to be in the Wingina Gorge, but Drewry had been anxious about this quiet little settler's safety. He had started a place at Mt Barnett by the Hann River away behind the eastern limits of the Leopolds, in extreme isolation. If Pigeon's threats to wipe out the whites were in earnest then Barnett by the Hann, Joe Blythe and son Charlie at Brooking Creek, Charlie and Willie Collins by the Oscar Range, and the MacDonald brothers on the Margaret were expected to be the first to go.

Drewry led his patrol among the foothills well clear of the Barrier Range, then camped to tryout a little scheme. For the trackers too had now received a "whisper" that Pigeon was in the Wingina Gorge, the message "sent" by an old tribesman named Cadwarry, who swore Pigeon had stolen his daughter Cangamvara.

Drewry persuaded six of Barnett's most trusted boys to attempt a deed of derring-do among Pigeon and his gang. If they succeeded their deed would be "sung" throughout the Kimberleys. Besides which, the promised rewards from settlers and Government produced grunts of eager acceptance.

17

ELLEMARA THE CUNNING

THESE six were warriors, and events proved them worthy of the title. They were to dress up in full war regalia and locate Pigeon, to capture him or put him out of action, and Captain and Ellemara too if possible. Failing this, they were to assure him they had killed Barnett and had come to help him kill more white men. Then await their chance at night, suddenly seize all the firearms they could, smash them on the rocks and escape.

With the plan carefully assimilated and rehearsed, the six warriors eagerly left camp to attempt the ruse. They were not envied by the dubious trackers.

If the six could only cripple Pigeon and Captain, explained Drewry to the patrol, his influence would be broken at the outset and lives on both sides would be saved.

The six warriors stepped out towards the bluff ramparts of the Barrier Range. They were feeling lonely now, on a desperate mission drawing them farther and farther away towards the dangerous "Pigeon country". It had felt different back there among that big, encouraging patrol, more police and white men grouped together than they had ever seen before, more men and guns and horses and trackers than they had ever imagined. But now, with every step they were leaving all this authority and armed friendship behind.

But gamely they carried on.

Within twenty-four hours they had definitely located Pigeon.

Chests proudly out as needs be for warriors who had allegedly killed a white man, they were walking down Wingina Gorge not feeling nearly so martial as they looked. Yet they were already heroes, yelled to in shrill tones by Pigeon's women scouts from the heights as they passed down below. Now and then they passed a group of armed warriors squatting by the water's edge, or lazing on the warmth of boulders long since fallen from the cliffs; silent warriors whose fierce, black eyes watched them unwaveringly. And there was guttural, questioning talk when they had passed by. Ominously plain was the fact that they would have no hope of encountering Pigeon and Captain alone.

By native etiquette, they could not greet these groups yet. They must first state their business, not in this case to the Council of the Old Men, but to the dreaded Sandamara whom the white men called Pigeon.

They found the gang down by the big waterhole, now very beautiful with its shadowed reflections of cliffs and trees, clean and white the warm sandbanks, a carpet of green the grasses by the water's edge and growing up between the slabs of grey, fallen rock. Pigeon was sitting quietly there, a rifle across his knees, two bandoliers slung criss-cross over his naked chest, a cartridge belt around his waist, and a lurking devil in his eyes. Captain was there too. A powerful six footer this Captain, overbearingly confident now with sinewy hand warm on his Schneider and longing to use it, even though very willing to welcome killers of white men. Ellemara was standing up, all six feet of brawny chocolate-black of him, naked and painted in warrior design, his war spears handy upon the rock beside him. But his sinewy hands held Richardson's double-barrelled breech-loading gun, a full bandolier was around shoulder and chest and in his cartridge belt a hunting knife looted from Edgar's wagon.

The six feared the expression in Pigeon's eyes though they gazed steadfastly at him. Mullenbuddin, whose spear stroke right through Burke's body was still acclaimed, squatted there grinning, his bushy black beard gaily threaded with scarlet, blue and yellow berries by an admiring young lubra. Carolan of the queer eyes was there, and Muckerawarra squatting beside Tilbomer. Byerbell and Fouringer with Teebuck and Tumanurumberry were gracefully doing nothing under the shade of a beautiful Leichhardt tree an easy spear throwaway. Luter, Putter, Tye-mering and Laweraway were squatting there fashioning one of Edgar's bullock-chain links into an iron spearhead. Wongamarra and Foe and Bundermen were nearby. And Lillimarra, his hand loosely on his Winchester and a look on his keen face as if he'd like to use it. There were other groups too, shaggy heads here and there amongst the rocks and bushes. Noted cattle-spearers and native killers all who had come seeking to join Pigeon's gang during these last few days.

For quite a time, a nervy time, there was silence as the six stood there gazing at Pigeon's cold eyes. For it was aboriginal etiquette that they must await the leader's pleasure to state their business. The only sounds were the sweet calls of birds, hum of insects in the humid November air and from away down the gorge a sally of childish laughter from piccaninnies down river playing at spearing fish.

Pigeon lifted his rifle to the crook of his arm, turned the muzzle towards the obvious spokesman.

"Speak!" he said coldly.

Unhurriedly they told how they had taken the white man Barnett by surprise and killed him, then burned his hut. That they had now come to join Pigeon and his killers and help them wipe out the white men.

Pigeon asked a few questions, which were unhesitatingly and convincingly answered.

Broad grins, guttural words of praise and pleasure came from the gang. Here was first clear proof that independent tribes, once encouraged by example, would rally round to kill white men in their own tribal country.

Ellemara the Cunning, Ellemara whom, so the tribesmen swore "carried devils in his eyes", Ellemara the Killer, lifted his double-barrelled gun to his shoulder, clicked back both hammers.

"Liars!" he snarled. "I'm going to blow your guts to the blowflies. You have killed no white man! You yellow-livered sons of dingoes! You would not have the guts to kill a crippled man unless you all fell upon him in his sleep. Liars and sons of liars!"

In the dead silence the six realized that Ellemara had seen through and through them. He had almost, but not quite. Perhaps it was through his queer gift that he had instinctively realized these men were liars. Or was he just trying a clever bluff?

Pigeon saw that Ellemara was right.

"Go!" he snarled, "go quickly and this time kill Barnett! Or we will track you down like dogs and kill you!"

Without a word the six men started back the way they had come. Every step must have seemed an eternity while they could feel those savage, vengeful glares, those deadly weapons at their backs.

It was extraordinary, the iron control Pigeon exerted upon himself and the ascendency he had gained in such a short time over this gang of ruthless fighters, now in a trembling fury to kill the six.

"Not now!" snarled Pigeon. 'When we have got all the tribes working on our side, then we will cut dogs like these to pieces. But not just yet."

But one thing neither Ellemara nor Pigeon dreamed of was that these six men were actually working for the police. Had they even guessed, they would have cruelly killed them. In the native vendettas that were soon to sweep the ranges two of the six were to be tracked down and pay with their lives.

The six were game, and for the time being anyway, very fortunate men.

18

RIFLE SHOTS IN THE DAWN

WHEN the abashed six returned to Drewry he sent his two most trusted scouts, in their war paint, to mingle with the bush aboriginals daily drifting in to Pigeon's camp. They were to locate exactly where Pigeon's own gang camped by night, then report back to Drewry who would meet them at the mouth of the Wingina Gorge on an agreed upon night. Cheerfully the scouts set out upon their hazardous job, even though it was night time which to the aboriginal is alive with spirits.

Drewry watched them go with anxious brow. The scouts, however, were experts and would find ample cover in the wild Wingina Gorge.

Throughout ages the Lennard River has churned this gorge through the Napier Range, the wet season floods pouring in torrents between hills and cliffs. During the dry season the river is quiet, the deep Wingina Pool peaceful and crystal clear, a lovely though savage scene hemmed in by the grey limestone precipices of the Napier Range. Elsewhere the range is turreted in castles, battlements, spires and pinnacles and grotesque shapes of weather-beaten limestone gashed by deep crevasses, pock-marked with blowholes and twisted pits.

Drewry rode the twenty miles by night to manoeuvre around to the north side of the gorge, while Cadden's patrol branched off to reach the southern end before break of day. The Queensland police boys with some of the Kimberley trackers were to climb the east side of the Barrier Range then down into the gorge by the only path believed possible. The plan was for the co-operating patrols to block all exit from the gorge, then creep along the big waterhole and hem in Pigeon's camp. Then, if the natives rushed to escape by the "goat" track up the cliffs, they would find trackers waiting for them on top.

But Pigeon was to prove far too cunning a leader to camp in any locality where, if surrounded, there was not an outlet of escape. The cards were slowly stacking against him though. Instead of the four or five rifles which he expected to ambush and wipe out he was to be surprised by three combined patrols. And surprised yet again for, by night marching, Drewry made his day lookouts useless.

Towards that sundown, Pigeon's lookouts withdrew and went chattering about their own business of the evening meal, scattering down along the gorge or along the river, or back down the other side of the range to rejoin family or tribal groups for the night.

Tomorrow they would return to their lookouts when Pigeon's gang and the warrior tribesmen again strolled back to their ambush positions, the remainder to their hunting, all eager for the new day to bring sign of the expected patrol. But now there was the sundown meal to be cooked to the exciting news of the day's hunt, followed by gossip around the widely scattered campfires, then sleep.

In warm weather the aboriginal sleeps deeply; particularly so towards dawn. They did not dream of patrols coming riding through the night.

In the dead of night, when nearing the gorge, Drewry's patrol halted, quietly dismounted. The horses were to be taken back a few miles under guard, for shod hooves on the rocky floor of a gorge make sparks and noise. Drewry's men took off their heavy Cossack boots, wrapped bagging and cloths around their feet, then walked quietly on. No man spoke unless necessary, then only in low tones.

It was slow, rough going in the starlight, over the rocks and grass winding amongst the timber-shadow men in the night. At long last, there was the black mouth of the gorge.

And then two blacker shadows joined Drewry. The scouts! They had located Pigeon's- own camp on a sandspit by the waterhole, just outside a few caves that opened out at the base of the cliffs.

Well pleased, Drewry pushed on. If he could pin Pigeon within those caves then Pigeon was his. It seemed all to depend now upon the timing and caution of Cadden's patrol, and of the co-ordinated movement of the Queensland blackboys.

It was 3.30 when Drewry's patrol crept very close to the hide-out. The scouts urged "halt". They waited, listening, staring towards the black cliffs with the gleam of still water below. Presently there was a guttural yawn, a grunt, then another. Several of Pigeon's men were stirring in their sleep across there on the sandbank by the base of the cliff.

In chill silence they waited, until at last appeared the first cold gleam of dawn. Drewry and Felix Edgar crept forward, believing they could see more clearly across the sky-reflected water-light than from back among the black rocks. High above, the cliff rim appearing in silhouette against the gathering dawn was suddenly made vivid by spurting flame as two shots rang out. Vague shadows leapt up across the water-vanished.

Pigeon's men had taken to the caves.

As the reports echoed along the gorge Drewry and Edgar crouched close together, peering across, trying to distinguish the cave mouths. There was a stab of flame as a bullet whistled between their heads.

Pigeon had missed a shot that might have made such a difference. Cursing, he fired again at where those two shadowy heads had been. As the light grew stronger came a fusillade from the caves, then snappy reply from the ridge behind the hidden patrol - it was the Queensland boys arriving right on time. Drewry's men fired rapidly at the caves to harass Pigeon's marksmen while the Queenslanders and trackers clambered down into the gorge. The light was still very bad, the police boys very quick, Pigeon's men very excited. Had they shot steadily at this stage they must have caused casualties instead of merely wounding one man.

The patrol, now rapidly strengthening, kept their heads well down, crouching amongst the rocks and trees which gave plentiful cover. The whites were astounded at the rapidity of fire from Pigeon's men, the whining of lead ricochetting off rocks, the soft pattering of falling leaves and twigs cut by bullets and shot, joined by the thunder of Ellemara's double-barrelled gun and the spattering whine of the pellets whenever he saw movement amongst timber or grass.

Ellemara, safe in his little cave hugging his big gun and ammunition, began to enjoy himself - for a time. That is, after he'd become partly used to the noise of this terrifying experience and remembered it was not the noise that could hurt him, though never in his life had he heard such a noise apart from a violent thunderstorm. And presently he became partly used to the constant, vicious smacks of bullets flattening on the cliff face, the comforting, throaty bark of Captain's 4.7 Schneider echoing above the sharp reports of the Winchesters. Warily he squinted from his little "dog-hole", eager for a shot. His quick eyes saw the crown of a hat cautiously creeping up behind a thick tuft of grass growing between two slabs of fallen rock. With a joyous leer Ellemara lifted his gun. He would wait until - now!

As the gunshot roared out the hat was blown sky high but Ellemara also saw the smashed stick flying from under it. It had been Alf Barnett's prized hat, slowly poked up on a stick to test whether he were under observation. He knew now. Chuckling humorously he began cautiously to crawl back into safer cover. Ellemara cursed bitterly at the trickery of white men, scowling heart-felt disappointment. He squinted out seeking another target when a bullet whistled past his ear to spatter in fragments along the cave walls. He nearly dislocated his neck pulling his head in. With thumping heart he crouched low, not enjoying himself quite so much. He lay low for quite a time, while early morn stole in beauty down into the gorge.

Ellemara was just beginning to believe that that bullet must have been a fluke. He thought he might risk peering out for a target again and did so as another bullet whistled in and spattered screeching fragments of lead all along the cave wall. Ellemara felt seriously alarmed; a white man would have expressed the sensation as "butterflies in the stomach"

The sunlight was bright outside now, the firing and thus the 'danger steadily increasing. More and more bullets would come flying into this little cave; he must inevitably be hit. Not so much perhaps by a bullet as by the screeching fragments that split on impact against the rock wall. This was only a dog-hole that he had tumbled into in his sleep-dulled urgency, whereas the dog-holes into which Pigeon and the gang had bounded close by had small passages that led into much larger caves and greatly added safety. With, above all, a getaway!

Ellemara's eyes blazed. What a fool he had been to jump into this trap half asleep on that first alarm! He knew what Drewry did not know, that from Pigeon's cave a tortuous passage led back towards the heart of the hill. And from there a network of passages led upward to end in a little dog-hole right up on top of the range. What a clever devil this Pigeon was after all! What fools the police and white men were to think they could trap him! But what a fool Ellemara was, to jump into this death trap!

Another bullet screeched into the cave and Ellemara leaped out from the dog-hole and was bounding for Pigeon's cave only yards away. It was sheerest bad luck for Ellemara that a distant marksman was sighting towards Pigeon's cave when he half saw the bounding figure and fired. Ellemara plunged convulsively into Pigeon's cave as the wire cartridge smashed into his back. A terrible missile. It had been fired from long range otherwise Ellemara would have fallen into the cave with his back blown away. As it was he lay groaning there in a dreadful mess and the sight of his bloody back did not help the morale of the tight-lipped men crouched within the cave.

A wire cartridge then was generally heavy shot or slugs bound tightly into a solid charge with thin lead foil, the lead foil wrapping used around the packets of tea. To be yet more effective and make the missile cling solidly together for as long a range as possible the shot pellets would first be rubbed with thick soap, then tightly bedded together by squeezing with the hands, then the solid mass of shot was bound around with the lead foil. Around all was wound and bound thin, cotton-like wire, the whole compressed to fit cartridge or gun barrel.

Such a "wire cartridge" would carry considerably farther than a charge of shot, before it disintegrated and spread out with range. Should it hit anything before it "burst" it made an awful mess of the object hit.

All the fight, all the forcible seizing of lubras, all the killing of aboriginal or anyone else, all the spearing of cattle, all the joy of being a greatly feared man, everything, except a determined spark of wonderful life was knocked out of Ellemara for months to come. The fact that he lived was an amazing tribute to the virility of the bush aboriginal.

19

THE FIGHT IN WINGINA GORGE

As morning drew on, the firing grew steadier. In the first ten hectic minutes both sides learned quickly. The whites realized that if they did not take every advantage of the plentiful cover some would be killed; they learned that a few determined aboriginals armed with firearms and sheltered in caves were a very different proposition to spearmen out in the open bush. While Pigeon's men learned that it was not as easy to kill armed white men born to the ways of the bush as to kill men when they slept, or innocently walked into an ambush. Yes, shooting these expertly sheltered bushmen was different indeed to shooting or spearing a lone horseman riding out in the open.

The police boys engaged took every care not to expose themselves, though delighting in the use of firearms which, incidentally, they could not use any better than Pigeon's men.

Drewry wished to avoid all possible loss of life. His orders were to keep under cover yet fire steadily at any target offering. That, and to keep the gang hemmed within the caves until they surrendered.

That they did not surrender caused him growing concern as the day wore on.

Meanwhile, in awed groups, for miles along the range were natives listening to the sounds of the fight. This was not the ambush they had so exultantly prepared for, while all these men and horses were far more than they had expected. And now they were isolated from Pigeon. They could only squat and listen.

These groups and many others, as Pigeon later explained, were the men he would have used to outflank patrols, also to attack their horses in similar fights. But he had not had time to train them. Also, in this fight the night march had taken him by surprise and with his groups well scattered.

In growing belief that the fight might develop into a siege, Drewry and Constable Brice from Cadden's party snaked their way around to the police boys to encourage them and work them into a better position, also to make arrangements for the bringing up of cooked food and water. Drewry also sent Special Constable Price away to bring up the horses, an all-round trip of eighteen miles. Drewry then directed steady firing into the mouths of the five caves - not the easiest of targets when his men must care for their own heads, for the cave mouths were but small, and low down at the base of the cliffs. As he wrote later in his report to the Commissioner in Perth: "They

[Pigeon's men] were at a spot where it was almost impossible to hit them. There were flat rocks in front of the passages and the ground sloped inside so that a great many shots only hit the sloping roof."

Drewry hoped that in time some of the ricochetting lead must find victims within the enclosed spaces, and that is what happened.

Pigeon, crouched back in the gloom of the main cave, was taking the brunt of it, fighting like a veterans in the face of heavy rifle fire. The vicious spattering of bullets on the cliff face, the far worse hiss and metallic wail as bullets zipped into the cave itself and splashed in pieces from wall to wall, would have daunted many a white man. But Pigeon kept firing, risking his life again and again in striving to glimpse some living target amongst that confusion of rocks and water, sandbanks and trees and grasses outside. And Pigeon had soon learned of a fact he had overlooked when choosing this almost perfect hideout.

The cave mouth was small, and right down by the base of the cliff. Pigeon and his men could see only a few yards' width of irregular outline of boulders and bank and grasses to their immediate front. Yet spread across that front for two hundred yards and more were men now directing their fire at the mouths of the five little caves. True, each enemy could only partly see indistinct, dark little openings shadowed by the dull grey walls and bushes. And of Pigeon's cave most could only see the edge of the sloping roof. But all could see some portion of a cave mouth. More and more their bullets were beginning to whizz in. And they were all firing from different angles.

Those bullets coming from directly in front hit the roof of a cave and splashed downward. Those coming from the right flank would hit the left wall and splash. Those whizzing in from the left flank would hit the right wall and flatten or smash and whine in fragments to the left. So that Pigeon's men crouching back in the narrow cave must inevitably be hit sooner or later. This increasingly accurate fire had another bad effect also on Pigeon's inefficient marksmen. For no matter how they sheltered, should they peer for sight of an enemy target bullets would whizz past their faces or spatter the wall beside them. Few men can coolly seek a hidden target when lead is flying past the face like that. But Pigeon stuck to his guns throughout.

The whites in the patrols, when describing that fight, were grimly enthusiastic about the gameness of Pigeon that day. Sub-Inspector Drewry in his long report of the affair to the Commissioner of Police in Perth wrote: "I am of the opinion now that there were not more than nine men and their gins in the gorge this day. Captain did not show himself. Pigeon was the only really plucky one; other natives were in other parts of the ranges."

The sub-inspector may have been unintentionally unfair to Captain. For Captain was certainly doing his part in the shooting, as survivors of the patrols describe in referring to the constant bark of his Schneider. Ellemara had fought until twice wounded, for it was found afterwards that as well as the wound in his back he had a revolver bullet in his shoulder; while several of the settlers enlisted as specials particularly noted Lillimarra taking risks from time to time in seeking a target.

If there were only nine men within the caves (it was proved eventually there were more), then each must have done his bit. For in his own report the sub-inspector states: "The murderers kept up a more rapid fire in ratio than my party" - a remarkable statement with which those settlers present fully agreed. If there were only nine of the gang then the combined patrols considerably outnumbered them for Corporal Cadden's patrol alone was of ten men including his trackers, while Lukin had referred to the thirteen whites who camped that night at his station, exclusive of their trackers. So that for nine aboriginals to outfire that combined volume of fire was not only a remarkable effort, but proof that each one of Pigeon's men must have been doing his uttermost.

The fire of the patrols from the very start was by no means slow. The sub-inspector's report reads: "At break of day the Queensland boys skirmished up to top of opposite side to ours and Pigeon began firing. I kept up a very quick fire to allow the Queenslanders to get down into the gorge which they did, passing within 70 yards of Pigeon's rifle and lining out."

Taking into consideration the fact that the fight lasted from break of dawn until just after two o'clock in the afternoon, then the few of Pigeon's gang who were cornered must have put up a remarkable fight.

As the morning wore on, Ellemara recovered sufficiently to begin to crawl back along the dark passage leading in under the range. He was helped by a lad, and by Wondaria, his Laughing Waters, who was to stick to him through thick and thin. Sorely wounded indeed, it was to mean a long, painful crawl for the groaning Ellemara, and a long, tortuous climb upward, his clawing hands sticky from blood. He would not be pulled moaning to the range top until starlight bathed the range that night.

Soon after Ellemara had crawled away Lucullia reeled back with a strangled grunt. From startled eyes he stared into nothingness a moment then sank back with a gurgling cough. Lucullia was sorely wounded indeed. After a time, a frightened lubra and a boy began to help him, too, back along the gloomy, narrow passage.

"Pitt!", "Pitt!", "Pitt!", "Pitt!" as the bullets flattened on the cliff face. "Hisss!" as one whizzed into the cave and tore into fragments along the walls. "Hisss!", "Hisss!", "Hisss!" as three at once fluted in, to a startled exclamation from Lillimarra, who reeled back in shocked surprise. The others glanced around to stare as he crouched in questioning alarm on the cave floor. Slowly, straight across his black forehead, appeared a thin red line. It swelled, then a film of scarlet dye began draining down to his eyes. A splinter of lead had cut straight across his forehead like a knife slash, neatly slicing the flesh to the bone.

Lillimarra now would have a new warrior weal of which he would become very proud. Far more admired it would be by the young girls than any warrior's weal cut by a stone knife.

Lillimarra soon recovered. With a broad, relieved grin he pawed the blood from his eyes, then crept very cautiously back towards the cave entrance, a glint in his eye showing intense eagerness to get even one shot at a visible target "Pitt!", "Pitt!", "Pitt!", smacked the bullets and "Hisss!", "Hisss!" those screeching into the cave.

It was midday when to a sound like a hammer blow Pigeon was knocked back into the cave. A bullet had thudded through his shoulder and ploughed out under the lower breastbone, carrying away flesh from his back - a shocking wound.

He recovered sufficiently within ten minutes to come crawling doggedly back towards the cave entrance. With ashen fury on his face he commenced worming himself into a position so that he could still use his rifle. Again then the gleaming eyes of his gang peered out across the cave entrance. Pigeon's action showed them the fight must be carried on.

He had gained a miraculous influence over his men in a very short time to keep them fighting under such conditions, unparalleled to the best of my knowledge in the annals of the white man and the Australian aboriginal. Sorely wounded too by now, he could have retired with ease. For he had only to grunt and they all would have been crawling back down the passage and into the safety of caverns into which neither white man or black would have been foolhardy enough to follow. They would then at leisure have climbed up through the blowholes and out into the open air and sunshine, far from the patrol down the gorge.

But Pigeon fought on.

20

RETREAT IN THE CAVES

PIGEON fought doggedly on, disappointed every moment that the caves were not rushed. For he had a few spearmen hidden waiting behind him. In a concerted rush on those narrow little openings the attackers must then inevitably be cut up by bullet, shot, and spear. But the long expected rush did not come. Instead, there was a groaning, then an agitated slithering from a passage overhead. And Pigeon's men knew that yet another one of them was crawling away, or being dragged back by the women.

And still the expected rush did not come.

Mullenbuddin looked so comical that Captain indulged in a grim joke: "He would make a saddlecloth for old man Burke." The others chuckled while Mullenbuddin grinned his appreciation. For when his spear had gone through Burke the saddle-cloth and horse's mane were splashed red with blood. And there was Mullenbuddin crouching with his thick lips grinning and big black eyes gleaming at the joke, his bushy black beard dyed scarlet as the mane of Burke's horse. But Mullenbuddin was not hurt at all, it was merely that three times now a splash of flying lead had flicked across his big face and slashed it like a razor.

Mullenbuddin grinned yet more broadly, at which Lillimarra chuckled: "We'd be safe in that cave. And see! the drip from the roof!"

They laughed uproariously at the simple joke. For Mullenbuddin's huge mouth was a cavern indeed when he grinned like that, and a drop of blood had dripped down into it, just like the drip of water from the cavern roof.

It was an hour later that Pigeon shivered convulsively and his rifle clattered to the cave floor. He had been hit again. He lay there awhile, his hand clutching his side which was dyed red, a questioning stare in his eyes. Then he nodded to Captain to hand him up his rifle. He tried to use it again but couldn't.

After awhile, he tried again. Only then, in dumb despair, did he jerk up his chin.

Immediately then his men were crouching away back into the cave. A frightened stealthiness was in their retreat as if they were creeping up in the open, sunlit bush, instead of away down here safe in the bowels of the earth. The only sounds were whisperings through the gloom and the distinct drip of a water drop swallowed by silence. Through the grey ghostliness of limestone, the coolness, they crept; on into deeper blackness; to places where a man might bump his head, other places where empty blackness went up to unknown height. Outstretched feet probed uncertainly for an invisible pit in the floor. The faint splash of some subterranean stream could be heard in the distant darkness as they crept along tortuous passages through which a river once ran, frightened eyes gleaming, the odour of naked bodies and the chill of dark water underfoot. A spear scraped against the wall, the dull thunder of rifle fire echoed far away behind, a man moaned, crawling away into the dark to die, a lubra whimpered. The heavily breathing, unseen bodies groped their way like stricken bats, with hoarse whispers, and an animal snarl from Pigeon as with bloodied hands he felt his stumbling way along the limestone walls.

It was about two o'clock in the afternoon when Drewry managed to get cooked food and water up to his men, who had been crouched in their firing positions since dawn. It was shortly afterwards that an excited yell came from the Queensland boys:

"Pigeon him dead!" As if this was the signal for the rush all hands leapt up and were racing for the caves. As whites and trackers closed in near the entrances black arms shot up and clawed ankles, bringing men in startled confusion to the ground, especially the trackers and police boys, several of whom lay stunned amongst the rocks. Amid startled oaths, hysterical screamings, wild scufflings and isolated shots the others flung themselves at the cave mouths.

Those clawing arms snatching up from the grass were lubras, hidden there by Pigeon no one knew how or when. Game were those women and girls; two paid for it with their lives. What unexpected confusion there would have been, and what lives Pigeon and his gang would have taken had all his men been there, or even had Drewry rushed the caves early in the fray.

The patrol found the caves abandoned. It was not until all the excitement was over that someone suddenly asked, "Who shouted out that Pigeon was dead? And why? Even if he was dead, no one could have seen him dead in the cave!"

There was no answer to the question. Several of the Queensland boys had shouted out, "Pigeon him dead!" Sheepishly they explained: "We shout out because we hear him 'nother feller man shout out, 'Pigeon him dead!'" The mystery remained unanswered for months, until several of the gang were captured. The answer was that Pigeon had sent a tribesman to crawl out unseen among the women hidden waiting in the grass. This man was to worm his way near the nearest trackers and shout out, "Pigeon him dead!"

Pigeon hoped this would result in the rush he had prepared for. And it had. But the man, who may have been confused as to the timing, had lain there two hours before he shouted out. And that was just after Pigeon had commenced the retirement.

Cautiously the disappointed patrol examined the cave entrances.

Sub-Inspector Drewry's report to the Commissioner in Perth states: Where Pigeon stood there was a lot of blood on the ground and blood all round where he was leaning when he supported himself with his hands when getting away; the marks of his hands in blood showing. One gin stated he had been holding his wound to stop the bleeding. We recovered a Winchester rifle and one muzzle-loading gun and one box of Winchester ammunition unused lying on a ledge where he was firing from. There was a lot more blood in a passage above this one where one of the other natives got shot. Price and myself thought we had some of them in a cave but on fetching them out they were only six gins and three children. Farther on we recovered a further 150 Winchester bullets, 3 tins of gunpowder, a quantity of shot, tomahawk, billy-cans, adze, clothes, blankets, police pistol and holster, 2 cartridge belts, tins of dried potatoes, 3 half chests of tea, 3 half sacks of flour, tobacco, matches, Gibbs' watch (going), bullet moulds and reloading apparatus, three handcuff keys, and other articles.

As far as I can find out (from the gins) Pigeon was shot through the shoulder blade, coming out near the lower breast-bone and underarm, carrying away the flesh over the other shoulder blade. And probably shot through left shoulder in front with a revolver. The last shot the gins did not see. Ellemara got a wire cartridge over the whole of his back, but I am afraid at too long a range, and a bullet through the shoulder blade that the gins state did not come out.

Meanwhile, while searching the caves which outwardly appeared like little dog-holes under the cliffs, but opened out to much larger caves behind, Felix Edgar, Alf Barnett and their blackboys found neatly stacked on a great shelf of rock a ton of flour and large quantities of foodstuffs, ammunition and tobacco, all loot from the Edgar brothers' wagon.

"It's a crumb left from the wreck," growled Felix. "I'll take it away right now."

"Leave it until tomorrow," suggested Drewry. "It's getting late and we've plenty to do before sundown. Just take the ammunition and tobacco; the blackboys can bring the rest out tomorrow morning. There won't be a nigger within miles of this place now.

At dawn next morning Felix Edgar and Barnett strolled across to the cliffs to start their boys bringing out the flour and goods.

"Crack!" "Crack!"

There was a spurt of flame from the cliff top while Edgar and Barnett leapt for cover, as did the startled patrol having breakfast by the river. A few more shots, then as dawn brightened all became quiet. The natives had disappeared.

So too had that ton of flour and every scrap of the foodstuffs.

A contemporary view of the attack on Lillamaloora police station, on Nov 3 1894.

21

ELLEMARA SCHEMES, FIGHTS FOR LIFE

DREWRY, though bitterly disappointed at not capturing Pigeon's men when it appeared he had them hopelessly trapped, consoled himself with the captives' definite statement that Pigeon was dead. And they believed Ellemara would die also. They maintained a sullen silence as to others. As Drewry wrote in his report: "There is great difficulty in getting any of these natives to mention the dead by name, it being against their customs to do so."

Drewry divided his men into three patrols with orders to ride swiftly northward, cut the tracks of Captain's men and hunt them to earth before they could reach the Leopolds. A stiff order, considering this wild country and the perfect bushcraft, speed and almost tireless endurance of the bush aboriginal when alert and hard pressed.

Two patrols hurried out to ride the negotiable country along the Oscar, Barrier, Lennard, and Napier ranges, while Cadden rode west to the Barker River, thence to Wambarella Creek, to block a pass which led through to the Leopolds.

Cadden's patrol rapidly travelled two hundred and eighty-six miles, thirty of which they had to walk, before reporting back that they had seen no natives. But plenty had seen them, among whom were Captain, Ellemara, Lillimarra, Carolan, Tickbuck, Frankey, Langeroo, Wongamarra, Langooradale, Lucullia, Mullenbuddin, Canada, Demon, and others of the gang. A dangerous combination, for four were ex-police boys, still armed, though they had now lost their big reserve of ammunition. They wished to fire on Cadden's patrol but Ellemara dissuaded them, forced to use all his sinister influence, coughing blood as he was, racked with pain, bent almost double, clinging to his two friends, his gun and Wondaria, fighting for life with the deepest cunning within him. Gasping, scathingly he impressed upon them that now they must conserve their ammunition until all the gang could get together again and raid a white man's station and take more. That if they fired on this patrol it would only bring other patrols upon them. That it was sound sense to let this fool patrol ride past for they would then think there were no tribesmen running for the Leopolds this way, they would ride away back again, leaving them here in a secluded valley alive with game, a perfect hideout for the scattered gang to rally to.

Ellemara did not explain that if they fired upon this patrol then he, Ellemara, was done. In a frightful state from his wounds, even with Wondaria's help only with pain could he hobble along, now only a very few miles a day. He knew that in a fight with a patrol he must be shot or captured.

That such must inevitably happen to Lucullia also he did not care a rap. He thought nothing of the sorely wounded Lucullia, but he thought a great deal of Ellemara.

Drewry's patrol spent a busy two days tracking along the south side of the gorge, for the Barker near Lillamaloora is so rough that tracking is almost impossible. They found numerous tracks of native groups breaking away in haste from the Barrier Range, but the trackers failed to pick up tracks of any of the gang. They recovered several sacks of rice and flour, blankets, tin dishes, and a cheque book, more spoil from the raid on Edgar's wagon.

Drewry then for the next week set both police and trackers combing the summit of the Barker Range from dawn to dark. But the experienced bushmen amongst them found there to their surprise a landscape on which tracking was impossible - bare limestone rock, criss-crossed by innumerable deep gutters and crannies, jagged with fantastic pinnacles of rock, in wide areas covered with sharp "nails" of limestone so dense that to rest in such a place a man had to smash the points with the heel of his boot, then lay the rifle butt upon the spot and warily sit upon that. Their heavy cossack boots were cut to pieces within the first few days. Even where there was vegetation it was but scraggy clumps of wiry spinifex and needle-pointed speargrass. Again and again they marvelled how even bush natives with foot-soles like bullock hide could possibly walk over such fiendish country. They returned to camp utterly worn out each night, to find but little sleep through the necessity of guarding against surprise. They must take especial care of their horses too. Trackers and police boys were nervy and liable to fire at a shadow. Such false alarms did not help sleep.

Drewry frowned when his trackers sullenly announced that their feet were cut about so badly that they must have a day's spell, and vaseline for their torn feet. That the trackers' complaint was justified is borne out in an extract from Drewry's own report to the Commissioner:

The place Pigeon was in in the Wingina Gorge was nothing compared to the more recent camps of these natives. You could mark out an acre and put a large and smart party on it and after searching that ground all day they would not be in a position to swear they had been all over it and that there were no natives in that tiny area. There are too many springs and holes about also (ideal hiding places, apart from the rough country).

Many things hampered the party from the commencement.

Showery weather enabled the natives to get away from us several times, added to the great extent of country where tracking was impossible; it would require a book to explain what the Barrier Range is like. But shortly, it rises out of the plain like a wall (on the south side); this was the side we had to operate on principally. It is composed of carboniferous limestone which stands up in millions of pinnacles as sharp as knives. The action of water has in course of time formed thousands of caves, underground passages, crevasses, etc., with lots of soaks known to the natives. This limestone is of the hardest description. A piece as thin as the blade of a knife will carry a man without crumbling. Tracking on it was an impossibility. The only indications [of the presence of natives] we often got was by articles which had been thrown away by the natives.

So that the trackers, even though in mortal dread of running into the guns and spears of the scattered gang at any moment, were justified in complaining that their feet were cut to pieces by the country rock.

Drewry gave them a day's spell, but insisted that the patrol divide into twos, scatter away down the gorge and examine the caves. That evening, they enjoyed a campfire laugh at the expense of Constable Pilmer.

Pilmer, rifle in hand, set off jauntily in company with his favourite tracker Big Ned. Presently he took pity on the limping, barefooted tracker and ordered him to hide himself in some quiet spot and just sit down and keep his eyes open. Gratefully, Big Ned found a shady, secluded nook, and promptly fell asleep.

Pilmer pressed on and presently came to the mouth of a cave by which there were numerous tracks. Eager to prove his mettle, he cautiously entered the cave, and crept on into the deepening gloom, listening intently now and then. He was about to give it up when he saw a faint glimmer of light far ahead. He pressed on, and the light grew stronger. Presently he knew it was sunlight filtering down through a deep crevasse. Soon he could dimly distinguish black mouths of caverns branching to right and left, several faintly illuminated to show shadowy stalactites and stalagmites, and dull pools of water. Like a cat on hot bricks he crept on past the shaft of sunlight but again the cavern grew darker until only blackness loomed ahead. He stood listening in the deathly silence, wishing he had had the sense to bring Big Ned for company. He turned to go back and as he did so thought he heard a muffled, shuffling sound, eerily magnified from some dim recess. He stood stock still, finger on trigger, hair on end. There was not the faintest sound now except the anxious thumping of his heart. Cautiously he began creeping back towards the sunlight filtering down the crevasse. And then . . .

A blast of fire, a volcanic roar reverberating down the cavern as a bullet whizzed past. He jumped almost his own height then, lowering his head, raced down the cavern, to pull up dead at the sight of Sub-Inspector Drewry standing inside the cavern mouth, rifle in hand.

"He almost got me!" stuttered the agitated Pilmer. "Did ... did you get him?"

"No," replied the inspector coolly, "I missed."

"Who ... who did you fire at?" gasped Pilmer. "At Pigeon?"

"No. I fired at you!"

Pilmer gaped in open mouthed astonishment then howled.

"At me?"

"Yes."

"Why ... why did you fire at *me*!" yelled Pilmer.

"I thought I saw a figure moving away in there by that shaft of light."

Then Pilmer regained breath and nerve and cursed his superior officer with might and main. The swarthy, thick-set inspector stood grinning until Pilmer paused for breath. Then he grinned still more as he quietly said, "There is only one thing saved your life, Pilmer,"

"And what was that?" demanded the aggrieved Pilmer.

"My secret sorrow in the fact that I am a damn bad shot." Slowly Pilmer grinned, sheepishly shook hands. The little incident was to cement a life-long friendship.

From 19th November onward Drewry's patrols harried the natives from the Barrier Range to the King Leopolds, for a long time without finding even tracks of any of Pigeon's gang. Even though yet again a patrol of nine men rode past Captain's hideout.

This was on 22 November, a steaming hot day with thunder in the air. That patrol travelled two hundred and thirty-seven miles from the main camp, sixty-seven on foot, to the Leopolds barrier via the Richenda River. They too crossed Wambarella Creek and returned to report no sign of natives.

They would have had a surprise to report, had it not again been for Ellemara, so cunningly nursing his wounds and resting, while slowly recovering. Thus he could receive his share of food, which he for the time being was incapable of hunting for himself. He had his young lubra Wondaria to fetch and care for him. Wondaria was such a great help, but such a danger to him, though apparently he did not notice the savage glances the others cast at her. He just lay there or squatted in shelter for hours, grinning inwardly at the glances lingering on the girl and scowling at the double-barrelled gun always handy across his thighs. His trusty spears had always been his favourite weapon but he grinned now as he thought that it was the white man's gun that would save his life. He was helpless to use his spears but he could use the gun. Cangamvara, Pigeon's young lubra, was now with them too. Many were the ominous glances cast at her but Pigeon's name was still dreaded. They were not certain yet that he was dead; they knew nothing of what fate had befallen him except that the police had not found his body, either dead or alive. Oh yes, Ellemara knew full well that sooner or later, and it was coming soon, there would be a fight amongst these killers for the two young girls, and others here too. Ellemara would hold it off as long as possible, and keep the others here as long as possible, for each day he felt warmly within him the surety of returning life - only given time, rest and food.

But Ellemara was desperately hard pressed on this occasion to hold off the glowering Captain and his men from firing on this second patrol. His most persuasive words, deeply impressive manner, his cynical, knowing grin, the mesmeric fire in his eyes only just managed to hold back their itching trigger fingers, their wommera hands.

It was only a few days later that the little crowd of killers sat glowering and sullen by the Barellam Spring. Carolan was absorbed in a job, squatting there with his shaggy head bent over the task his cunning, claw-like fingers were doing so well - expertly binding kangaroo sinew around revolver bullets, to "fatten" the cartridge case so that it would fit into the larger bore of a rifle.

Carolan of the corrugated brow was also experimenting. For around other cartridges he was tightly binding neatly cut strips of paperbark, the soft, pliable bark that is so like paper. When Carolan had finished a dozen of these cartridges he would try them out in the rifle, those bound with kangaroo sinew, and those bound around with paperbark. Whichever material proved the best, then that material would he use for all the revolver cartridges in his possession.

It was an unusual job of improvisation for a Stone Age man to think out and attempt to "fatten" modern revolver bullets so that they could be fired from the larger bore of a rifle. Strangely enough, in three different parts of the ranges three members of the gang was attempting the same thing, unaware that the same thought had been born in others. For the gang had split up into three, a cunning move to scatter the police patrols. Had the gang stuck together and their tracks been picked up then every patrol could have concentrated upon the one chase.

The complete gang (excepting for the time being Pigeon) was, however, always within smoke signal, each section within an easy day's march of the other two. So that if there was need of mutual help against hostile tribesmen resenting trespass on their tribal grounds, or for any other reason, then they could quickly come together. This, with other cunning safeguards, had been thought out beforehand for the gang by the vanished Pigeon.

Increasingly the patrols, as the chase became hot and natives were surprised, would come upon cartridges bound with sinew or paperbark, telling their own tale of a shortage of ammunition, and the occasional loss of a rifle. It was proof also of an adaptability of the aboriginal in something which keenly interested him within his own environment.

Members of the gang still had a fair supply of revolver ammunition, but had lost most of the rifle ammunition during the surprise and fight at the caves and the ensuing scattering towards the sheltering Leopolds. *

*Author's Note: Felix Edgar assured me that in his brothers' wagon were 4000 rounds of Winchester ammunition alone, apart from Schneider, revolver and shot-gun ammunition, and abundant material for refills. Apart from this Pigeon and Captain and the original gang had all the ammunition, rifle and gun and revolvers of Constable Richardson's patrol. The far-sighted Pigeon had secreted a large quantity in some deep recess in the caves, which indeed was to come in very handy for his "rainy day".

A Nor-West police patrol investigating the killing of Thompson and Shoesmith (Canning Stock Route tragedy, 1912).

22

INTRIGUE AND DEATH CAMP WITH CAPTAIN'S GANG

THIS morning it was a "sulky" camp. No hunting had been done the day before for that day had been "sulky" too. Hunger had been added to vengeful frustration, uncertainty, and wrathful jealousies. And now they sat there brooding, thunder-black of brow. Ellemara, seemingly noticing nothing, squatted there with that double-barrelled gun across his thighs; quite unconcerned he seemed, and as if not nearly so weak as he knew he was. Among the women present was Pigeon's lubra Cangamvara, and Ellemara's Wondaria of the Laughing Waters. Both, with the others, should have been high up the hill behind the camp, on lookout. For Captain now copied Pigeon in using the women as lookouts. And Cangamvara and Wondaria had the keenest eyes of all, and could always be depended upon. But Captain had not ordered them out this morning. So with the other women they squatted. quietly there, grinding pintubi seed into flour ready for the baking, roasting the parsnip-like yardamarra and boora roots, sensing full well that what was coming was coming soon.
Lillimarra's spear hand was twitching. Carolan was fingering the stone dagger at his belt. Towerdine was glaring towards Ellemara, sudden hate in his eyes.

Suddenly Tumanurumberry leapt up and seized Cangamvara.

Captain was upon him on the instant and both crashed down, clawing and gouging and biting as they rolled across the camp-fire in fiendish fury. Both leapt up and snatched dowicks but Captain's club struck sickeningly first. Tumanurumberry dropped to his knee but sank his teeth in Captain's stomach and Captain yelling gouged at his eyes. Both men leapt away, Tumanurumberry with his left eye hanging out as blindly he snatched for spears. But again Captain was quicker and his spear pierced Tumanurumberry's ribs. Again Tumanurumberry dropped to his knees, frenziedly breaking the spear haft. As Captain leapt in to finish him Tumanurumberry's hand flashed out from behind him. He fired full at Captain's face with a revolver-and missed. Captain bounded back, leaping from side to side to avoid the second shot. Tumanurumberry was up and racing for the rocks as Captain leapt aside for his rifle, snatched it up and fired. But he missed the leaping man; both were far too excited to use firearms. Like a pack of dogs they chased Tumanurumberry then, a howling mob rattling their spears, leaping in the air, chewing their beards in frenzied excitement. But two more bullets whistled amongst them and they crouched low behind trees and rocks, afraid as always of firearms.

Tumanurumberry got away, mainly because Captain thought of the camp and the lubras and Ellemara squatting back there with the gun. They followed Captain hurriedly back but Ellemara and the women were still there. Panting from excitement they glared around with eyes animal-mad. Then ...

Lucullia saw it coming, he stared helplessly at all those savage eyes concentrating upon him. He was fast dying of his wounds anyway. If only they would give him a few hours longer!

They fell upon him, killed him, cut him up, cooked and ate him.

Ellemara ate his share. Knowing, while he ate, that he was eating to gather strength so that he would not be killed and eaten in his turn.

Rarely does the aboriginal eat his fellow man, excepting always the kidney fat of a warrior, and several other morsels. But under stress of various circumstances it happens occasionally.

They feared Ellemara, Ellemara who "carried devils in his eyes", as they feared no man except Pigeon. Ellemara knew well that each man there was ravenous for his kidney fat. For by eating it each implicitly believed that he would imbibe and develop Ellemara's spearcraft and notorious cunning. U-ai! he who could kill Ellemara the Killer and eat his kidney fat, would become himself the Killer - and would take the young girl Wondaria also.

Yes, Ellemara ate to live. And he knew that to live he must retain possession of Wondaria. As he ate, one hand never left his gun. Though he did not seem to notice anything, nor betray concern.

But they feared "the devils in his eyes" - and the hands that held the gun.

Tumanurumberry got clean away, though badly hurt. It had been a cunning thought of Tumanurumberry to secrete that revolver behind him in his human hair belt. But when the time came he had been too excited to use it immediately, and Captain too quick. But it had saved his life, all the same.

Tumanurumberry took sanctuary in the Leopolds, in the wilds of Mt Broome, second highest mount in the Kimberleys. There to hide like a wild dog, all alone, and recover from his wounds, until such time as Fate should catch up with him.

Thus, one by one, Pigeon's best men would be killed, captured, perish, or vanish; by bullet or by spear or club in fights amongst themselves, or in native intrigue and bitter vendetta.

Captain claimed Cangamvara. And as he glared upon them with his rifle at the ready none dared say him nay. But he knew by their grim faces that he must be ever alert to fight. He did not care.

It was not long afterwards that Drewry's patrol in the Barrier surprised a party of natives roasting a bullock. They scattered and vanished, abandoning several quart pots, dishes and dog chains, most of the links of which had already been made into spear tips, and in a dilly-bag, Richardson's pocket book. Curiously the patrol riders examined a handful of revolver bullets wrapped around with kangaroo sinew to make them fit a larger weapon.

Next day, however, while making across more open country towards the Barellam Springs, Drewry knew he was on the scent of the real quarry. There was great excitement among the trackers riding ahead. They had cut the tracks of Captain, Ellemara, Lillimarra, Pyabarra, Carolan, and others of the gang, and found a little farther on, some empty revolver cartridges where they had been firing at kangaroos. Still farther on, used Schneider shells again confirmed the presence of Captain.

The quarry had grown careless as so often happens when the aboriginal considers himself safe.

Drewry's patrol spread out and hurried on fast as the eager trackers could follow the tracks, making towards Barellam Springs. With increasing excitement Drewry began to believe the wanted men might be camped at the springs. If only he could surround the springs unseen, then close in and rush the camp!

Cautiously they did so. But to their bitter disappointment they were too late. There was plenty of evidence of their quarry, including the bones of Lucullia. Broken spears and empty revolver and cartridge cases showed evidence of a fight, confirmed when the trackers excitedly pointed out marks on the earth and broken vines where men had struggled and wrestled. Fresh tracks led out from the springs. As quietly as possible, intensely alert, the patrol filed out on the tracks.

Captain and the crowd were not far away, squatting around the cooking fires at the base of a spur leading up a hill that merged into a rocky, thickly timbered range. Close behind them was plentiful natural cover leading up the spur. Just the drowsy hum of insects, birds whistling up on the timbered hill. The gang, full bellied and seemingly content, were taking it easy. Just the steady grinding as here and there a man bent over his task of fashioning a fragment of iron into a precious spearhead, the slow, patient job of grinding it to shape with stone and sand and water. Others were squatting there smoking, for they still had tobacco from Edgar's looted wagon. Wongamarra was scratching his tangled beard, his envious eyes on Ellemara's gun.

Ellemara knew those eyes were on the gun. Wongamarra had not been able to keep his eyes from the gun for days past. Ellemara grinned deep, but inwardly. He knew just what he would do, should the big trouble come. He would instantly shoot Captain, the most dangerous man, then give the other barrel to Wongamarra, fair in the belly. He chuckled; he could vision the pained surprise in Wongamarra's eyes when he received the coveted gun that way. Whilst he, Ellemara, would reload and be facing the startled others before they could recover from the shock. He was sure he could then work his will upon them. They must stay beside him until he fully recovered. And he would become leader of the gang.

He glanced at Wondaria. Impassive of face she squatted there, roasting a fat carpet snake in the ashes for him. He knew that her alert mind, quick eyes and understanding were guarding him against any treachery that he might not see. Yes; should the trouble come, he knew he would win.

The women had not gone on lookout yet this morning; Captain had not given the signal. But now he half glanced at Cangamvara. She rose and the other women and children with her and walked towards the spur to climb the hill. All except Wondaria. She had almost finished cooking Ellemara's carpet snake. She would give it to him, accept her share from him, and eat it as she climbed the hill to keep the other women company on lookout.

A few moments dreamed by, then ... a long, piercing scream.

They all froze, eyes staring questioningly. Again rang out Cangamvara's urgent warning and with it now came the thud of galloping hooves. In an instant they had snatched weapons and were on their feet as a thunderbolt hurled itself upon the startled Ellemara and snatched the gun. They were racing for the sheltering spur to the yells of white men and trackers, thundering hooves, "Crack!", "Crack!", "Crack!" of revolver shots.

His wind knocked out, Ellemara clawed for his spears as Wondaria helped him up. "Quick! Quick! No, this way!" And she half raced, half pushed him through the bushes, then flat down into a little grass-lined gutter near by as horsemen came galloping through the camp.

23

CAPTAIN FLIES FROM GALLOPING PATROLS

CANGAMVARA'S warning had come but in the nick of time. Minutes later a ring of horsemen galloped straight into the hastily vacated camp. One glance and they galloped on up the steep spur, but the fleeing natives here outran the horses while the boulders and timber sheltered their flying bodies from bullets. Within minutes all had disappeared. The only capture was a terrified lubra, Terawarra.

Ellemara, crouched under the bushes in the gully, was feverishly anxious to crawl out and hobble away after the horsemen had thundered by.

"No, no," insisted Wondaria. "Lie here in safety. To run away means death; you cannot run. The trackers would find your tracks, hunt you down and shoot you. Stay here. They are chasing the others up over the hill now. They will follow their tracks; they will never think Ellemara remains hiding away back here; they will believe you have escaped with the others."

Panting, Ellemara fought for his nerve. The surprise, the galloping hooves, the loss of his gun all in the one shock had panicked his crippled system. Fighting that desperate urge to hobble away, away, away, he agreed to stay.

After the quietening influence of many hours of safety Wondaria prevailed upon him still more. Ernestly she urged that he remain right here. She would bring him food and water. Each day he was growing stronger, his wounds could only heal with food and rest. And now he would be free of worry from his fleeing fellow killers. The patrols would never dream that Ellemara had remained in hiding at the Barellam Springs camp; they would now seek him anywhere but here.

And thus Wondaria of the Laughing Waters saved Ellemara the Killer - for the time being, until he finally regained strength.

As for the sorely disappointed Drewry, the routine resolved into the same hard riding, rougher "foot walking", ceaseless patrolling of a dozen ranges, right back to the ramparts of the Leopolds, The quarry were silent and elusive as the mountain dingo; or suddenly appeared to yell hilarious insults from a mountain crag and then vanish, as if the canyons of the Leopolds had swallowed them.

Yet again a patrol would ride a couple of hundred miles or more with no sign of man, not even the distant, long drawn out "Yack-ai!" of a hunting call. Just a whisper of insects through the sunlight on the flats, the rustling of a snake through the grass, the "thud!", "thud!" of a bounding wallaby, the trumpet call of brolgas dancing by some lily lagoon. Or, in the ranges, they would hear a tremulous sighing growing into heavy murmuring of wind in a gorge, splashing of water over a waterfall, moan of tortured tree limb rubbing against its fellow, sharp fall of a rock from some nearby height, splash of tortoise into a pool. Now hot, deathly silence, then low growl of distant thunder. From the patrol would come the murmur of hooves, clink of quart pot or hobble chains on a pack animal, snort of a horse. And over all the call of birds.

But no sign of Man.

The first storms of the near Wet broke in thunderous fury that rocked gorge and cliff and rolled out over the plains, black sky and gasping earth sizzling from lightning. The murmur of mountain streams swelled into joyous, growing life. Soon would come the raging torrents.

Then the bogs! With weary men urging the horses on.

Tired animals floundering, bogging. Hiss of icy rain. Dark bundles upon the earth of nights that were men in the sleep of exhaustion, rolled up in sodden blankets.

And this was but the start of ceaseless patrolling. It would have been interesting had a record been kept of the many thousands of miles of patrolling before Pigeon's race was run.

After the disappointing raid on Captain's camp at Barellam Springs Sub-Inspector Drewry received some little consolation from the terrified lips of the captured lubra Terawarra.

She was given in charge of Tracker Peter, to win her confidence. And after twelve hours the still frightened but very relieved lubra muttered her story, as reported by Sub-Inspector Drewry to the Commissioner in Perth on 23rd January 1895.

Terawarra who was questioned quietly by assistant Peter for a day states: Sandamara alias Pigeon died after the first day's shooting at Wingina Gorge. She did not see him. Pigeon ran away by himself but when he did not come to join the others they went to look for him and found him by the smell. They put him in a hole in the limestone and put some earth on him. She heard them talking about it and has not seen him since.

She went on to describe some of the men at present with Captain, who were already fighting amongst themselves for Pigeon's lubra. She told the story of the eating of Lucullia, and the fight of Captain and Tumanurumberry. The report goes on to state: "The lubra says 'Ellemara's back is bent like a bow (from his wounds) with matter coming out all the time'.

"But," writes Drewry, "as he has lived so long he will probably recover."

Drewry would have been deeply chagrined had he known just where Ellemara was "recovering".

In the raid on Captain's camp Drewry had recovered Burke's blankets, canvas hammock, jackets, knives, cooking utensils, more gun cartridges, powder and shot; Constable Richardson's handcuffs and keys, a purse containing a sovereign and small change. They smashed numerous native weapons abandoned in the sudden flight.

Thus Pigeon's gang were slowly but surely losing their spoils though escaping, in the main, with their lives. Just one "going out", here and there.

Wongamarra for instance, he whom white men called Foe, he who had snatched the gun from Ellemara. In the escape from the patrol none had been so fleet as he - clutching that coveted gun. And he had kept on running when his friends, once in safety, had stopped and come together to jeer furiously at the outdistanced patrol. But Wongamarra had wanted to be quite alone - with the gun. He barely slept that night, for admiring it. He was still admiring it next morning, a delighted grin on his shaggy face as again and again he pulled back the hammers to listen to the little "click!", "click!" that seemed to talk to him. Standing up, he peered down the muzzle of each barrel in turn, his deep lined brow puckered up. He wondered and puzzled what was away down there; he couldn't see anything, it was dark, just like looking deep into the black nothingness of a cave. But he knew full well there was a "something" down in there, a great magic that was now all his. He knew that though it was so black and dark and quiet now, there was really a blazing fire hidden there, and a thunder noise, and sudden death. And now it all belonged to Wongamarra. It was all his, Wongamarra's!

As he lowered the gun the butt struck a rock. The jar fired the hammers and the gun blew his head off.

Thus yet another of Pigeon's men "went west".

Captain and his gang, having exhausted their fury and every native curse they could think of against the police, strolled casually across the range with ever-roaming eyes ready for sign of wallaby, or carpet snake, or agile goanna, or scratch on a tree that would betray the home of a mountain possum. They believed themselves quite safe, unaware that another surprise was coming, for the trackers were clinging tenaciously to their tracks. During the following two days Captain crossed a valley and with his comrades sauntered into the foothills of the adjoining range.

Next day the gang were unconcernedly squatting down in good cover, planning to return to friends in the Lennard Range. They planned to spear Lukin's cattle and if opportunity occurred carry out the long-discussed plan of shooting Lukin and looting his station. Idly Captain stood up and climbed a rock to gaze back over the country. He nearly fell back in surprise as he whipped up his Schneider and fired. It was the two trackers gazing towards him not a hundred yards away who fell back in fright.

Instantly the gang took to their heels to the sound of urgent shouts close to and almost around them. Men were leaping up on rocks and racing to vantage points to the crack of rifles and revolvers, the whine of bullets ricochetting off rocks. But as the reports died away the gang vanished among the boulders like flitting shadows as birds rose in alarmed flight.

Yet again Chance and a few precious moments had cheated Drewry of his quarry.

"On the 13th," he wrote in his report, "Captain fired one shot from the Schneider at Friday and Lumpy [the trackers] at about eighty yards. They were standing exposed at the time. I am of opinion they are very short of ammunition or they would not have missed such a chance, firing only one shot. The party fired about twelve shots but owing to the nature of the country none of the gang are believed to have been wounded."

Captain certainly was short of ammunition but it was the utter surprise that caused the gang to take instantly to their heels. They would have been foolish not to have done so, not knowing whether they were even then completely surrounded.

In deep chagrin Drewry carried on with his patrol. Meanwhile Cadden's patrol had been working from west to east along the tangled valleys from the Barker, while Pilmer eastward of Drewry was working his way west along the Upper Oscar, again hundreds of miles on horse and foot with not a sign of a native. Yet sometimes, when they'd ridden by, grinning tribesmen would swarm out from caves. Or rise up from the Hat tableland of a range and come swarming down hill or cliff like a mob of chattering monkeys - warriors, women, and piccaninnies in hilarious mirth at trackers and patrol.

Meanwhile Constable McDermott's small patrol by a round-about way was making for the Geikie Range north of the Oscar and north-east from Fitzroy Crossing. McDermott was really making for the Geikie Gorge, believing that in this wild fastness he would stand a likely chance of surprising some members of the gang and their cattle-spearing friends. In this he was backed up by Joe Blythe, father of Charlie, Archie, and Joe, each name writ large in Kimberley pioneering history. Blythe was then pioneering Brooking Creek station just south of The Crossing. His station boys, harassed by the cattle-spearers, swore that one of their main camps was within the Geikie Gorge. And Blythe as a "special", with his faithful stockboy Wisego, again rode with the patrol.

Thus McDermott's patrol doubled back towards the gorge, riding quietly by night. An hour before dawn they arrived near the gorge mouth. McDermott sent Tracker Shadrack to ride a mile back to safety with the horses. Stealthily then the patrol entered the gorge on foot. They crept on over the rough ground, cautiously creeping on into a blackness becoming as the darkness of the pit as the gorge narrowed between walls of cliffs.

Still no alarmed snarl from a dog, no dull glow from the nearly dead coals of a campfire.

Geikie Gorge.

24

THE FIGHT IN GEIKIE GORGE

JUST before dawn, the trackers hissed warningly, sniffing. In the moveless air they had caught the taint from the naked bodies of wild men and women, warrior bodies heavily rubbed with rancid fats and with the sun-melted fats dripping from the bodies of dead warriors.

Whispered words, and the patrol crept on, McDermott in dread lest an excited police boy discharge his rifle by accident. It was just at the break of dawn that they crept into position, and waited. Before them, the dull shadows of shrubbery framed by black wall of cliffs. Silence. Then a groaning grunt as a man turned over in the chill sleep of dawn. A cough, followed by another sleep-deadened grunt farther out there to left and right. Every now and then the sounds of a big camp in sleep.

Peering out towards the camp as trees and bushes took clearer shape the patrol silently waited for light and sight of life. Orders were that as soon as it was light all hands would rush the camp while the natives still slept, the trackers to swiftly recognize any wanted men and point them out. McDermott would call for surrender. There was to be no shooting, unless they showed fight.

It was breaking dawn when a prowling mongrel came sniffing along their tracks, right to the feet of a hidden tracker, Leaping back snarling, it raised its head and yapped the alarm. Inquiring heads showed here and there away out in front, then a lubra yelled piercingly.

Instantly men, women and children were running for the cliffs though here and there a group of warriors leapt up and stood their ground, shipping spears as the patrol jumped up and raced towards them.

McDermott's shout to "Stand! drop him spears you feller boy or we shoot!" was greeted by a shower of spears and the patrol opened fire. Jaduwall fell, then Biritbeer sprawled grotesquely upon the grass as spearmen ran for the cliffs. But other spears came whistling from the left and the patrol opened fire on this group. They too fled when two were wounded, leaving Congolo breathing his last. But now spears came viciously from the right. Had these three groups of spearmen acted in concert and stood their ground the small patrol must have been wiped out.

It had been a lively few minutes.

"Watch him!" yelled a tracker, "lookout longa stone!" and the thud of a falling boulder echoed the warning cry as they leapt back under a shower of rocks and spears.

"Back! Back! Quick feller!" yelled McDermott as more rocks and spears came whizzing from the sky.

The cliffs were black with yelling men, women and children hurling rocks and spears, while others pushed over heavy boulders that came out into space to strike bottom and bound out in flying leaps towards the party running back across the gorge.

Out of range, they turned around breathlessly to gaze up at the exultant black figures. Warriors were now leaping high, to spin around, bend and heartily smack their backsides towards the patrol, while the women shrieked yet heartier insults.

"Phew!" breathed McDermott. "That was a hot spot!"

"I'll say!" agreed Blythe, "but if it hadn't been for that mongrel giving the alarm we'd have been right in under that cliff and copped the lot."

"Yes," agreed McDermott thoughtfully, "that little ambush has been well planned. The camp site to lure us on right under the cliff, those boulders and heaps of rocks stacked along the cliff top beforehand."

"Langooradale!" yelled a tracker excitedly.

"Ah!" exclaimed McDermott, "*he's* our man. Can you see him, Blythe? Look! Yes, there he is, yabbering to that crowd in the centre. You're the best shot! Let him have it if you can."

But immediately Blythe's rifle was levelled the group fell flat to the ground while a derisive yell came from other natives.

"The cunning devil," said McDermott, "he's been training them too!"

"Those ex-police boys of yours," said Blythe grimly, "are going to do a lot of damage with these *munjons* if we don't break them up quickly. I hope to goodness it's true what Drewry believes that Pigeon is dead."

"I don't like this!" exclaimed McDermott. "These fellows may be only holding us. If their lookouts locate our horses they'll send a mob around to spear them. Come on, we're getting out of this - quick feller!"

They made their way back up the gorge, the derisive howls growing fainter. It was rough going, and they wasted no time. The natives disappeared. Toward its head the gorge narrowed considerably. McDermott was just breathing a sigh of relief when the gorge head sprang alive with yelling figures as boulders, rocks and spears again carne whizzing down.

"Back!", "Back!" yelled McDermott, but the cliff head behind them echoed to exultant yells as another shower of stones carne at their backs.

"Take cover!" yelled McDermott. 'We must fight our way out, Do your best, Blythe. Shoot straight!" he shouted to the excited trackers. "Take good aim! Steady feller now!"

To a crackle of rifle fire and the thud of falling boulders Tronkey high on a cliff edge poised a moment, then over he came like a hurtling black cornet. There was a howl of fury from both sides of the gorge as showers of stones came flying. The natives were not hiding themselves now.

"Pick off Langooradale!" shouted McDermott. But it was Wonawona who next came hurtling down.

A moment later and Langooradale leapt back with a Besh wound and from then on he kept back. Very probably the temporary loss of their leader saved McDermott's patrol. McDermott glanced over his shoulder at a thud and a grunt then a cry from Wisego and there was Blythe sprawling in the grass, his face a bloody mess, Wisego anxiously bending over him. The wound looked worse than it really was. One cheek had been laid open by a Bying stone that luckily struck only a glancing blow. The howl of exultation changed to a wail of lament as Conunwarra carne tumbling down, followed almost immediately by Mungulla. There was sudden silence as the natives disappeared.

McDermott jumped to the partly dazed Blythe.

"Quick!" he said. 'We've only a three hundred yards' run and we're through the gorge. Help your boss, Wisego! Come on boys, quick feller now."

They got through, then to McDermott's immeasurable relief a mile farther on he found the hidden horses still safe. The patrol would return to Fitzroy Crossing. Blythe could have his face stitched up there with what needle or thread the boys possessed, or ride down the Fitzroy the two hundred and ten miles to Derby and a doctor.

Meanwhile Cadden was patrolling the Barker River to Cowlera and Tehangaroo while Pilmer's patrol doubled back for the Oscar. All along that abrupt range they found stone ovens which the tribesmen had built for the cooking of the good fat beef, taking tribute from the stations of the Fitzroy plains with a vengeance. Even the patrol, men well used to evidence of beasts killed and roasted, were startled by the number of beasts they saw had been killed along this range alone. And they knew that for every one seen killed ten others not seen was a fair calculation. The aggressive example of Pigeon had been taken up by the tribes with a vengeance.

The wildboys of the hills were not afraid of the white man either. For the patrol found a beast killed, roasted, and leisurely eaten within four miles of John Collins's homestead.

"It might have been me," said Collins philosophically. And he looked well to his weapons when the patrol rode away leaving him alone.

No lack of tracks but - never Pigeon's track. Nor had any other patrol seen the track of the most notorious man in all the Kimberleys, the most discussed amongst both black and white. It appeared certain now that Pigeon had died of wounds received during the fight at the caves, as all natives questioned swore he had. Nor could the trackers now find Captain's track. For the very good reason that Captain, Lillimarra and their hearties were away back in the Leopolds, deep in the gorges of the Precipice Range, carrying out a little private war of their own. Later; the tribesmen swore they had shot twenty natives during that time, warriors who dared stand against their demands. The dreaded Ellemara's tracks were not found either, for Ellemara was still in his hideout at Barellam Springs, faithfully tended by Wondaria of the Laughing Waters. Ellemara's back, which had been "bent like a bow" from his dreadful wound, was much straighter now. But he was ribbed like a poor goanna, no longer the fine strapping athlete fearing neither police, white man nor black. But he was recovering rapidly, nursing his strength, and nursing his fury too whenever he thought of his gun and Wongamarra, He would reach out clawed hands for his spears, gritting his teeth, a fiendish light in his eye every time he thought of Wongamarra.

He was unaware that Wongamarra was now but bones picked clean by the dingoes.

But Pilmer's patrol rode across tracks of other members of the gang, among these the tracks of Langooradale. And by the tracks the trackers read that he was suffering from a wound, the wound received in the Geikie Gorge fight. They lost the tracks in a violent storm that drenched range and plain.

But Vengeance was catching up with yet others of Pigeon's old gang. Vengeance that sometimes works slowly, sometimes swiftly, but that, once started, inevitably strikes.

One morning Constable Pilmer reined back his horse in startled surprise as a tribesman rose from the earth right before him. A *munjon* this fellow, a wild bush native in war paint and feathers, carrying war spears. Obviously afraid of the patrol but standing there motionless as a rock. And vengeance was upon his brow.

This man was Ballacot, a warrior pledged to bitter vendetta.

With solemn gaze, spears with their butts to the ground, the weapons held upright by his left hand, wommera in his right, in guttural sentences he explained that he knew where to find the tracks of Langooradale. Langooradale who had deserted from the police, had tried to kill his patrol officer and release prisoners at Mt Abbott police camp;

Langooradale who had taken to the bush, had led the Geikie Gorge tribesmen and had rolled rocks down upon the police and thrown many spears; Langooradale who had rallied many tribesmen around him, who threatened that if Pigeon were really dead he would take his place and surely kill the whites at Fitzroy Crossing, and along the Margaret and Louisa also. With Langooradale were also Elgally and Wingelly, great spearers of cattle who had also attempted the lives of white men. With them were others too, all wanted by the police. He believed he knew where all the mob would be camped even now. He offered to track Langooradale to earth, whether or no.

And thus Pilmer, quietly sitting his horse, heard translated a simple tale of native vengeance.

For Langooradale, like Pigeon, Captain, Ellemara, Lillimarra, Demon, Pyabarra and other members of the gang, had used their firearms against natives to even up old vendettas, or out of sheer bravado, or to take women or anything else they fancied. Ballacot had suffered deeply at the hands of Langooradale and from Elgally and Wingelly also.

Grimly Pilmer nodded to the *munjon* to guide the patrol.

Ballacot set out with long, sure strides. Thus Vengeance now travelled fast on the tracks of Langooradale.

It was on 26th December that Ballacot led the patrol, now cautiously advancing on foot, on the last stage, To Langooradale's present camp - his last camp, in the last dawn.

It was a perfect surprise. The patrol was so close that Langooradale, Elgally and Wingelly were covered before Pilmer rose up and shouted them to lie still, not to attempt to touch their weapons. Just one startled moment, then fifty tribesmen leapt to their feet fitting spears to wommeras. Pilmer shouted "Fire!" and Langooradale dropped but was on his feet on the instant, bent double as he raced to escape. Elgally launched his spear, then dropped and lay still. Langooradale dropped again, yet again staggered to his feet. Women and children and some of the men were running and when Wingelly fell, shot through the head, the remaining warriors also fled. Langooradale was almost in safety when he dropped yet again. But still he managed to crawl away to die.

Seven were shot. Thus Ballacot was avenged on Langooradale, Elgally and Wingelly.

Up to 13th January patrols rode the Oscar valleys, the Barker, the Barrier and the Lennard, with the horses rapidly growing leg weary, the country boggy in places from the storms. The wet season was starting in earnest. Drewry, convinced that Pigeon and a dozen of his gang were dead and that he had driven the remainder back into the shelter of the

Leopolds for the Wet, returned to Derby on 16th January 1895. He reported to Headquarters: "With the ammunition that has been recovered at various times and what they have fired away, I am of opinion that the murderers have only some revolver cartridges left, and during the wet season it is probable that some of the weapons will get out of order through the carelessness of the natives. Then again the woman question will crop up and there is a chance of the other natives killing Ellemara. It will be against all tribal customs if they do not kill Captain."

Which was sound reasoning based on a knowledge of native customs. For Captain was a "foreign boy", an aboriginal of the faraway southern coast. But allowance was not made for the fact that these men were feared as ruthless killers. In small bands, they stuck together, ever alert against treachery. Always some among them were armed with rifle, gun, or revolver, welcoming the least chance to use them. Knowing the "white man's ways" they sneered at native custom. They went where they willed, took what they wanted. Also, they were heroes far and wide.

So that while they stuck together there was no body of warriors of any single tribe numerous and game enough to attack them for tribal trespass. And it is rarely that aboriginal tribes combine.

None knew that the most feared of all, Ellemara, he who "carried evil spirits in his eyes", was crippled and hiding alone, cared for by but one native girl, with devotion and extreme cunning. For it was Wondaria who had to move about, to hunt for Ellemara as well as find food for herself. Had she once been seen, had a single track been found by some wandering hunting party, it would have been all up with the crippled Ellemara, his enemies would have cut him to pieces with fiendish pleasure.

Drewry strengthened the few isolated police outposts, then returned to Derby to reorganize during the wet season. Meanwhile Headquarters in Perth ordered Inspector Lawrence at Roebourne, seven hundred miles south down the coast, to proceed north at once to Derby, organize a strong posse, and disperse the outlaws. No excuses whatsoever to be made of shortages of men and horses, wet season or no wet season.

It was necessary, though a "tall" order, considering the few whites, and the distances, the extreme ruggedness of the country, the hardships of a wet season, the numbers of the natives and their proved intelligence and boldness, now spurred on to emulate little hero bands of killers scattered here and there for hundreds of miles amongst them.

And they had tasted blood-white man's blood, and were seeking more. Long Frankey had even deliberately sent in word that he was coming in to burn the Fitzroy Crossing telegraph station, and the new police station that Constables Pilmer and McDermott and their six trackers were so busy building between patrols. And, Long Frankey boasted, he was going to kill every white man in the place and every police boy. He hungered, so his messenger repeated, for their kidney fat. After which, he added, he would loot both stations, then burn them.

It was evident that the goggle-eyed native who came running to gasp out the message fully expected that Long Frankey would carry out his boast.

"I only wish he'd come and try!" said Pilmer to McDermott. "So long as we are here!" replied McDermott grimly.

Long Frankey was a notorious cattle-spearer, a killer too of stockmen game enough to stand in his way. With Long Frankey's band roamed Waggarrie, a beetle-brewed cattle-spearer who had killed a lone white settler on the Margaret River and so far had defied capture. The scattered settlers east of Fitzroy Crossing were considerably perturbed by the depredations of Long Frankey's "mob". Their black stockmen were terrified of them. The result was that now Long Frankey raided the herds almost with impunity.

Raiding from just west of The Crossing but with his hideout in the ranges north, was a similar little band led by Big Paddy. A recklessly fearless, exceptionally powerful tribesman this Big Paddy, another notorious cattle-spearer and killer of native stockmen who had dared stand in his way. Big Paddy had proved he was not afraid of white men. Only eighteen months previously, single-handed and alone, he had tackled Charlie Blythe. Blythe with his team and boys was driving his wagon along the Fitzroy. Charlie Blythe was a lad six feet two inches, rapidly developing into the powerful man he was to be in coming years. But Big Paddy deliberately picked a quarrel with him. After a desperate struggle he got him down and was throttling the life out of him when Blythe's teamster boys threw themselves upon Big Paddy and tore the two apart.

In a maniacal rage Big Paddy defied them all, threatening that the first time he saw Blythe in the bush again he would kill him for sure. As to the yellow dingoes of teamster boys, he would catch up with each one of them in time and rip out his kidney fat and eat it before his living eyes. Foaming awful threats Big Paddy strode back into the bush to rejoin his gang.

Since then Big Paddy had increasingly harried the cattle and also speared three station boys who he swore failed to send him information of movements of police patrols that had ridden by their stations.

If both "mobs", Long Frankey's and Big Paddy's, combined to attack Fitzroy Crossing the result could prove serious. Telegraph station and police station were on opposite banks of the river, more than a mile apart. Each little building could be attacked at once, or separately.

At the new police station either Pilmer or McDermott with four trackers had been away on constant patrol seeking Pigeon and Captain. Should events necessitate that both constables and trackers be called away at the same time . . .

Small wonder that Jack Scott the telegraph operator and Abe Harris his assistant slept fitfully of nights, fully dressed, firearms beside them.

Little wonder that the stockboys on stations in the vicinity of these killer bands went in fear of their lives.

Constable Johns with three Aboriginal trackers.

25

LONG FRANKEY AND WAGGARRIE DIE FIGHTING

INSPECTOR LAWRENCE rode from Derby with a strong patrol, heading inland along the Fitzroy. He was pleased to have Joe Blythe riding with him, his wound received in the Geikie Gorge fight still a bit raw. Blythe had penetrated portion of the country over which Lawrence hoped to travel.

While Drewry and his patrols were combing the southern ranges from the Lennard to The Crossing, Lawrence's ambitious plan was to travel north through the eastern limits of the Leopolds from The Crossing, then westward around the great range if possible. Thus to surprise the wanted tribesmen, placing them between Drewry's patrols and his own.

Such a plan was a task for an army, let alone a patrol. Although Lawrence found the task impossible, it nevertheless proved an outstanding patrol, carried out doggedly in unexplored country which was a labyrinth of valleys and gorges, and cliff-faced ranges running like sheer rock walls, in places right to the distant coast. And this during the wet season when again and again every creek came pouring down and every mountain river was a torrent swirling through wild gorges to tumble into rock-walled valleys and rage westward to the cliff-walled fiords leading to the sea. But about the many patrols carried out during that hectic three years space allows but the barest mention here.

Past Fitzroy Crossing on to the Margaret River Lawrence found the few scattered settlers in trouble. Determined bands of marauding natives were practically everywhere, defying white and black stockmen alike, allowing them to ride almost to spear throw while they squatted around cooking fires gorging on roasting bullocks, daring the uneasy stockmen to come but a little closer and they would spit them on their spears and roast them too. The black stockmen when working alone kept their distance from such mobs of howling taunters.

The natives along the entire Margaret now claimed all the cattle on their lands; boasted they were going to eat them - and the whites also.

And, as settlers impressed upon Lawrence, "So they can - as soon as they start in earnest. If the ringleaders are not cleaned up soon then this means the abandonment of the Kimberley cattle lands."

All believed that Long Frankey and Waggarrie's gang would start the bloodshed of whites here, backed up by Big Paddy's gang farther west. It would mean disaster if Captain's mob joined up with them first.

In deadly seriousness, they inquired if it were definite fact that

Pigeon was dead. Lawrence assured them it was firmly believed so.

"How about Captain?" they inquired, "and that long swine Ellemara. And Lillimarra and Mullenbuddin and Pyabarra and Towerdine? Fouringer too and Byerbell and Demon and Canada and all the rest of the cut-throat mob?"

"Driven right away back into the Leopolds," replied Lawrence confidently. "A few have been captured or shot, more killed in tribal quarrels. Ellemara when last heard of was a cripple and desperately wounded."

Lawrence carried on up along the Margaret to Fossil Downs station where Charlie and Willie MacDonald gladly greeted the patrol. Their news was that the local tribesmen with bands from the hills were now in scattered groups marauding all up and down the Margaret. Lazy and fat-bellied and contented, for now there were numerous patches of boggy country into which cattle could be easily driven and speared at leisure. Long Frankey the ex-tracker and the white killer Waggarrie were the main dangers here.

Long Frankey was urging the Margaret natives to combine with the Mueller Range and Geikie natives to make an all-out attack on Fitzroy Crossing while the patrols were absent chasing Captain's gang. But the local natives, lazy with the easily got tucker, argued that it would be better to attack Fossil Downs station first. It was much closer, and easier too than Fitzroy Crossing where the white men were now building a police station. After looting Fossil Downs they declared they would all go down river and attack The Crossing. To which Frankey was fiercely arguing that once Fitzroy Crossing was wiped out the isolated stations along the Margaret and Louisa would be cut off and completely at their mercy. Which was quite true:

They were still arguing, all along the river. "But believe me," impressed MacDonald, "when the Dry comes and the natives have to move about for their tucker there is going to be real trouble. If Captain's gang then comes out of the Leopolds and joins up with Long Frankey and Big Paddy, then you can say goodbye to the settlers in the West Kimberley. And the trouble will spread to the East too."

Two blackboys came galloping to the homestead with exciting news. Bush blacks had jeered at them that Long Frankey was camped only a day's walk up-river. He was gathering the blacks for an attack on the homestead. Soon they would come down-river and cut out the kidney fat of whites and "tame" blacks alike.

Lawrence's patrol rode fast and surrounded the unsuspecting camp before dawn. Then at break of day Blythe with his shadow Wisego and five trackers galloped upon the sleeping camp calling upon all to sit still and surrender. The natives leapt up and scattered, then turned and hurled spears. Immediately they were fired upon by the encircling patrol. They stood their ground a short while then broke and fled, but not before their leaders had been shot. The trackers and the MacDonalds' station boys identified these as well-known native killers and cattle-spearers, But to Lawrence's disappointment neither Long Frankey nor Waggarrie was amongst them.

An excited shout brought them hurrying to a tracker scouting on the outskirts. And there plain were the tracks of Long Frankey and Waggarrie among a dozen others. Tracks of yesterday, leisurely making back to the hills.

The patrol mounted in swift pursuit but a prolonged storm washed out all tracks. Lawrence divided his drenched patrol into small groups with orders for each to scatter, ride swiftly and try to cut the tracks. If unsuccessful, to still ride on and reach the sheltering hills before the quarry if possible. To post lookouts there and try to ambush Long Frankey.

Not two hours later Blythe's little company picked up fresh tracks. They followed swiftly for the tracks were plain; Long Frankey and his friends were just lazing along, quite unaware of the swift advance of a patrol.

Before sundown, Blythe camped under cover near the mouth of a narrow valley. The tracks had gone straight up the valley. At midnight, taking a chance, he left the horses in charge of one scared blackboy while he and companions cautiously commenced stalking up along the gorge.

When three miles up the gorge an excited tracker located the wanted men by smell - the tang of rancid human and animal fat upon living human bodies warmly coiled around the dying coals of a hidden campfire. The taint, wafted by a faint, moist breeze came to the tracker's keen nostrils from a low hill directly ahead.

Blythe and his eager men crawled a little way up the hill, then took cover until daylight. Shortly after dawn, a tribesman stood out plainly halfway up the hill. He yawned broadly as sleepy-eyed he gazed down the brightening valley. Then a tall, painted figure appeared beside him.

"Long Frankey!" hissed a tracker.

"Waggarrie!" hissed another as a thick-set, black-bearded tribesman appeared beside Long Frankey.

Soon there were a dozen of them yawning in desultory talk, gazing down the valley back along their tracks.

"Long Frankey! Waggarrie!" shouted Blythe. "Stand proper feller quiet feller! Quick feller now or we shoot him you!"

For a moment they stood amazed, staring down at the heads behind rifles now poking up at them from the grasses. Then leaped back and vanished as they grabbed spears and fitted them frenziedly to wommeras. Almost instantly they bounded into sight again launching spears to furious yells. The rifles cracked and Long Frankey came grotesquely diving downhill spreadeagled like a great flying bat. Almost instantly Waggarrie pitched forward after him, then another fell, tearing up the grass as he rolled. The others disappeared.

Thus Fate caught up with Long Frankey and Waggarrie, avenged too the killing of a lone settler. And robbed Pigeon of two useful ringleaders and the mob who would have followed them.

26

TROUBLE AT OOBAGOOMA

BEFORE getting fairly started on his Leopolds patrol Lawrence was called back to the Fitzroy River to one of the very few sheep stations. Sheep were being driven away in little mobs to be killed. Several station boys had lost their lives through attempting to intercept the killers. And now Big Paddy had organized these particular marauders and things looked desperate.

Lawrence split his patrol into swift riding groups to try and stop this sheep killing up - and down-river.

One brilliant morning a party of trackers rode upon tracks of a mob of sheep being driven towards the hills by twenty tribesmen. The horsemen caught up with the little mob close by the river. Big Paddy was the leader; it was for him that the trackers were all eyes.

The trackers reined up just out of spear throw, called upon the sheep stealers to drive the sheep back to the station homestead. Which brought hilarious laughter, followed by jeers.

"Come and take them back yourselves!" yelled a tribesman. "Yes," they howled, "you've got horses! It's easier to ride than walk! Come and drive them back yourselves."

"Come on, you dingoes! What are you frightened of?"

"We've got spears! You've got guns but no guts! Come and take them!"

"What's it got to do with you anyway?" yelled a tall young warrior. "These are not YOUR sheep! They're OURS. The food they eat grows on our country, and they're ours!"

Big Paddy had neither jeered nor shouted. He stood there upright, lightly holding his spears, the cicatrize of warriorhood across his brawny chest standing out lividly in the brilliant sunlight. But his wommera hand was twitching, his deep-lined face a study in ebony, his black eyes gleaming as he calculated distance. They were only just out of spear throw. With one swift rush ... Would there be time to get near enough? To fit spear to wommera and aim and balance and throw? Their horses, alert eared, quiveringly expecting action, were poised there just a little side-on ready to charge or gallop away, the riders now part crouched over the saddle, left hand through rein gripping the threatening rifle ready to whip up to shoulder, right hand gripped behind the trigger guard. Would there be time? If they all bounded forward together?

The leading tracker half raised his rifle to shoulder. "Throw down your spears, Big Paddy! Surrender!"

Instantly Big Paddy leaped forward with a roar answered by one wild yell as they all bounded forward. As Big Paddy threw back his arm for the throw each rifle was levelled straight at him - Big Paddy had left his decision but seconds too late. Each rifle seemed to crack at once and Big Paddy in the final attitude of a spear thrower held his poise one shattering second before he crashed to earth.

Instantly each raider leaped around and was racing for dear life for the river bank. They were into the water before the excited trackers could curb their horses and follow.

Long Frankey and Waggarrie and Big Paddy were gone. And the settlers along the entire length of the Margaret and farther breathed a sigh of relief.

Lawrence's patrol then rode north into the Wild Lands but again and again were blocked by the ramparts of the King Leopolds, again and again hemmed in by cliff and precipice, again and again turned back or Aside from the route they tried to take. It was to be years yet before the few narrow passes through those ranges would one by one be discovered. They tried to penetrate the Precipice Range but struggled into .an area where for thirty miles sheer perpendicular cliffs from six hundred to eight hundred feet high hemmed in the rocky gorge. Their horses were soon forced back. They tried to force the Charnley Range but were soon driven back by the torrents of the Charnley. Just as well, for if they had penetrated the gorge they might never have come back. In one area the gorge runs for forty miles between cliffs five hundred feet high, and the wet season was soon to bring the Charnley roaring through the gorge in foaming spray through and over the fantastic channels that ages of water have cut through the solid rock. Had they and their horses been caught deep down there, hemmed in by those sheer cliff walls...!

The King Leopolds with their parallel ranges seldom reach even a paltry three thousand feet in height, but for impassability and ruggedness their seas of peaks and flat, cliff-faced ranges are of a pigmy grandeur.

The patrol battled their way twelve hundred miles in three months throughout the wet season. Here and there they clashed with *munjons* (wild natives) disputing their right of way, but whether these were actively connected with the trouble away to the south I have no record. It certainly eased the situation a lot down along the Fitzroy and along the ranges south of the main Leopolds. But the patrol saw no sign or track of any of Captain's gang, nor of Demon's, Pyabarra's and Canada's "mob". As to Pigeon, the whites in the West Kimberley were mostly sure now and fervently hoped that Pigeon was well and truly dead.

Not so the tribesmen in the wild country around Oobagooma.

Only eighty miles nor-west of Derby itself, just the station track led to Oobagooma, with unbridged rivers to cross (there are no bridges in the Kimberleys). The rough homestead lay amongst a tangle of timbered little hills leading swiftly back into one of the wildest patches of country in Australia. No habitation north, just the fastnesses of the Leopolds, the Precipice Range, the Charnley, the Glenelg, the Prince Regent, and the rock-walled fjords of the coast.

Young Gus Rose, as manager, was battling desperately to make a cattle station out of this wild area. He was destined not to succeed, not just here. Particularly wild country, cattle-spearers, and distance to market eventually caused the area to be abandoned, as it has been several times since. But in 1895 the tribes were wild indeed and the triumphs of Pigeon's gang had spread like wildfire from inland right back west to the coast, many a crazy corroboree urging the warriors to emulate Pigeon's deeds. So that even while Lawrence and his patrol were hunting Long Frankey and Waggarrie and Big Paddy along the Margaret just over 200 miles to the east, and the Drewry patrols were seeking Captain between the Barker and the Leopolds, big trouble was gathering around Oobagooma, away back on the coast quite near Derby, the Kimberley Police Headquarters.

When the natives began spearing the precious station horses right up against the homestead Gus Rose sent a trustworthy boy riding to Derby for help.

Constable Spong rode out with a patrol in pouring rain, with three flooded rivers to swim. There was tragedy for Tracker Peter when swimming the Townsend, for a packmule that carried among other equipment Peter's treasured riding-saddle, rolled over and despite Peter's frantic efforts was drowned and vanished below the brown torrent. Woebegone Peter! Through no fault of his own he had "lost face" as well as the mule and his treasured saddle, in addition to his fifty Winchester cartridges and forty Webley revolver cartridges in the saddlebag.

They carried on through the grey, rain-soaked bush, a miserable ride, every flat a bog in which laden packhorses and riding horses floundered wretchedly. They swam the Robinson, a vicious brown stream tearing at the trees along its banks as it hissed its way to the angry waters of King Sound. And still it rained until at last they rode wearily to, the horse paddock fence by the rough little homestead. The horse paddock fences were the only ones in the Kimberleys, practically the only fences today.

They crowded the little homestead and verandas, the small patrol, with Rose and Tom Jasper the white stockman and Rose's most trusted station blackboys. Spreading out the gear, praying the sun to come soon so that every sodden thing would dry.

For that is how the Wet sets in in earnest in the Kimberleys.

Maybe a week of steady rain followed by humid sunshine. Or a fortnight of steady rain followed by a week of sunshine. Very much like that, after the storms, for three months.

At the homestead the station blacks were frightened, expecting an all-out attack. They had been warned that, if they did not turn on the whites when the attack came, then they too would be killed.

"But what really bothers me," explained Rose, "is that the boys say the two main ringleaders of this dangerous mob are Sambo and Captain with the ringleaders of the mob that killed Plummer and Peyton a few months ago. If so they'll have firearms if they haven't used up their ammunition; they've been using it freely on the cattle. They threaten to wipe us out as Pigeon did Richardson and Burke and Gibbs."

"I only wish they would try," replied Spong grimly. "We'll fix them!"

"I doubt if they'll attack when they learn that a patrol is here," said Rose, "although I don't know. The example of that wretched Pigeon back along the Fitzroy has made the Oobagooma hill blacks much more venturesome and defiant than before. Even my best stockboys are scared to ride more than a few miles from the homestead unless Jasper or I ride heavily armed with them. Even then, they're ready to turn tail and gallop."

"This Captain is not the Captain of Pigeon's mob, worse luck," said Spong.

"No. He's a cunning devil though; he is even working upon the name. He could be as dangerous as Pigeon's Captain. Both he and Sambo worked here as stockboys and thus know the run of the place, which makes them all the more dangerous. Sambo is a surly, husky brute who boasts he is going to be the 'Pigeon of Oobagooma'. And this wretched Captain boasts he is going to be the 'Oobagooma Captain'. The trouble is, the idea has caught on with the local munjons; the hill natives are all for it."

The sun did come. And stockyard rails were draped with drying saddlery, saddlecoths, blankets, all the gear of a thoroughly drenched patrol.

There were three days of sunshine. Then, in the sleep deadened early hours...

All hands sprang up and grasped rifles to a frantic clatter of horsebells, stampede of hooves, then the high, piercing scream of a stricken horse.

They dashed out into the night, firing in the direction of triumphant yells.

Too late.

They listened to the sound of vanishing hooves where the terrified horses had crashed through the fence and galloped into the bush.

27

THE OOBAGOOMA WARRIORS STAND GAMELY

THEY stood by until daylight, then walked across the paddock in black anger. Every bushman loves his horse. But in the Kimberleys where horses were so valuable and the dreaded Walkabout disease took such toll ...

Five horses lay dead, the long spear hafts sticking up from their ribs. Rose's favourite horse Ned was down, gazing up at its master with questioning fear in its big brown eyes - it was dying fast. Spong cursed bitterly, for his best riding horse Florin stood trembling and drooping with a deep spear wound in its shoulder. One of the trackers' horses was hobbling on three legs. The station boys quickly picked out the tracks, among others, of Sambo and Captain. Despite the presence of the patrol they had come right up to the very homestead.

Little wonder that Rose wrote bitterly to Drewry in Derby.

"Seven spears were sticking in one mare, Ned dying three hours later. Would rather have lost any other three horses. Spong's best horse also with spear in shoulder, nasty wound. I consider the police should be better equipped. Am helping all I can with horses but considering various misfortunes I won't have any myself shortly."

Tom Jasper the stockman, a good man in the bush, immediately went out on the tracks of the horses with trackers Paddy and Billy and stockboys. He succeeded in rounding them all up before nightfall, except four others that had been killed and soon would be eaten.

With sombre brow, Constable Spong wrote the brands of the four missing horses in his notebook, for every precious animal must be rigorously accounted for to the Heads "down South":

"Chestnut: O C near shoulder. 4 W near ribs. Bay: O̱ C̱ nr. sh.

Black: O C nr. sh. Grey O C nr sh."   M

    C D 5   7

When reorganized, the patrol rode out from the homestead to try to break up the local Oobagooma cattle-spearing gangs. Constable Spong and four trackers, Rose with stockman Tom Jasper and half a dozen stockboys. When ten miles from the homestead a station native came running through the bush, his eyes sticking out like pickled onions, so excited he could only yabber incoherently.

"Big feller mob!" he pointed behind him. "Big feller mob he come! Altogether plenty big feller mob! Killem altogether longa station! Killem white man!"

His news was that a large mob of warriors was coming to wipe out all hands at the station. To loot and burn the homestead, then drive all cattle and horses back into the ranges and roast them at leisure. Then when the Dry came they would join up with Captain's mob and kill all the whites in the Kimberleys.

"A tall order!" laughed Spong grimly.

"Yes," replied Rose seriously. "All right for you fellers in Derby, but nervy for isolated settlers. What sort of a position would Jasper and I be in now, for instance, if your armed patrol had not arrived."

"Come on," replied Spong, and rode on.

They were riding through bush parallel with the densely tree-lined bank of the Stewart River. A mile farther on they rode out on to a long open flat, green as a lawn from the young grass of the Wet. In startled surprise they reined up.

Coming straight towards them was a mob of painted warriors, the upright hafts of their long spears a little forest. A fairly compact mob of eighty warriors right out in the open on the little green flat. They halted, glaring towards the horsemen. Then their leaders turned and with waving arms yelled orders. The mob ran together, a compact mob of heavily armed warriors, now silently facing the horsemen. A wild picture of the primitive was that now solid little black crowd with their grotesquely painted bodies upon the intense green of the young grass, enclosed by the dull bush timber to the one side, the dense wall of river timber to the other. On their bodies broad bars of white and yellow war paint, vivid feathers in their headbands, dangling from every neck or from the human-hair belt at the waist a stone dagger and tuft of cow tail. Around the waists of some were from six to a dozen tufts of cow tail. For this, as it was learned afterwards, was a picked mob. Every man among them who was not yet a man killer had had to prove that he at least had been game to kill a white man's beast.

Straggled out behind the mob, now poised like black statues, were numerous women, each with as heavy a bundle of spears as she could stagger under upon her shoulder. They had carried those long, heavy bundles for many miles, "spare ammunition" for the warriors.

"Phew!" breathed Rose, "they've enough weapons to tackle Derby-let alone a lonely homestead defended by only two white men and a dozen frightened stockboys."

"We'll see what's doing," said Spong, "but ride easy. Come on."

"They'll open fire if they've got any ammunition left," suggested Rose.

"We'll soon know," replied Spong.

As the little troop came on at walking pace the tribesmen's leaders turned again and shouted to the mob. There answered an upthrust of many spearheads, clattering of wommeras, then the thunder of stamping feet in unison to deep-chested roars of "Huh!", "Huh!", "Huh!"

The faces of the trackers twitched uneasily to the excitement of their horses, the faces of Rose's stockboys changed to a dirty colour, their eyes began to roll.

"You savvy, boss, what name him feller talk?" inquired Tracker Peter easily of Spong.

"No," answered Spong, "what name him feller talk?" Tracker Peter explained that the leaders were exhorting their men to stand steady, to wait until the horsemen came within spear throw. Then each man was to leap forward and hurl one spear. Then all would run forward to hurl spears while the fleetest raced around the horsemen's flanks and encircled them.

"We'll see about *that!*" said Spong, and reined in his horse. Casually but carefully he impressed upon the trackers, and especially the station boys, that there might be trouble, but if they did exactly as he told them none of them would get hurt. He was going to ride to within shouting distance, he explained, then call upon the tribesmen to lay down their arms and give up any wanted men amongst them who had broken the Law. The rest must turn back, but could go free. If, he explained to his attentive listeners, they refused to lay down arms then the patrol would pretend to charge them. If the mob did not break and run, then he would rein up just out of spear throw and try again to induce them to give up the wanted men. If they still refused and attempted to fight, then on the order each man was to fire into the crowd. If they still came on then the troop would wheel and gallop away, only to wheel around and order surrender again. Spong impressed upon the black boys that, if necessary, they could fight all afternoon like this and not a man be hurt if they obeyed orders and were not cut off. It did not matter about the numbers of the others for they were on foot and out in the open while all the patrol were mounted.

The fear in the faces of the boys changed to relieved grins. "Now spread out!" ordered Spong. And the little line of horsemen advanced steadily again.

When within easy shouting distance Spong reined in and called to the waiting mob to lay down their spears, and give up the wanted men. A howl of derision was the answer. Spong waited for the hubbub to die down, then gave Tracker Peter instructions to shout the order in tribal lingo. A roar of execrations and insults was the reply, warriors leaping into the air, waving spears and chewing their beards in rage, challenging:

"You dingoes, come on and fight!"

Spong then impressed upon the patrol that he intended to make a sham charge. That, whatever they did, they must watch him. For if the tribesmen did not break and run then he was going to rein in just out of spear throw, and try for surrender yet once again.

"Come on!" and Spong leaned over the saddle, the troop behind him at the gallop.

A roar from the tribesmen, the leaders bounding out ahead with spears at full balance.

Spong reined his horse back on its haunches. He had hoped they would break and run for cover. A blood-curdling yell went up as the horses reined in. Men came bounding out from the compact group.

Spong whipped out his revolver and stood in the stirrups. "Drop him spears you feller! Quick feller now!"

But their roar of defiance was nearly drowned by their stamping feet.

"Aim for those six leaders!" called Spong to Rose and the trackers, "but don't fire until ... !"

"Crack!" It was Spong's revolver for with one roar the whole mob bounded forward with spears at the throw. The crack of the rifles sounded as men stumbled or fell. There was no missing that dense crowd as the horses wheeled away followed by a shower of spears.

"Back!" shouted Spong and the excited horses galloped back only to turn and come plunging almost to within spear throw again!

"Drop him spears quick feller!" yelled Spong again.

A moment's hesitation now for four of their leaders were down, then half the mob came bounding forward.

"Fire!" yelled Spong and this time six men stumbled or fell to the crack of the rifles. The whole mob now hesitated and Spong yelled, "Keep firing! Quick feller!"

To the crack of revolvers five more men were hit and there was a distinct wavering in the mob.

"Come on!" yelled Spong and they galloped straight at the mob that turned and raced for the river, yelling horsemen at their heels.

28

THE CAVE OF THE BATS

SPONG wheeled his men back from the danger of that wall of river trees, whence the tribesmen could safely hurl a vengeful spear, while behind them awaited their ever-ready protector, the water.

He ordered Trackers Paddy and Billy to circle out and see if they could pick up any wounded or prisoners while the patrol rode back to the black figures lying sprawled at the scene of the fight, Sambo and Captain prominent amongst them.

"We have avenged the deaths of Peyton and Plummer," said Rose soberly, "and this should also mean at least a breathing space for Oobagooma."

The lubras, dropping their spear bundles, had fled also. The patrol burned many hundreds of spears alone.

The trackers returned with three limping men and some frightened lubras who had been helping the wounded away.

With practised fingers Spong dressed the wounds. They were not very bad; the constable knew in his heart that in a couple of months or so these men would again, but much more cautiously, be running around spearing cattle. They were then all questioned through Tracker Peter. A lubra named Gunbunger proved the best witness, telling how they were all going to Oobagooma to spear the white men, then the station boys, then the horses, loot the homestead and burn it, then drive the cattle far back into the ranges.

Spong impressed upon them to tell all natives far and wide that if they speared white men, or station boys either, then many police would surely hunt them down and avenge the killings. But if all men went back to their hills then all would be well.

Inspector Lawrence's patrol returned to Derby during the middle of March 1895 to refit, then ride again. For Captain and Ellemara, Carolan and Demon, Lillimarra and Fouringer, Mullenbuddin and Tilbomer, Muckerawarra and Bundermen and Byerbell, Pyabarra and Canada and others of the gang, apart from other scattered local groups, were still boastfully active.

The settlers greeted the end of the Wet with relief. They could return to outdoor work again. With the added relief that Pigeon was long since dead.

If only they could have seen within the Cave of the Bats!

I have not been into that particular cave but when riding with a police patrol in 1932-3 we camped in the vicinity with old Felix Edgar, who was mustering his cattle. Felix rode with the patrols throughout most of that wild three years and here is his campfire description of the cave:

"It's a weird place, Jack," explained Felix in his slow, deep voice, "this aboriginal Cave of the Bats. Only a score of miles from here, just north of the Horseshoe, where the Mount North Creek comes through a natural tunnel under the Napier Range to flow into the Lennard. The water, ages ago, churned out this subterranean course for itself, right under that portion of the range. The cave opens out into a huge cavern, then closes again to a tunnel through which to walk a tall man must bend his head. In places the water is shallow, elsewhere it is deep enough to swim. A man wading through the pools takes the chance of putting his foot upon a river crocodile, though they are only from four to six feet long. A streak of daylight shows at the west end of the cave. Here is an old aboriginal burying ground, the 'Death Ground' of Pigeon's tribe since probably the Dream Time. Musty skeletons of all ages lie everywhere.

"Where the creek emerges on the western side of the range it joins another and plunges into a wild ravine in which grow gorgeous Leichhardt pine, native fig trees, gums and many trees, shrubs and grasses in what you writer men call 'riotous profusion'. Snakes there too. One day there I saw the largest rock python I've ever seen, the great lazy mass of him coiled up like a mighty turban. He was on top of a grey granite boulder surrounded by greenery. The sunlight poured down upon him, the big thick coils of him were gleaming with black and gold. I've never quite forgotten that big old-man snake, he was a beauty."

Felix paused, leaned forward and with practised fingers flipped a live coal from the fire to his pipe bowl.

"Yes, Jack," he puffed, "it's a weird place, the cave and its surroundings too. The day I saw the snake I climbed down the ravine where it tumbles into the gorge. Many of the trees down there were festooned with countless 'ropes' of flying foxes; there must have been vast hordes of them."

Such was Felix's description in part. And now, in March 1895, when the settlers believed Pigeon dead, here was a fire far within the Cave of the Bats. And crouching over that fire was - Pigeon!

A wonderful hideout, this Cave of the Bats. Not only was a hunted man in there invisible. Not only was he safe, for who would dare to enter even though they found the cave and suspected that someone was within? Not only was a hunted man perfectly safe in there, but he could choose whichever side of the range he wished to emerge upon. He had only to walk and wade through this tunnel cave. Whereas pursuing horsemen must ride twenty-five miles to get around the range just there, the man in the tunnel could, if he wished, remain deep within the cave. Or walk out of one side of the range and vanish into ravine and gorge. Or walk out of the other side.

And Pigeon was there now-deep down under the heart of the range.

A sullen Pigeon this, the dim fire glow turning to bronze his brooding face. Hunched up there, he was no longer the well-conditioned athlete who rode in Constable Richardson's patrol. But he had regained his health and much of his strength, and his wounds were healed, though there were two bullets in him yet. For Pigeon had received four wounds, not three, two from rifle bullets, two from revolver.

It was his big mother Jinny who had helped him into this cave, to live or to die. No one else would he trust with his life, only his mother Jinny. Even his favourite lubra Cangamvara was not to know yet whether he was alive or dead.

Only his mother he trusted with his life. She was the only soul in the world who knew where he was.

The Council of the Old Men of his own tribe were sure he was still alive, because his mother had not, in accordance with tribal law, reported his death. But even the Council did not know where he was, nor did they ask.

As for the rest of the tribe, if questioned, they shook their heads with downcast look.

This meant that Pigeon was dead. For it is not lawful to mention the dead by name.

Cunning Pigeon! Even when he knew he was very near to death, he gasped out his command to Jinny his mother bending over him: "Tell tribe-say I'm dead! When white man ask then say: "Pigeon him dead! We put him longa hole! We know him dead by smell!"

And Jinny had obeyed as she did in all things. She had tended his wounds, fed him, guarded him, crooned over him as he raved, brought him back to life. And brought him the news.

For long now he had crouched in the Cave of the Bats, brooding. In the cool, deep silence, a silence that was frightening as Time brooded on. Ah! a faint splash, somewhere - in some black pool. Silence. Presently, away in under the range, a "Drip!", "Drip!", "Drip!", growing ominously distinct only to fade into silence.

Ah! Mother Jinny was coming. Pigeon looked up. He did not see, for she was black as the cavern. He did not hear, for she was silent as the silence. She squatted down beside him. Coughed.

Weird echoes went sighing down the cavern. Thus Pigeon brooded.

For long now, while recovering, here he had crouched in the Cave of the Bats, brooding. Brooding over what he believed could have been. Brooding on the present, but particularly, with crinkled brow and snarl on his lips, brooding on the future.

At any time he would be a hunted man again, to be shot, or hung if caught. He knew so well! How many times had he hunted for the hunters! And he had seen men hung.

If they caught him alive they would hang him. They would never cease hunting him until he was dead. He knew! He had killed white men; the black did not matter now. And he had urged the tribes to kill all the whites. They would hunt him, not with one patrol but with many, season after season, until they caught or shot him. If ... ! Ah!

Pigeon was going hunting too. While the patrols were hunting him, he would hunt white men. He would surprise those patrols: he would be both hunter and hunted. More than that, he would end up by being the hunter!

Fiercely, with gathering strength, he brooded there, planning to make it all come true. To gather together what remained of his gang, to raid a station for firearms, then add to his gang other men who could use firearms, raid yet another station until he had gathered the fighting men of all the tribes together to wipe out all the whites. He would do it yet.

A very shrewd aboriginal this Sandamara, called by white men Pigeon. Sandamara the ex-police tracker who knew so much of the white man's ways.

So he brooded in the Cave of the Bats, fast gathering strength.

He would soon get in touch with Captain and Ellemara, Demon and Lillimarra and Coiro and make his first swift raid.

A huge, grotesque black shadow appeared on the dull grey walls illumined by the firelight. It was Mother Jinny, bringing good beef freshly speared, her dilly-bag stuffed with vegetable foods that her hero son might eat and grow ever stronger until he became a killer again.

29

THE "RESURRECTION" OF PIGEON

IT was in March that Constable Pilmer from Fitzroy Crossing was riding just out from the big old trees of the Fitzroy River, riding alone. Except for worrying over certain urgent commands from distant Headquarters as to the dire necessity of arresting certain native outlaws, Pilmer felt contented. The little police station, its timbers hewn from the bush, was beginning to take form, despite patrols and the Wet. And, thank heaven the Dry was coming at last. This urgent patrolling throughout the Wet had knocked the stuffing out of police, men, and horses. But now the Dry was here; a clear blue, cloudless sky, sparkling sunlight that invited all to breathe deep of new young air of life. All was now full of life, life just "busting" to spring up and live and grow. Green young grass was everywhere, green of hills and valley, of plain and range. Beside him amongst the luxuriant undergrowth and big river trees rose a ceaseless shrieking and cackling and chattering of bird life, at times in vivid, whistling swarms. Away out on the plain too a lively line of brolgas were trumpeting and pirouetting in fantastic dance, in the joy of a new-born year warm with life. Yes, young Pilmer's horse felt good this morning and so did the rider, taking it easy. Away back at camp the boys were shoeing horses, repairing saddlery, giving themselves and the animals a few days' much-needed spell. Pilmer, for some unaccountable reason, had felt the urge for a ride along the river. He might cut tracks, so Excuse whispered. Though it was known that all wanted local men were away back in the nor-west hills, most were back in the Leopolds. Idly Pilmer was thinking of Goiro, and his savage brother "Doctor", two of the local native terrorists. They were not afraid of the whites either for they had threatened both McAtee and Gregory to their faces that they would "bring a mob and kill them!" And these settlers had impressed upon Pilmer in no uncertain terms that this was no idle threat. Their station boys went in fear of the two wild brothers, not daring to interfere even when they rode upon them red-handed while spearing stock. If and when Coiro attacked the lonely homestead it would mean only a matter of time with his mob behind him.

Pilmer was riding past Cingarra waterhole, about 200 yards to his left. Between him and the heavily timbered waterhole stood a solitary line of trees. Idly he turned his horse; he would have a look at the placid old waterhole, now alive with waterfowl.

He rode through the trees and there, in the open right before him, was Coiro casually walking towards the waterhole. Instantly Pilmer leant over his saddle as Coiro glanced over his shoulder. One frozen moment and instinct carried Coiro's legs at the bound for the waterhole. But the horseman was too close, headed him off and wheeled his horse right across his path.

"Drop him spear quick feller now, Coiro!" shouted Pilmer. Coiro with startled eyes leapt back, trying to ship the long spear, but the horse plunged straight at him. He lunged as Pilmer ducked and snatched the spear from his hand. With a snarl Coiro whipped a tomahawk from his belt but the horse swerved and the tomahawk whizzed over Pilmer's back. Coiro kept backing from the plunging horse, whipping out his throwing club which Pilmer warded off to a glancing blow across the back. As Coiro snarled back from the plunging hooves he jerked back his arm for another blow but Pilmer whipped out his revolver and shot him through the heart.

As his plunging horse circled around the prostrate figure Pilmer gasped in great breaths. Phew! what a close shave it had been! If Coiro had heard him he would have waited behind those trees. Phew Pilmer! you must never, never go to sleep like that again. Otherwise you will sleep-just as Coiro is sleeping down there!

Almost on that same day, 17th April 1895, about 100 miles farther north, Constable Dave Brice from the Lennard was on patrol near Mt Broome.

This well-liked patrolman was known far and wide as the "Boney bream". About forty years of age, tall and thin, dreamy-eyed, quiet and unassuming, he would suddenly "come to life", though, on the rare occasions when he lost his temper, or found himself in a hot spot. He was a good bushman, a good horse-man, a good revolver shot, and a good fellow. Although well able to look after himself he was somewhat of a fatalist and did not seem to care overmuch for his own life, nor for anyone else's if there was nothing he could do about it.

He had chummed up with his "opposite", Special Constable James Price, who had been a fencer on Meda station before volunteering as a special when the Pigeon trouble became acute. Jimmy Price was an ex-naval man of stocky build. Always ready for a laugh and a joke, as noisy as Brice was sometimes taciturn. Jimmy was a poor bushman, a poor horseman, a poor shot, but a good fellow. He was very handy during the arduous work of the patrols in that he was always ready and willing to tackle any uncongenial job-and there were plenty. Jimmy was the reverse of a fatalist and cared a great deal about his life. All these short-comings of Jimmy's, Brice took with amused tolerance. The long and short man, the quiet and noisy man became firm friends, to the amused asides of their patrol mates.

But on this brilliant morning away in the loneliness of the Leopolds Constable Dave Brice was on his own, except for Trackers Davey, Billy and Drake and the patient horses. They were climbing up among the ridges of big Mt Broome. Presently, choosing the easiest spur he could find Brice was riding steadily upward. This was the second highest mountain in the Kimberleys, rising up out of the southern edge of the Leopolds. Soon, they had to dismount and lead the horses.

Brice was not following tracks, for the patrol had seen no sign of natives for days. All the way from the Lennard police outpost they had sought to cut the tracks of Captain or any others of the gang. In vain. The thousands of natives in all the Leopolds and beyond seemed to have vanished.

Constable Brice determined to climb the mountain, if only for the view of the crags and valleys, the table tops and pinnacles, the rivers and unexplored gorges he must glimpse from there. Surely he might see at least some hunting, or smoke signal.

The patrol trudged on until near the top of the mountain, but saw no sign of smoke, let alone track of man. Near by, a steep, grassy spur rose up towards the blue sky. Brice sent trackers Davey, Billy and Drake to walk up there and see what they could see. Brice stood by the horses watching as the three dark figures slowly toiled up the steep spur. They had almost reached the top when Brice gasped and snatched for his holster. A naked tribesman had stepped from behind a boulder and was shipping his spear to throw at the unconscious Davey only fifteen yards away. As Brice yelled came the report of two rifles and the tribesman threw up his arms and staggered back, falling out of sight.

Trackers Billy and Drake had seen him and fired on the instant.

The dead man was Tumanurumberry.

While his wounds had slowly mended after the fight with Captain at Barellam Springs he had hidden here all alone. And now, though with but one eye, he was fit and well again, planning to go down into the valleys and seek his revenge.

But this warm morning, when danger seemed so far away, he had fallen asleep upon his own lookout. Yes, and now Tumanurumberry-slept!

During Constable Brice's following patrol he was riding back among the ranges between the Barker and Lennard rivers, back to the little Lennard River police outpost. His trackers suddenly broke into a gallop and soon ran to earth a *munjon* tribesman named Uldigee. In panting fright he gasped out startling news, that Pigeon had "come to life again". That he had come into the ranges and met Captain. That there had been a "big fight". That the tribesmen had taken all the women from Pigeon and Captain and Barney, had speared Pigeon in the wrist and put two spears into Barney's back. That Pigeon and Captain and Barney had then started south for the Fitzroy to kill white men.

Brice sat his horse in silent perturbation while his trackers questioned the prisoner. But they could get nothing more of sense out of him; he was frightened into a yabbering confusion.

Brice swiftly pencilled a report, adding "this information may not be reliable". He sent a tracker riding in haste with the news to the Lennard River police outpost. From there, in disbelief, Sergeant Cadden forwarded it by swift rider to Derby.

Superintendent Lawrence received the news in disbelieving consternation. But in a matter almost of hours he received confirmation that electrified every patrol into swift action.

The tribesman Uldigee's information was partly true. Pigeon had appeared and joined up with Captain and the gang with phantom swiftness. They immediately turned on tribesmen within reach and evened up scores, shooting eight in revenge for vendetta and women troubles. Then they had in fact turned south for the Fitzroy, desperately short of ammunition. But the widely scattered patrols did not as yet know this. Until ...

One glorious morning a patrol was leisurely riding towards the Barker Range. A tracker riding away out in front reined in his horse, leaning over its neck. Then slipped to the ground, kneeling. Leaping bolt upright he waved and yelled piercingly. The constable thought he had been bitten by a death adder. Another tracker came hurrying. He too jumped off, looked, sprang up and yelled. The two other trackers came galloping. They too looked, then all four yelled and waved excitedly to the patrol.

The patrol officer rode up to find his trackers in almost hysterical excitement, their eyes bulging as they pointed downward and yelled.

"Pigeon!", "Track belonga Pigeon!", "Pigeon!", "Pigeon!"

For another two years every tracker, no matter how experienced and sedate, would again and again go wild with excitement at sight of the tracks of "Pigeon!", "Pigeon!", "Pigeon!"

The patrol officer disbelieved, yet knew it must be true. For the bush natives, let alone trackers, never forget the individual track of a man, or horse, or any other animal.

The patrol gathered silently as the trackers pointed at tracks, shouting "Captain!", "Barney!", "Towerdine!", "Lillimarral", "Til¬bomer!", "Bundermen!", "Mererimerl", "Pyabarra!", "Demon!", in rising excitement as they recognized the tracks of old members and notorious newcomers to the gang.

In vain, though, they looked for the tracks of Ellemara. Ellemara, now recovered though with a back that never would be quite straight again, had heard the news of Pigeon's coming and emerged from his hideout. But he would not join Pigeon right away. Those whistling bullets and the thud of hot lead into his back were still tender memories, while his weakened legs still trembled to his nightmares of the thud of galloping hooves.

With his faithful little Wondaria of the Laughing Waters trailing behind, carrying her dilly-bag packed with food and her master's spare spears, Ellemara followed slowly on the tracks of Pigeon and Captain. From afar, he would await and see what happened in Pigeon's first clash with the whites. If all went well, then Ellemara would be on the scene in time for a share in the glory. If not, then he would be discreetly in the rear with a flying start from those galloping hooves.

The patrol officer sent a galloping messenger to the Fitzroy police station. From here, the news would be telegraphed to Derby. Yes, faster this news than the wild man's smoke signals, though only along the length of the Fitzroy and into the East Kimberley wherever the wires went.

The patrol followed on along the tracks of Pigeon and Captain and the gang. Away back in Derby Inspector Lawrence sent warnings far and wide to every settler within reach; in mortified tribulation wired the ominous news far south to Police Headquarters in Perth. Then with feverish activity he set about getting in touch with his scattered patrols, ordering them to concentrate towards the Fitzroy.

The settlers one by one heard the news with troubled brow.

And this news, for some strange reason, swept throughout the thinly settled parts of the West Kimberley as the "resurrection of Pigeon."

30

PIGEON MOVES TO ATTACK THE SUPPLY WAGON

IN great spirits, Pigeon and the survivors of his reunited gang strode south through the bush towards the Fitzroy road. In no hurry, for the scouts had reported to Pigeon that his intended prey, the supply wagon to Fitzroy Crossing, was seven suns' camp away, just slowly toiling up the road from distant Derby.

Pigeon had again organized his women lookouts, through Mother Jinny, He had sent her out a week ahead to collect them, before he left the Cave of the Bats to rejoin Captain. He wanted only those lubras who could be swiftly gathered. A swarm of eager warriors and women would gather around him immediately news of his big "come-back" swept across ranges and plain.

Pigeon had planned carefully those last few weeks within the Cave of the Bats. Urgently he desired to attack Collins's Oscar Range station and seize the much-needed guns and ammunition, loot the homestead of stores and fire it, then retire back into the hills and pick the best from the cattle-spearers who would come to join him. Then he would make another lightning raid for yet more rifles,

But Mother Jinny had warned him that there were two white stockmen now working for Collins. That the stockboys were armed and more numerous, and "cheeky" too. That day and night a strict watch was kept around the homestead. Her spies amongst the station lubras had whispered to her that there would be no chance of a surprise. Added to this, sometimes now a couple of well-armed settlers camped at the homestead, men who came riding along the Fitzroy road to The Crossing and beyond, or came from there to pay attention to their own stations for a few weeks before riding back or away again to rejoin the patrols. Men such as Blythe, and Felix Edgar, and Green, and Barnett, and Black, and Rose, and other white men. Collins had never quite believed that Pigeon was really dead. Fearing an attack on the station, he had asked that police stay there permanently.

Mother Jinny's information was remarkably accurate. Collins had written urgently to Inspector Lawrence at Derby that a constable and trackers be permanently stationed at the homestead.

Reluctantly Pigeon had given up thought of attack for the present, knowing through Mother Jinny how short of firearms and ammunition Captain and his men now were.

In scowling thought, he had pondered deeply, by the fire within the Cave of the Bats, in the deep, brooding silence, with not even a murmur from the steadily burning fire.

A very game man was Pigeon, despite his knowledge of the white man's beliefs, and his own despising of many tribal beliefs. For the Australian aboriginal has a traditional dread of deep, dark places, where dwell the spirits of the night, and of the underground.

But the ancestral tribe, or at least their Council of the Old Men, had dwelt here, maybe only as refuge or perhaps more truly during periods of sacred ceremony, for their crude drawings adorned the dull grey walls as deathless witness.

Maybe it was the spirit from their ancestral past that one night breathed into the brooding mind of their tribal son.

"The supply wagon!"

Of course! Pigeon drew a long breath, his eyes grew big and glassy as suddenly he crouched forward, glaring into the fire.

Of course! the supply wagon to The Crossing from Derby, two hundred and ten miles up along the Fitzroy River. Meandering along there through the bush out from the foothills, by the river at the edge of the big old Fitzroy plains.

The supply wagon to the telegraph station and newly built police station would be loaded with at least six months' supply of stores, with firearms and ammunition. There would be plenty of ammunition now for the patrol stationed at the Fitzroy would be needing it, needing more too for the other patrols that rode back from the ranges to the Fitzroy. More rifles and guns and revolvers and plenty of ammunition for the settlers too, clamouring for more firearms for protection against the native troubles.

Pigeon raised noiselessly laughing face to the cavern roof and felt awe within him.

Yes, the supply wagon. His spirit ancestors had answered him, answered him from far back in the wonder days of the Dream Time.

So now on a beautiful morning they strode along under the bluest of skies, the riot of tall grasses even now turning golden brown, a light breeze idly whispering among the trees, sighing down in the valleys. A tree-clad, precipitous little range lay before them. The mob was in great form, laughingly excited at joining up with Pigeon again, hilariously excited at thought of ambushing the supply wagon, certain of another but much greater victory than the successful attack on Fred Edgar's wagon and cattle and the killing of Burke and Gibbs. Pigeon and Captain strode along ahead carrying rifles, the sun gleaming on their chocolate-bronze bodies newly scarred with wounds, wounds from both white and black. Just behind them were Lillimarra and Mullenbuddin, behind them Demon with his grim face set in an unholy light of anticipation of a big kill and probable fighting over the spoil afterwards. Teebuck and Byerbell, Fouringer and Bundermen, Pyabarra and Yarramarra and Murrarnin, all those still alive of the old gang were there, with eager newcomers to treble their numbers. What a great mob he could arm when he took the arms from the supply wagon, then the rifles and guns and revolvers and ammunition from The Crossing.

Pigeon, feathers of the killer hawk bedecking his hair, breathed deeply of the air of his native hills as he strode along in the lead. Life was giving him yet another chance, a big chance.

They had barely a dozen firearms amongst them now, while for several rifles the ammunition was revolver cartridges bound with paperbark to fit the rifle breeches.

Pigeon grinned to himself at the pleasant surprise he was about to spring upon his men. He led them to Wingina Gorge. And here, in the caves, he unearthed a few packets of Winchester bullets and revolver cartridges and cartridges for Captain's precious Schneider that he had secreted during the "fight in the caves".

Cunning Pigeon. Grinning, he accepted their acclamations of delight. Yes, their Pigeon was a leader indeed, he thought of everything, he could even do that wonderful thing, think a long way ahead, could think as well as the white man - better! as they would soon prove to the whites.

31

ELLEMARA FEELS UNEASY

THE remainder of this quite formidable little band were armed each with a bundle (which their womenfolk must carry of course) of long, heavy war spears. And with dowick or whackaburra and short throwing club. And every spearhead was the cruel "shovel-blade" which gave those greatly envied warriors who possessed one such great faith in their own armed might. The dreaded "shovel-blade" spearheads were broad assegai heads of iron that could (and today also do) kill a bullock.

This fact gives an interesting sidelight on the initiative and adaptability of the wild Australian aboriginal. For the first settlers had come into the West Kimberley but a bare fifteen years before these events, while they and their scanty goods were in very small numbers and supply. Yet the Stone Age men had almost immediately realized the uses of iron, and more interesting still, had evolved an entirely new and murderously efficient spearhead, immeasurably different to their spearheads of the ages past. The "shovel-blade" was so called because it was first cut from worn-out, discarded or stolen shovel blades. Then from any occasional shovel or saw or piece of flat or part rounded iron that could be stolen. Flattened, cut and fashioned into a long, broad, assegai shape, the only tools ingenuity, patience, stone, sand, elbow grease, and water, such a spearhead could kill a man within three or four minutes, while an expert could kill a bullock with one throw. Other efficient iron spearheads were fashioned from worn-out horseshoes. These the settlers used as hinges for gates. At nights, the abos would lift off the gates and remove the hinges from gate and gate posts. They would trail a horseman for many miles if his horse was shod, seeking the opportunity to spear the horse for its shoes. Any scrap of iron of any sort which station natives could be coaxed or bullied to steal was an envied prize to the *munjons*, the wild men.

Other iron-tipped spears of Pigeon's men were fashioned from chain links, and other iron relics from Edgar's wagon. Sharp, strong, iron spearheads were capable of doing infinitely more damage than spearheads of stone or wood or bone.

Pigeon camped his eager mob by the foothills facing the plain, with the dense line of Fitzroy River trees only a few miles out in front. Just there, the rough bush road to The Crossing wound along parallel to the river.

Pigeon was puzzled when the lubra lookouts scattered along the range parallel with road and river continued to send word that the team remained camped away back along the road. Pigeon put it down to the terror of his name, and grinned, frowning uneasily all the same. Possibly "bush telegraph" had spread word that Pigeon and his gang were on the warpath again. But the wagon must come on now, it was much too far along the road to turn back. Still, he did not like it overmuch. He knew the patrols were far back in the Leopolds searching for Captain and Ellemara and the supposedly still scattered gang. Still, if a patrol captured any bush natives who had heard the news and in fear blurted it out ...

Pigeon believed the scattered patrols were a long way away.

Still, he knew well how fast and far a patrol can travel when it picks up a scent.

Pigeon's gang also knew that Ellemara was dawdling along a day's march behind them. They wondered that he had not caught them up by now. Pigeon guessed. After a while he grinned. Then he sent two lubras back to Ellemara with a message telling him that he was going to attack the Fitzroy Crossing supply wagon, that he knew Ellemara would be interested, for one of the boys travelling with the wagon was his old friend Danmarra the stockboy, he from whom Ellemara had taken Wondaria of the Laughing Waters. As an afterthought, Pigeon advised Ellemara that perhaps it might be best that he should leave Wondaria behind in safe hiding, lest Danmarra take her back again. A shame should that happen to her warrior, for then Laughing Waters would laugh no more.

Ellemara chewed his beard in snarling rage when he received this message. But there was nothing else for it. He picked up his spears and nodded curtly to Wondaria. He must join Pigeon's gang straight away, otherwise he would be laughed at by the women, jeered at by men who were game enough, would be cursed as a dingo and every man's hand would turn against him.

Taking his time, Ellemara followed along Pigeon's tracks. They were easy to follow, the tracks of this compact little mob, travelling straight south towards the big river. The merest child, thought Ellemara absentmindedly, would have told by the tracks that this obvious war party were making for a definite locality, with a set purpose in view. No scattering into small groups, no deviations, no straying from the main tracks for a little hunting, and not the slightest attempt to disguise the way of their going. Idly as he strode along, Ellemara read the tracks, nodding to each name as if he were greeting a friend. Pigeon, Captain, Lillimarra, Fouringer, Wonginn, Luter, Mererimer, Boll, Mullenbuddin, Warramarra, Bull, Woinmarra, Pyabarra, Canada, Rowally - he knew the tracks of every man, woman, and child in the crowd. None were strangers to him. He recognized the tracks of their individual dogs also.

As the warm morning drowsed on past midday, Ellemara frowned thoughtfully. Pigeon should really have taken just a little more care, even though he believed he would have to wait but a few hours for the wagon, then would be able to make a quick getaway. He really should have arranged this march as usual: the band to separate into fours, each four wide apart, by devious routes making their way to the meeting place. Easy thus to lure away pursuers if being tracked, while warning the scattered ones by runner or signal smoke. But these broad tracks! They were plain for any stray stockmen or tribesman hunter to see and comment upon - or any enemy.

Of course, the fool patrols were away back and far to the north-west searching among the Leopolds. Pigeon was travelling south in the very last area where they would expect him to be. He would strike quickly, then get back to the sheltering hills with the loot long before the vengeful patrols would know, much less be able to take action.

Ellemara grinned. Once back in the hills, all would be safe.

If danger threatened the hangers-on, of whom there would be plenty by that time, they could swiftly scatter in little fleeing groups. The gang meanwhile would disappear into the caves; Pigeon the crafty would be sure to make back to within striking distance of some favourite caves before he paused to divide the loot.

Ellemara grinned, striding on reassured. Pigeon certainly was a crafty planner; he always made sure of a line of retreat, with certain escape offering should need arise.

Yes, Ellemara strode on reassured. His dark thoughts had set his frightfully scarred back a-twitching, for it was not so very far from here!

Yes, once in the caves they would be safe. Only in Pigeon's caves, of course. Many a cave was only a hole that "went in", and "stayed there", whereas those caves that Pigeon knew and loved "came out". You could go in, a long way in, to other caves, then climb up, up, and come out into lovely daylight, while the stupid patrol would stay waiting for you away back where the hole "went in". There were other caves too that Pigeon knew, caves that went right through the mountain and came out the other side. You simply left your enemy waiting for you at the mouth of the cave, while you walked through and came *out* at the other end. And enjoyed a great laugh, and strolled away about your business.

Yes, those favourite caves of Pigeon's were lonesome but very comforting. A warrior was safe from the hardest riding patrol if he were within easy distance of those gloomy black dens.

Ellemara disliked the caves, loathed the deep ones. Even with reassuring torches of pandanus-palm leaves, or snake-wood. But without them ... ! He hated the groping through the darkness down there where no dull shade of light came from deep cracks high up; he hated particularly the wading when a cave floor would dip below water level; wading, spears tight clenched in one hand, the other groping along the cold wall, up to the waist in icy water and the dread of stepping on a crocodile which had come crawling along some subterranean stream from the river. He hated the climbing, groping up and down, never certain despite Pigeon's sneer, that he might not be stepping down into some deep, black hole, like the holes that the piccaninnies playing far away up in the sunlight above would throw stones down into and listen to hear them strike or faintly "plop!" into water far below.

Yes, Ellemara detested the caves, but loved their safety. Now, if Ellemara were only leader of the gang it was far back into the Leopolds that he would By after a foray. Into the safety of the mountains, the Precipice Range for instance, the Charnley and the Isdell; into the deep gorges, the rocky fastnesses parallel one with another, stretching far back to where there were no white men at all, only wild *munjons*, hostile tribesmen. But with an armed gang he could laugh at such enemies, if ever he had need to penetrate their fastnesses.

"True!" frowned Ellemara as he plodded on, "the patrols now ride the valleys between the deeper Leopolds and the white men in the Fitzroy."

Before reaching the Leopolds the gang must pass back through country ridden by the patrols. Some patrol would almost inevitably cut their tracks even though the tracks were days old and they then in safety.

Ellemara frowned. Tracks! The tracks of the gang were plain to see, coming right down here, obviously making back to the Fitzroy. Now if ... !

Ellemara stopped dead in his own tracks. If those tracks were seen by any wandering stockmen, let alone tribesmen like Danmarra the stockboy or Marawon the warrior from whom Pigeon had taken Cangamvara . . . or by any tribesman nursing a vendetta against the gang, then they would hurry to the nearest settler who would send a rider galloping to get in touch with a patrol!

Ellemara thought deeply. Ah yes! they were safe, those caves of Pigeon's. Pigeon did not have to reach the Leopolds to be safe. For the first time, Ellemara felt grateful to Pigeon for being the crafty leader he was. But Ellemara was cunning too. Those plain tracks, and the thoughts of the trackers and Danmarra and the many blood vendettas now caused by the gang, brought a worried frown to his deeply corrugated brow.

He was climbing a gentle spur leading easily up to the summit of a line of hills. Once up there he turned and stood, gazing thoughtfully back. Back along those tracks was some five miles of level country, scantily timbered to a parallel line of hills over which the gang and he had come. No sign of life but birds, and a mob of lazily grazing 'roos.

Ellemara turned to Wondaria. GrufHy he ordered her to stay there, day and night, and watch back along those tracks until he sent for her. But if she saw any man following along the tracks, either black or white, she was to come for him like the wind. She knew exactly where Pigeon was awaiting them.

Wondaria nodded obediently, sought cover, and squatted down quietly to commence her lonely vigil. Ellemara grunted and strode on alone, feeling greatly relieved.

He reached Pigeon's camp before sundown, was greeted boisterously by the gang, in silent dread by the occasional tribesmen and women beginning to drift in. Cheerfully he replied to Pigeon's veiled sallies, sensing that Pigeon had something more serious on his mind.

The wagon was toiling slowly along. But now there were two wagons travelling in company. For The Crossing wagon had waited for a station wagon to join it. With each wagon were three mounted white men, well armed, four blackboys and three dogs. Six white men, eight stockboys, six savage dogs; well prepared and alert - a tough nut to crack. And Pigeon had but a dozen men with firearms and scant ammunition.

But he was determined to attack. He must gain firearms and a success before the patrols got on his track. Besides, he would seize the loot of two wagons now, instead of one. Long into the night they sat, intently listening while Pigeon impressively explained to them his plan. It was a clever plan, too; even Ellemara grudgingly admitted it must succeed.

Some of the Australian aboriginals, at least in those localities where varied and plentiful food supplies have built up the native physique in their own environment have proved by no means the fools that many have believed them to be.

Next day at midday the wagons toiled past along the road, one close behind the other, watched from far back by many hidden eyes. But the teamsters had seen no sign of a bush native for weeks past.

Pigeon knew almost for a certainty where the teams would camp. Nearly all here knew every inch of this country.

That evening, Pigeon and his gang would follow on. They would attack at dawn. The fighters of his gang would make a sudden concentrated rush upon the white men while the others scattered the riding horses. The rest would be easy.

The wagons had barely disappeared, creaking along the road, when the whole mob seemed to stiffen in expectant silence. Yet there had been no unusual sound, merely the contented midday call of birds, the vanishing shout of a teamboy calling to his team. Moments later Wondaria appeared racing among the trees to sag to her knees panting amongst them. For minutes she was unable to speak. Then she gasped out that a police patrol was coming. She had seen them riding down over the hills and on to the flat from where Ellemara had left her. Once on the flat the tracks were so plain that the trackers had leant over their horses' necks and the patrol was coming cantering along. Wondaria had come swiftly to warn them; she had run all the way. Pigeon leapt up, his face twitching with fury. He would fight the patrol. But Wondaria gasped out that there were "plenty white men" coming with the patrol. "Plenty feller!", "Plenty feller!"

So there were, comparatively speaking. For two patrols, riding towards one another from different localities, had met almost exactly where both cut the tracks. And with each patrol there happened to be riding three specials.

Pigeon yelled to the tribesmen to scatter and run far and wide, to try and lure the patrol away on a false scent. With a nod to his own gang he was running straight back towards the foot-hills. He knew that he must waste no time for they had to run almost directly back upon their tracks for some miles before getting near even the first series of caves.

They did not quite make it. They were hurrying upward to cross the foothills when two horsemen appeared over the summit ahead. Recognition was mutual. A yell, and the horsemen were galloping down towards them. A moment's hesitation, then Pigeon kept running. More horsemen appeared. Pigeon dropped to his knees, aimed and fired. The horsemen scattered, though still galloping on as Captain fired. Pigeon fired again but two of the horsemen jumped from their horses and knelt down to fire while others came galloping on. A bullet whipped up the dust right beside Pigeon, another whined off a rock from behind which Captain was firing. A policeman whipped out a revolver and started firing as he came galloping, yet another did the same. Pigeon leaped up and raced for cover with Ellemara at his heels, Ellemara whose frantic back was a bow again as bullets came whistling by. The mouth of a large, sloping cave opened up before them. Ellemara actually bounded past Pigeon and was into the cave to fall with rattling spears and outspread limbs a-sprawl in the sloping darkness. They all bunched up while plunging into the cave with the hoof-beats almost upon them. A man screamed to a "smack!" and went plunging and writhing sixty feet below, followed by a comrade with a bullet through the heart. A mass of falling, writhing bodies and clattering weapons, they tumbled down amongst one another to the bottom of the sloping cavern.

32

CAUGHT LIKE RATS IN A TRAP

WITH the galloping patrol almost at the cavern mouth Tracker Billy reefed his horse aside as a bullet fired from below zipped away his hat, while another ploughed along the neck of the following horse. Lucky indeed were both riders that Pigeon and Captain had not had time to recover from their tumble down the cave.

"Gallop all around quick feller and find any outlet from the cave!" shouted a constable to the trackers. But a station boy of Edgar's excitedly yabbered to Felix Edgar that there was no outlet. He had been here before when hunting.

"Then we've got them!" exulted the constable. "Caught like rats in a trap!"

Well back from the entrance, by standing in their stirrups they could peer about ten feet down the sloping funnel of the cave, sunlight shining full upon and down it. It sloped down just under the brow of a grassy knoll, about halfway up the slope of a steep spur rising from the river.

"There's not the faintest hope of escape," declared the delighted constable. "What a catch! Pigeon and Captain and Ellemara and the gang caught like rats in a trap! And like rats they must be feeling right now. We'll just stay put and starve them out - they *must* come out in time. But don't take any risks unless they rush. It would be a shame to have a man killed needlessly."

The horses were taken down the slope of the hill under cover in charge of a tracker and three blackboys. Each man of the patrols picked his own cover close to the mouth of the cave until they three parts encircled it. The knoll rose straight above the lip of the roof - no need for men there. With rifles ready and eyes to the cave mouth they took out pipes and smoked, in laughing excitement awaiting a possible rush, though not expecting it until well into the night. After a while Felix Edgar cut a long sapling, fastened his hat to it, and poked it out towards the edge of the hole. A bullet from below flipped it into the air.

"They'd really shoot a man," grinned Felix, "if he put his head over the hole."

As the afternoon wore on a constable grinned in the throes of a brilliant brain wave. He ordered the trackers and horseboys to collect armfuls of stones and lay them in heaps near the mouth of the cave. While this was being done he explained to the patrols:

"We'll fix them! Every man of us will throw stones down the cave - a hail of stones. They'll have to surrender quick and lively or take their chance and rush up the cave. So when we start keep your rifles handy to block the rush."

All agreed this brainy plan must flush the quarry. Willingly they set to work collecting and piling heaps of stones three parts around the cave mouth. When all was ready every man crept forward and began hurling stones out into the cave mouth. Two rifle shots were the immediate result, then silence except for the terrifying clattering of stones bouncing down the walls of the cave. But no cry of surrender, no upward rush of demoralized men. Soon, every stone had gone. They gazed at one another questioningly, the senior constable glaring at the boy who had been down the cave before. And this boy, grinning from ear to ear, burst out into hilarious laughter.

"What name?" demanded the constable sharply.

"No more t'row 'im sthone!" chuckled the boy. "No blurry good!"

"Why not!" demanded the constable.

"Plenty feller big feller hole down below," laughed the blackboy. "Boy down there he run along under roof under hole. Stone no more can hit him!"

"Then why the blazes didn't you tell us in the first place, you stupid bonehead!" swore the irate constable, "instead of grinning there like a Cheshire cat! You've got less brains than a porcupine," he added disgustedly. "And stop that hyena laughter," he added again, "or I'll chuck you down the cave."

In the general laugh, the constable grinned resignedly. "Oh well," he said, "they've got no water, and no food. They must either perish, or crawl up and surrender sometime."

But the abashed stockboy was muttering to Tracker Billy. "What name that blurry fool talk 'im now?" demanded the constable.

"Him say plenty water down longa hole."

"Well then tell him to explain to you all about the cave," ordered the policeman, "so that we know just what it looks like down below!"

The tracker explained that the blackboy said the cave opened out below into a cavern, running a short way into the hill, and a little way back towards the river. That there was plenty of room down there and a pool of clear water towards the hill end of the cavern. That was all.

"Oh well," said the patrol officer, "they're all caged down there anyway. There is no exit, no food. They must either starve or come up."

He ordered the blackboys to collect firewood and pile it near the cave entrance; the trackers to bring up the packhorses with the food and blankets and camping gear.

That night a goodly firelight brightly illuminated the mouth of the cave. Four men remained on watch, two hours at a time. The patrol rolled themselves in their blankets close behind them, rifles to hand. If the men below came creeping up the sloping cave then at the instant alarm every rifle would be pointing at the cave mouth.

Throughout the night an occasional shot came thundering up the cave funnel. And throughout the next day, just now and then. And throughout that night also. And throughout the next day.

It grew wearisome, waiting up on top, alert every minute of the day and night for the forlorn rush that must come some time. But all hands were almost hilariously bucked up by the knowledge that they had not only Pigeon but all his gang safely caged. What a triumph for these two patrols, what a relief when the news should spread throughout the Kimberleys.

But while those on top were nervy under the tension of constant waiting for the expected rush, it was nothing to the sickeningly dismayed feelings of those trapped down below.

After the shock of tumbling down into the safety of the cave the gang crouched aside under the sheltering roof, drawing panting breaths as they glared at the two dead men, then listened to ominous sounds up the sloping tunnel of the cave. Pigeon and Captain crouched there, firing up occasionally. Like staring up a long, sloping funnel it was, every grass blade around the rim of the cave mouth clearly distinct against the blue sky.

After the rain of rocks came a deathly silence as full realization came upon them that they were hopelessly trapped.

Hours dragged by.

Pigeon felt Ellemara's burning eyes upon him. Pigeon scowled back, uneasily looked away, down at the dead men. But Ellemara still stared from those vindictively accusing eyes. Pigeon, his senses acutely sharpened by disaster, presently sensed that Ellemara was trying to make him do something, trying to force him to do *something* that they might escape from death to freedom.

Pigeon was desperately thinking too, but when night came and light came glowing down the cave from a fierce watch fire above, Pigeon knew it was hopeless. No chance now of a stealthy crawl upward, then one plunge as every man leapt out into the darkness and raced through the patrol and away. Up there now awaited certain death for all. To wait down here meant slow starvation - or surrender for all.

Sullenly Pigeon gave up, sneering down at the two dead men by his feet, the two men whose troubles were over. Just before dawn came Pigeon would order his gang to creep silently up the cavern, then leap out and kill every man they could before they were killed.

But that accursed Ellemara would not let him give up. Ellemara, squatting there, staring, staring, with his snake's eyes.

Staring. Staring.

Snake's eyes. Snake's eyes.

Staring. Staring. From those eyes that "carry evil spirits". Silence.

Breathing - breathing. Frightened men softly breathing the deathly hours away.

Staring. Staring.

Snake's eyes. Snake's eyes. Staring ....

Pigeon glanced over his right shoulder, into the blackness of the cavern. The blackness went quite a distance into the hill. The waterhole was along there.

The waterhole was along there! Staring. Staring.

Snake's eyes ....

Pigeon, rifle clenched across his knees, stared down at the dead man by his feet. His feet were resting against the now cold body. Pigeon's fierce eyes, so used to real darkness, could see the body quite plainly, the cicatrized weals and scars of warrior-hood upon chest and shoulder muscles and thigh and back all puffed up, already swelling. From the watch fire up top a . little glow came right down the cave funnel, making a devil's light in those black eyes of Ellemara opposite.

Staring. Staring. Devil's eyes.

Curse Ellemara and his evil, spirit eyes. Staring. Staring.

Snake's eyes. Snake's eyes.

In glowering despair Pigeon glanced into the blackness at his left. There was nothing there, he knew. The cavern extended a hundred feet or so along there, then gradually tapered down to nothing. Only to cold stone.

Pigeon squinted up the cave funnel, fired, reloaded, resumed his staring at the dead man.

Enemara's snake's eyes. Staring. Staring.

Presently, Pigeon glanced along to his right again. The waterhole was along there.

Ellemara's eyes. The waterhole was down there.

Pigeon glared down at the dead man. Not one of the gang had spoken a word for hours. They just crouched there in the silence - breathing, breathing. Presently, Pigeon glanced down to the right again. The waterhole was along there!

The waterhole was down there!

With a puzzled frown Pigeon stared down at the dead man, then up at Ellemara's eyes-stared at Ellemara's eyes ....

Staring. Staring.

Glittering now, like a snake's eyes when fiercely alive .... Staring - staring.

Pigeon scowled down again at the dead man but glanced again to his right - the waterhole was along there.

The waterhole was down there!

Pigeon stared for long, hard moments in puzzled fashion, almost in a pained sort of way, then sighing stared down at the dead man again. Yes, the waterhole was down there ....

He glanced to his right ... the waterhole ... Staring, staring.

Snake's eyes staring. Pigeon gazed again to the right towards the water pool as if striving to detect a phantom down along there, a phantom that was not there - the waterhole ...

He turned and sighed as if weary from some nagging ache, impelled again to stare across at Ellemara's eyes.

The waterhole ...

Suddenly Pigeon sat upright, his eyes startled as if gazing into a great distance, then snatching a spear he was groping away along the cavern, down towards the left . . . the left!

Soon he was stooping, then groping on hands and knees in pitch blackness, then crawling until his outstretched hand was blocked by cold stone. He drew up the long spear under him and broke off the spearhead, the spearhead that was a two-foot length of hardwood, the sturdy spear point half a straightened horseshoe cemented to the spearhead with spinifex gum, the iron spearpoint ground to a double-edged blade tapering to a sharp point. A deadly weapon the complete spear in the hands of a good man, and now, a sturdy tool!

Pigeon drew back his hand and jabbed hard at the stone wall.

The iron bit in. Pigeon wrenched - a little flake of stone dropped out! In the darkness Pigeon's eyes gleamed exultantly, his mouth widened in a long-drawn, animal-like whimper of joy. Again he struck - struck hard, again and again. The faint patter of the falling chips was Dream Time music to his ears.

Away back in the cavern eyes had glared towards eyes at Pigeon's sudden departure, tense ears had pricked to that first low, distant "thud!" Ellemara's body seemed to tauten, his eyes, his face, his ears a tense concentration of questioning listening, his heart thumping painfully. At the second muffled "thud!" his chest breathed deeply, he grinned with a queer, whingeing sound of breathless joy. The others listened tensely, reading the answer in Ellemara's fevered eyes. There was not a word but a great indrawing of breath and uncontrollable twitching of fingers. Then tense silence as Pigeon noiselessly returned and, picking up his rifle, squatted again beside Captain. His face had grown young again teamsters had seen no sign of a bush native for weeks past.

Pigeon knew almost for a certainty where the teams would camp.

Pigeon sat, gently twirling the spearhead in his hand, his eyes glaring now at Ellemara's eyes, the shadow of a strange grin at the corners of his tight-shut mouth. Then he threw the spearhead at Ellemara's feet, with an upthrust of his chin towards the left.

Ellemara snatched the spearhead and vanished straight down the chamber. All eyes followed him. Then "thud!", "thud!", "thud!", "thud!", "thud!", and they knew as with deep hisses and low, guttural growls they turned crouching towards one another, grinning as men grin at the last moment's reprieve.

Pigeon nodded. In an instant they were scrambling among the spears, snatching at those with the more solid iron heads. "Snap!", "snap!", "snap!" as they snapped the spearheads from the hafts. In murmurous eagerness one by one they began to grope their way towards that "thud!", "thud!", "thud!", "thud!"

Yes, they knew now! They would dig their way right through the solid stone to the big waterhole in the river, now that their cunning Pigeon had thought of it and found that the stone was soft enough.

It would seem an almost impossible distance. They never thought of impossibility. All they could see was what they had often seen before - the big waterhole in the sunlight far away through the wall between them and it. They could see the little cliff, running straight down into the edge of the waterhole. They would dig right through and the hole would come out through the cliff right at the edge of the water. In black night, one by one silently they would worm their way out along the hole, slip noiselessly into the water of life and away.

"Thud!", "thud!", "thud!", "thud!"

"Ha!", "ha!", "huh!", "huh!", "huh!", "wah!", "wah!"

How those fools away back up the hill by the cave mouth would wait - and wait - and wait!

"Thud!", "thud!", "thud!", "thud!"

33

THE ESCAPE

THAT tense digging went on ceaselessly minute after minute, hour after hour, in the pitch darkness down there throughout the following days and nights, the "thud!", grunt, "thud!", grunt, "thud!", grunt, "chip!", grunt, "chip!", grunt, "chip!", grunt, "thud!", grunt, "thud!", of rough-hewn iron biting into stone, hiss of outflung breath, grunt of desperate worker. Each man dug with concentrated urgency until he felt the first ache in his muscles. Immediately then he would worm his way back and another man would crawl on chest and belly up into the hot, black, stilling little hole so painfully, so slowly, yet so surely eating its way farther and farther into the limestone wall towards the waterhole! When the stone chips and rubble cluttered the way the digger would lie on his side and his hand would scoop the rubble down past his belly. Another hand would come groping up beside his legs and pull the rubble farther back to yet another hand until finally it was thrown back into the cavern.

"Thud!", "thud!", "thud!", "thud!"

Not one ounce of surplus stone was dug from that tiny round tunnel. How human beings, even though tough Australian aboriginals, could work and live and breathe in it is one of the miracles of the miraculous human system.

"Thud!", "thud!", "thud!", "thud!" was drowned by reverberating rille reports as now and then Pigeon or Captain fired up the shaft away behind.

Back in the cavern in the dull light where Pigeon and Captain kept ceaseless guard up the shaft, men feverishly kept the spear blades sharpened, grinding with other blades and stone and sand and water from the little water pool away up the cavern - the little "waterhole" to the right.

Every moment, hour by hour, day and night, but so far away and muffled now that Pigeon and Captain could barely hear it came the "thud!", "thud!", "thud!", "thud!", "thud!"

Desperately they listened. For limestone varies considerably in hardness and sometimes in sudden changes, from soft, through varying degrees of hardness until there comes the steely hardness that demands explosives to fracture it. Yes, desperately all listened. If there should come a steel-hard band in front of the man digging the hole . . . !

"Thud!", "thud!", "thud!", "thud!"

It was in the small hours of a morning that a spearhead at last crunched through. There was the faint plop of chips falling into water, sweet breath of night seeping into the wee hole.

Pigeon and Captain waited far back in the chamber by the shaft while with fierce care the diggers enlarged that first tiny hole. Then the digger, a black worm wriggling from black cliff out into the night, lowered his head into water and slid down, silent as an eel.

Ellemara's nerves were a-quiver to be following him. But he squatted back there throughout the long, shuffling minutes as man after man, head to feet, head to feet, squirmed into the hole and wriggled along it. Then Ellemara hurried back to Pigeon, nodded, and immediately returned to the hole. Pigeon nodded, and Captain followed Ellemara. Pigeon lifted his rifle, aiming up at the rim of the shaft. The continuous fire glow from away up there came softly down and bathed the now deeply chiselled brow, the glistening eyes, the triumphantly cynical leer on the stubborn face of primitive man.

Pigeon fired. The bullet whistled up the shaft and the report reverberated in thunder down in the cavern.

The watch up above wearily wondered yet again how long this was going to last, how much ammunition they really had, how many more monotonous days, nights, hours it was going to take to starve them out. Or how long it was going to take them to die. Or how many were now dead. They should have been all dead by now.

Pigeon deliberately waited a little longer. Then fired again. The report was still reverberating as he crawled into the little hole with his eyes aglow at the faint breath of open night and freedom far, far ahead.

34

THE ELUSIVE PIGEON

ALL but Pigeon fled back to the Leopolds, a Bight this time in grim earnest. When the aboriginal is really scared he travels night and day to reach sanctuary and can travel for an amazing length of time and at amazing speed. And Pigeon's gang had been badly scared when apparently entombed within the cave. They barely paused for imperative rest until far away within the frowning gorges of the Precipice Range. After a desperately needed rest they separated into three groups, Captain leading one, Ellemara another, Lillimarra the third. Thus if they were tracked - which appeared and was impossible, the pursuers would be in a quandary. No patrol had yet penetrated here. In the unlikely event of one doing so it would have to be a large patrol indeed with sufficient numbers to split up and follow the three sets of tracks, which if necessary would split up again. The three groups, though setting out in different directions, would, after feeling sure they had lost any possible pursuers, then take an agreed course which would bring them within distance of one another should mutual protection demand it. They would then take things easy and let time dishearten the patrols until such time as Pigeon should send for them again.

As usual, Pigeon vanished as if the earth had swallowed him.

Which it had, in a manner of speaking - within his old ancestral sanctuary, the Cave of the Bats.

Long before the ceaseless pursuit of the next two years was finished Pigeon became famous for his "vanishing act". Time and again a patrol would be hot upon his tracks but Pigeon would simply "vanish". At times, he left his tracks so plainly that the pursuers knew he was laughing at them, that sneering laugh of his. For Pigeon, when he wished, could cover his tracks so well as to bewilder the best trackers in the land. Occasionally he would leave tracks that a white man could follow, but always, both tracks and Pigeon would vanish. And this though the best trackers in the whole vast State were brought to the Kimberleys. Always they rode farther north while trying to cut his tracks, always sure he had made deep into the heart of the Leopolds. Only to be amazed to learn a few weeks later that he was back on the Fitzroy spearing cattle again, occasionally taking a pot shot at a settler or lonely traveller along the Fitzroy road. The trackers began to mutter among themselves, to question whether Pigeon could make himself invisible, as it was whispered that Ellemara could do. The trackers began to wonder also if he could at night double back upon his tracks with the speed of a spirit flying through the air.

For just over two years the whites and trackers alike did not realize the full significance of a few of the cave systems in those areas of limestone country where the caves occurred. Naturally so. The Kimberleys were only being settled, new stations being taken up both in the West and East Kimberleys where water and land and availability made it the easiest to do so. The handful of settlers were not interested in caves, they had far more important matters to think about and contend with. As to the trackers, they would not know either for they were from districts often far distant from this, as much "foreigners" in this country as a German would be a foreigner in Tibet. More so. For, far from a local tribesman explaining to a "foreign" tracker any of the secrets of this, his country, it was tribal law that he should kill him if he could. It was only through bitter individual vendetta that a man would be betrayed. Though Pigeon had shot tribesmen he had not yet been betrayed, for it would be only the most vindictively brave who would dare attempt the life of the hero Pigeon. He had long been not only the hero of heroes of his own tribe, but of tribes for three hundred miles from west to east, and two hundred miles from south to north. Even so, Pigeon was very cunning, for his favourite hideout, the one he used in dire straits, was known only to Mother Jinny, If the elders of his own tribe knew, then never a word left their lips.

Captain, Ellemara, Lillimarra, Pyabarra, Mullenbuddin, Demon, Canada, Yarramarra, Boll, Muramin and the others were not so well protected from vendetta. Even now, Vengeance was dogging their tracks.

Thus, with a patrol hot upon his tracks, Pigeon would vanish, sometimes at the water's edge. When this happened the trackers would spend long, slow hours carefully examining the waterhole or river banks to find where he had come out. For he must come out somewhere. But, though they combed both banks up and down stream with the greatest patience, care and cunning, never could they find where Pigeon had "come out". To their intense mortification, and the disappointment and exasperation of the officer in charge of the patrol.

Pigeon had simply vanished again. They must seek him elsewhere. But where? In discouragement and puzzlement and chagrin the patrol at last would be forced to ride away on the seemingly hopeless quest.

The secret would be in a cave, which generally led into many caves. Maybe a mere hole in the ground among the bushes away up on top of a range. Or on the side of a hill. Generally it would be where a limestone cliff came down into a river, creek, or waterhole, so long as it was "cave country". Perhaps only a "dog-hole", so small that a man had to wriggle into it. But that dog-hole might open up into a cavern inside. Then again it might not-the police searched many such. Many might only "go in" a few feet, a few yards, a hundred yards. But one amongst them might go "right in", and lead to a honeycomb of caves.

Even so, there had to be more than this in it if Pigeon wished to escape, or merely to bamboozle and lose a troublesome patrol. For the caves he favoured must not only have an inlet, but an outlet. An inlet to disappear into, and a distant outlet through which to come out into the world again should the inlet be detected and guarded.

And here and there across his country Pigeon knew of a number of such caves, not many, but enough. Their systems of outlet differed. An innocent looking little hole might lead way back into cliff or hill and open out into a cavern, or a network of caves "one on top of the other". One or more galleries might lead up to the surface in the form of a dog-hole, or into some deep crevasse of weather fissured limestone.

Should Pigeon "vanish" there, it would mean merely that he had swum river or waterhole to cliff or hillside and hauled himself up into the hole, where traces of his wet feet and hands would quickly dry from the hard, bare limestone rock. He would grope his way forward into the darkness a safe distance, then calmly grope for a ledge where he always left fire-making sticks and torches of resinous bark or leaves, mostly the oily pandanus leaves for flares, snake-wood for slow burning "torches". In a few moments he would have a lighted torch. He would walk on, then finally begin to climb until light filtering down from crevices or blowhole or cave above would make a torch no longer needful. Pigeon would climb right up and calmly emerge in open sunlight right on top of the ridge or tableland; out into the peaceful bush among the trees and birds and glorious sunlight. With a contemptuous grin he would calmly walk away about his business, leaving his pursuers diligently, laboriously searching the river bank away below and a quarter of a mile or more behind him. He away and gone up on top of the range, and they behind him, scratching their heads, down on a waterhole bank.

The outlet of several cave systems was different. Some ridges in those areas ran for ten, twenty, thirty miles, but may be only two or three miles "through". In several such, Pigeon knew of a cave network that went right "through". He, and if the gang were with him they, would lose their tracks in water, then climb into an innocent looking hole and soon be walking and climbing along up and down caverns that led right through to the other side of the ridge. While the patrol were searching to pick up their tracks on one side of the ridge, Pigeon and his gang would emerge on the other side and calmly stroll across the flat or valley to the next ridge. Or calmly yarn as they walked along, then scatter, having agreed upon a rendezvous. Thus, if next day or any day a patrol should cut their present tracks then the puzzle would be which particular tracks to follow. Many a laugh did the gang have in disagreeing as to which would be the most important tracks, which 'would be the tracks the puzzled patrol would follow.

Ellemara would say: "They will follow Pigeon's tracks!" and the others would know he spoke truly. They would accuse Pigeon of being the favourite of the police, and of the white men, and of the trackers too. And would laughingly ask to know in what manner he had "crawled" to them.

"Ah!" Pigeon would chuckle, "it is because they love me so.

They are always chasing me, they want me to be always with them-in a little hole in the ground. They will plant you too like that when they catch you, so that you can never get away again. So take care and cover your tracks, always remember that your tracks are leading you to a little hole in the ground. Never take a chance, always cover your tracks. Otherwise they might track you while you sleep. And you will wake up with lead in your guts!"

There were several other even more perfect cave hideouts, differing yet again, scattered about Pigeon's tribal country, which stood him in good stead in times of need. The entrances to these particular caves were subterranean. He would disappear in river or deep waterhole and the sharpest eye could not have seen him come up again.

The reason was that he did not come up, he kept swimming under water into a subterranean cave mouth. He would swim along a little distance under the bank then come up into cool air and pitch darkness. Groping his way up into the cavern, he would find his fire-making and torch sticks, light them, then saunter along towards whatever form of outlet Nature had designed for this refuge. It might be right on top of the ridge, or out on a hillside, or down in an adjoining valley, or out into a gorge or creek, just as the vagaries of Nature and Time and long-dead streams had fashioned it.

Yes, little wonder that the trackers, though not daring to speak openly for fear of the scorn of their white masters, began to whisper at night that when Pigeon "vanished" it meant he had been transported into the 'World of the Spirits".

35

THE OLD SHEARER-PROSPECTOR

THE hard riding patrols drove the gang and the cattle-spearers who were keen to emulate them well back into the Leopolds and hoped they had more or less cleared the Fitzroy. But within a couple of months Charlie and Willie MacDonald of Fossil Downs, of Margaret River and Louisa Downs stations again reported to Derby wholesale cattle killings, intimidation of stockboys, renewed threats to burn down Fitzroy Crossing. Again trouble broke out at Jack Collins's Oscar Range station, at Blythe's Brooking Creek station, and away east along the Margaret and Louisa rivers almost to Hall's Creek in the East Kimberley. West of The Crossing, too, along the Lennard and Barker, and right back along the Fitzroy to Oobagooma, near Derby.

"This wholesale cattle killing along the Margaret can be attended to by the East Kimberley-Hall's creek police," wrote the overworked Inspector Lawrence to Perth Headquarters.

There were not the men in the East Kimberley to do it of course and certainly the West Kimberley patrols had their work cut out.

It was some months after the escape from the cave that the gang drifted back from the Leopolds to Pigeon again. Pigeon had been crafty as a lone wolf, but now he organized the gang again for a big killing, which was nipped in the bud by a swift clash with the police. Janmarra the stockboy, he from whom Ellemara had taken Wondaria of the Laughing Waters, was the vengeful listener who upset Pigeon's plans.

Constable Pilmer, riding back from Mt Abbott police camp to The Crossing, had 'barely unsaddled when that night a station boy (Danmarra) whispered to Tracker Ned that Ellemara was now camped away up the Margaret River, rounding up the tribesmen for an attack upon the white men at MacDonalds' station. Yes, he admitted that members of the gang were with him: Lillimarra and Demon, Pyabarra, Towerdine, Canada, Boll, Yarramarra, Woinamarra, Bundermen, Warramarra, Mullenbuddin, and others. But he shook his head at inquiry about Pigeon and Captain, mumbling that he did not know. When Tracker Ned hurried to report to Pilmer, Danmarra the stockboy disappeared.

Pilmer's patrol rode swiftly and to their delight a day later cut the tracks of Pigeon and Captain and all their gang. With haste leavened by caution they followed up.

Three days later before dawn they surrounded the camp on the bank of a waterhole. They charged the camp at dawn. Only thirty tribesmen leapt up where they had expected a hundred. One swift glance and the tribesmen plunged into the waterhole and swam. But those seconds of instinct and sight and sound had shown them the weakest part of the circle galloping fast around them. They dived like wild ducks as horsemen appeared on the banks with rifles at the ready. They emerged with incredible speed up the bank and out among the trees as rifle shots sounded. With savage yells each threw a spear, then ran. A horse neighed shrilly and plunged forward with a spear in its flanks, a mounted blackboy cried out and reeled with a long spear quivering through his shoulder. The tribesmen raced for some nearby hills, leaving two of their number gasping out their lives by the waterhole. Like wallabies they bounded halfway up a steep, rocky hill thick clad with bushes. And here they stopped and yelled defiance as the outwitted patrol came galloping to the foothill.

They put up quite a savage fight, from rock and bush hurling spears at the dismounted men who sought to climb up and dislodge them. When their spears were finished they hurled clubs, dowicks, quondis, and whackaburra fighting sticks at any enemy venturing to show himself within range. They were quickly joined by a yelling crowd of fifty tribesmen who came bounding over the hilltop and down among the rocks to their fellows, howling defiance at the smack of bullets ricochetting off the rocks. Several fell sprawling amongst the bushes, for despite their excellent cover they were extraordinarily reckless. Munjarri went to the Happy Hunting Grounds in company with Widali, Monboni, Coolya, Mulabia, Culcul, Calapi and Munger. Their comrades then vanished as if from the earth. But almost immediately a signal smoke ascended from a hilltop. And that thin blue wisp ascending straight up into the sky filled Pilmer with presentiment.

None of the fallen were of Pigeon's special gang, though each was a well-known local native killer and cattle-spearer. The patrol shot two of the wounded horses, roughly dressed the wounds of two trackers, then hurried back to the camp and quickly found the plain tracks of Pigeon and the whole gang where they had left the camp in a body the afternoon before.

Pilmer followed swiftly on the tracks, cursing that warning smoke signal ascending upon the hill behind.

Twenty miles away, Pigeon with Captain, Ellemara, Demon, Lillimarra and all the gang stood upon a hill gazing back towards the smoke wisp.

Ellemara looked at Pigeon. Pigeon shrugged expressively.

"Lose your tracks!" he growled.

With a grunt of perfect understanding they turned and in groups of four commenced quietly walking down the hill. They would separate, then travel on with that long, effortless stride that can carry the aboriginal so far and so fast, back to a beloved rendezvous in the Leopolds.

But Pigeon turned alone in an opposite direction-to the south-west. He would actually pass around the oncoming patrol, but the patrol would be unaware of it.

Black was the brow of Pigeon. For yet again his carefully thought out plans and preparations had been brought to nought. He had been almost ready to attack Margaret Downs station. Only one more "mob" he had to visit. He was travelling to them when they saw the warning smoke. Almost at the last moment an unexpected patrol hot upon their tracks!

As he strode along Pigeon ground his teeth in rage. Through his numerous native contacts he had thought he knew the whereabouts of every patrol. Some accursed enemy must have put him away!

Pigeon did not yet know that had not Ellemara taken Wondaria of the Laughing Waters from Danmarra the stockman so long ago ... !

Thus yet again Pigeon's mob was forced into hiding.

Time dreamed on. Long, long since the giant grass had fallen and gone to seed or up in rolling clouds of black smoke to the shrill squeaks of hovering brown hawks, the frantic rushing of smoke-blinded animals and reptiles, the exultant yells of hunting aboriginals. The river waters had long since dwindled down to gently Bowing streams, in other instances to chains of long, quiet waterholes. It was nearing the end of the dry season. Soon an-other Wet would come.

Pigeon and his gang had met again but only in cattle-killing forays. The patrols were constantly active, constantly moving. But at times Pigeon, Captain, Ellemara and Lillimarra had hunted alone in Pigeon's country. They survived narrow escapes, escapes that chilled Ellemara's back. Pigeon was long since convinced that someone was working against them, some hidden enemy who was all ears for the faintest whisper, some instrument of vengeance who passed that whisper on to the nearest patrol.

Captain and Ellemara and Lillimarra listened sullenly, knowing that Pigeon was right. But they could not pick this particular enemy. Each knew at least half a dozen who had a blood ven¬detta against him and each bitterly threatened that those men would die when they met them. Ellemara particularly wished to kill that dingo stockman Danmarra, though he could not say this was the particular enemy for he had taken other girls besides Laughing Waters.

A day came when they escaped from almost under the hooves of a galloping patrol. There was not the slightest doubt this time that someone had put them away.

Captain, Ellemara and Lillimarra, in sullen anger, hurried straight back to the Leopolds. There they would rejoin the gang and entice the patrols far back into the Leopolds again.

Pigeon "vanished" for the time being.

It had been an exceptionally hot day, with that breathless mugginess that compels a man to camp and smoke lazily, or sleep. The birds, even the leaves of the trees were enjoying a midday snooze; there seemed not a bird call in all the wide bush, every tree leaf dropped in moveless languor. The horses too. Tough old greybeard Williams yawned, while like all bushmen he was ever if but subconsciously listening for the tinkle of the horse bells, that occasionally tinkle or the lack of it or the clatter that can tell the experienced bushman much that he wishes to know.

In a bend of the Fitzroy Williams's tent stood out like a snow-white cauliflower down among the big river trees. Williams was lying on a sapling bunk, smoking idly, quietly listening for sounds that might tell him of the life of the bush outside human life, as well as the life of animals and birds, for there are certain birds that warn of danger or a stranger approaching. By his head, a shield against possible spears, stood his two big pack saddles. A loaded Winchester was beside him, a revolver at his belt.

Both police and settlers had urged him against travelling alone while Pigeon and his gang were on the rampage, though they were believed to be back in the Leopolds again. Williams had thanked them for the warning then had growled, "I've knocked about the Kimberleys long enough to know how to look after myself."

This wiry, grizzled old greybeard was a shearer and "part-time" prospector, as many shearers have been. At the beginning of the three-months or so shearing season the shearers would start from Derby and work their way up along the Fitzroy, shearing at the only half-dozen stations in the West Kimberley that (as today) stock sheep. The season over, they would return to Derby, then on to Port Hedland to shear their way down through the nor'-west, thence back home to Perth to await the next season. But Williams would carry on with his packhorses loaded with tucker and tools to Fitzroy Crossing and two hundred miles farther on to Hall's Creek in the East Kimberley. There he would quietly prospect, as inclination lured him, any likely looking country all the way back to Derby. He would arrive back in the tiny port in time to load up stores again and start the new shearing season, only to ride away again back to Hall's Creek and his beloved gold seeking.

And today he was camped west of The Crossing on his slow trip back to Derby to "put in the Wet", until the new shearing season would start. Yes, a warm afternoon indeed. He felt comfortably drowsy. He yawned, pulled the mosquito net down; he would enjoy a snooze. He fell asleep.

He was utterly unaware of hidden eyes that had been watching him for hours.

Pigeon's eyes!

36

THE GREYBEARD'S LONE FIGHT

PIGEON had been watching Williams for hours. Except for Cangamvara, his spear carrier, he was alone. Gloating. For here he had a white man's life utterly in his power. Pigeon had reached that stage in his career when to kill another white man had become an obsession. To kill another white man! And yet another! A good rifle to be seized here too, and revolver, and ammunition. A dozen times from his hiding-place among the river trees he could have shot the greybeard dead. But he gloated in the cool shadows of the big trees, with bright sunlight pouring down from the sky on to the open plain, turning the tent in the bend of the river a snow-white. The lone tent at the 67-mile with just the white man inside and Pigeon watching from behind this old tree, with his big-eyed little Cangamvara crouched beside him. The three were alone in the wild bush, with no sounds but a dreamy hum of insects and the sleepy clucking of ducks back there on the river waterhole.

Why should Pigeon waste a cartridge on this white man! The unnecessary report, too, which would roll far away on such a breathlessly still day. No, he would spear him. It would be pleasant to stand by and watch him writhe.

Beyond control now Pigeon stepped out into the open, walking towards the tent, fitting spear to wommera. He would not kill him outright first time. He would test his spear aim - it would be sport.

He noted the position of the sleeper within the tent, then stood aside so that the side of the tent was between him and the sleeper. He would tryout his aim. At quite long range he poised a moment, then the long spear flew out and up into the air, to come ripping with frightful purpose into the tent. There was a convulsive movement as Pigeon stepped aside so that he could see into the tent. The spearhead had plunged right through one thigh and transfixed the other. Williams convulsively jerked upward, his hands gripping the red hot thing pinning his legs that instantly seemed swelling to bursting point. His dilated eyes focused on a grinning black face out through the open door.

With gritted teeth he whipped up the rifle and fired. Pigeon spun around and fell, to leap up, spin around again and fall. But instantly he was up, crazily beating at his head. He leapt around in a little circle, dazedly beating his bloodstained head. Cangamvara ran out, snatched his arm and guided him back amongst the trees. Pigeon lay there gasping, holding his head as if fearful that it was his no more. Then he leapt up and instinctively took to the water, nor could the frightened Cangamvara urge him away.

The bullet, by a mere fluke, had struck Pigeon a glancing blow across the temple and temporarily stunned him, demoralizing thought and the power of controlled movement.

Back in the tent Williams reached down from the bunk and lifting up the filled billy-can almost drained it of water. Then, teeth gritting in pain, with a sheath knife he commenced hacking through the tough spearhead that skewered his legs together. Forehead beaded with sweat, sawing against time, he managed it with a groan of anguished relief. Then he snapped off the long haft, which was much easier. Thank the good God his legs were now free though an eight-inch length of spearhead remained embedded in each. They were one vast muscular pain, felt as large as houses, swelling to bursting point.

It had taken frantic, agonizing time during which the cool water on Pigeon's throbbing head had brought him to his senses. With the blackest murder in his heart he crawled out of the water and up the bank. With Cangamvara beside him he crawled back to his weapons. It would be the rifle this time.

Standing beside his tree he deliberately levelled the Winchester. Across the open sunlight he could see into the tent, the mosquito net torn down, the white man crouching up in the bunk. That tough old greybeard, quite unaware of how many natives were about, was agitatedly muttering: "I'd better fire a few shots, better fire, scare them away! Let them know I'm still alive and can fight. They won't know then how bad I'm hit!"

As Pigeon levelled his rifle towards the white man's heart Williams lifted his rifle and fired straight out the tent door. Pigeon spun round and flung himself flat against a tree trunk. He had been hit another glancing blow in exactly the same place.

There would be many who could see the hand of the Great Protector in this million-to-one chance. Whether or no, the old shearer-prospector was not fated to die this day.

Again Cangamvara had to guide Pigeon's erratic feet down to the river. On recovery, he had had enough. Something amazing had happened that he could not understand. Losing all control over mind and movements had terrified him. That it had happened the second time filled him with superstitious terror. He felt certain he could not kill this devil of a white man, was as certain the white man could kill him. Fearfully he sent Cangamvara back to recover his weapons. Then both stole noiselessly away.

Williams, quite unaware that he had hit Pigeon again, knew that he must make use of what little strength he had, and quickly. He must get out of the tent for it hemmed him in so that he knew nothing, could see nothing, while they could crawl right up to it. He believed there were a lot of them hiding among the trees three parts encircling the tent around the river bend.

In agony he not only managed to crawl out but dragged his shield of packbags with him. Out in the open, he sat with his back to a spreading Bauhinia tree. He dragged a packsaddle to each side of him, then, with rifle and revolver to hand, he grinned. "Snug as a bug in a rug. Now let 'em all come," he muttered to the wide, wide bush.

Every now and then he fired away into the trees, either from rifle or revolver. Afternoon merged to sundown with bird life noisy among the river trees. A mob of grey 'roos came hopping to the waterhole to drink, followed by a slinking dingo. Evening merged into night, and the stars shone down. Came the hoot of an owl, and such a long, long night. Next day was hot, sweltering, breathless. Came midday. The old die-hard began muttering to himself, just now and then. Came afternoon. Charlie Flinders the mailman on his monthly trip came jogging along the Fitzroy road. When just by the 67-mile a rifle shot startled him.

"Pigeon!" he thought and his knees gripped his horse, his hand whipped out his revolver. No further sound. Then his searching eyes saw the tent. Cautiously, he thought he would investigate that tent. And so found the greybeard semi-delirious under the old Bauhinia tree. As Flinders rode up and dismounted a cloud of flies buzzed angrily up from the stricken man. The blanket was soaked in blood, and flyblown. Flinders could smell things, and so could his snorting horse.

"I'm all right!" muttered the greybeard, "fighting fit! But - I could do with a drink!"

Flinders quickly put the billy on and the old man drank the whole billy of strong tea in deep, throaty gasps. Flinders bathed the wounds in hot water; the stench was awful, the wounds already flyblown. Flinders bandaged them, fed the old man, gave him another billy of tea, left him water within easy reach, made him as comfortable as possible.

"Keep your tail up," he said cheerily. "I'll travel like the hammers of hell. I might meet a traveller along the road; if so I'll send him straight to you. If not, I'm riding all out for the Lennard police station. We'll soon be back."

"You'll find me here!" grinned Williams, "sitting up and taking nourishment."

"I'm sure we will," agreed Flinders cheerily. "Pigeon won't come again now."

"It was not him I was scared of," said the greybeard soberly, "it was the ants."

"Ah-yes," said Flinders slowly.

"Yes, the meat ants. Me sit-me-down is the only little bit of meat I've got left. And it's a raw and bloody mess now you see."

Flinders shuddered.

"It's all right," chuckled the greybeard. "If the ants come I can put in time drowning th' cows with all this water you've left me."

"Have you any other buckets or billy-cans I can fill?" asked Flinders slowly.

"No. You've filled 'em all. And thanks."

"I'll fill my own billies and the meat bucket for you," said Flinders.

"No you don't! You'll need your billies for tucker on the road."

"To hell I will!" said Flinders, and walking to his packs took billies and bucket and filled all. Then he cleaned up every damper crumb and stray scrap of food from around the old man and arranged his food supply within reach but out of reach of ants. Then cut him a dozen leafy switches.

"This is what I call the 'ants' pants'," grinned the greybeard.

"You're leaving me enough weapons to fight all the ants in the Kimberleys, But there's one thing you've overlooked."

"What is that?"

"Them tiny little black ants. I'd like a few of them to come along."

"Why?"

"To eat the young maggots outer me legs."

It was in the early hours that Flinders reached the Lennard with the news.

"I think he'll be dead when you get to him. You'd better take a pick and shovel."

"Right-oh. It's stiff luck though," said Constable Buckland when the trackers were rounding up the horses. "Brice has just ridden into Derby on the best horse. I'll hurry Tracker Jacky in with word to send out a buggy along the Fitzroy road - just in case he's still alive."

It was four o'clock in the afternoon when the swift riding men came within sight of the white tent. The trackers sniffed, glancing expressively at one another. Then Buckland smelt it, and was glad he had brought that pick and shovel.

But the greybeard was still alive, part delirious and badly fly-blown now. "I was scared it was the ants was going to eat me," he chuckled, "but it wasn't, it was the maggots."

"We'll soon get rid of them for you," said Buckland cheerily. "If only the little black ants had come," sighed the greybeard wearily. "If only they had come not too much, I could have fixed these crawlers meself."

Buckland bathed the now awful wounds with hot water and Condy's. Many of the torturing worms came wriggling out. Buckland felt sick.

Buckland attended to him all that night and next day.

Next morning Williams insisted: "You're spendin' too much time on me. Put me on a horse an' we'll ride to meet the buggy. If you can only fix a sort of pillow between me legs and the saddle, I think I can manage it."

He did, in agony for twelve miles.

"I can't stand any more - not today," he moaned.

"Never mind, we'll camp here," said Buckland as he carefully lifted him off. "The buggy should be along any time now."

It was - at the gallop. In a cloud of dust with the horses in a lather of sweat.

Ten miles back the horses had been trotting along, Constable Brice driving, a tracker sitting beside him. A bullet whistled between the heads of the two men.

"Quick feller! Gallop! Pigeon!" yelled the tracker as he glanced around.

As the horses plunged forward another bullet smacked into the back of the buggy.

"Let him have it!" shouted Brice.

The tracker aimed a Schneider over the back of the buggy and fired.

Pigeon, on the prowl alone, had stepped out on to the road behind the buggy just within range. He had run after it a little way just to make sure, aimed, and fired. A near miss, the wonder is that he went so close as the buggy was trotting away over the rough track. He ran after it again, but it was careering madly along now. Still, he could run faster. Again he ran, stopped, aimed and fired. Then again he chased it.

The tracker with the Schneider in the swaying buggy had no chance of hitting Pigeon.

"I'll pull up around this next bend," said Brice furiously. "Be ready to grab the reins and hand me the rifle and I'll get this Pigeon!"

"No, no, boss!" urged the tracker. "Keep going quick feller, boss! S'pose 'im you sthop, all more better longa Pigeon! He catch up! He shoot 'em horses! Then he shoot 'em you! Then shoot 'em me quick feller! You no longa get buggy longa Cons'ble Buckland! Longa Williams take him longa Derby hospital! We feller altogether dead feller!"

The constable, his wrists now beginning to ache from the galloping horses, saw the cold logic in this urgent advice. He drove them not so much for his life as to bring the buggy to his superior officer and the wounded man. Which was why Senior Constable Buckland shouted to the trackers to run for the horses when he saw the buggy coming in a cloud of dust.

37

THE CHAIN GRIPS COLD UPON THE NECKS OF CAPTAIN AND ELLEMARA

BUCKLAND escorted the greybeard into Derby, to the little hospital.

Williams recovered with time; he was tough. But he would never shear again. His wounds had been terrible. He could no longer bend and manage the old blade hand shears, the tough and sustained physical work that shearers must do.

But he could still prospect. The great day came when he hobbled from the tiny hospital. Several weeks later he loaded up his trusty old packhorses and with a "Hell to you Pigeon and all your gang!" set off east along the old Fitzroy road, bound for Hall's Creek and the Golden Rainbow.

But Fate was catching up with Captain and Ellemara. With Lillimarra too. One sunny morning, strolling casually down a rocky gorge Captain and Bundermen stood as if frozen in their tracks, their eyes and surprised mouths absurdly comical as they stared into rifle muzzles.

Armed men had risen from their very feet - Captain gaped at the steely eyes of Constable Brice of the Lennard police outpost, gaped at the revolver muzzle within six feet of his body. Still shocked, they stood nerveless as the handcuffs were slipped on. Then the chain.

And for Captain the birds had ceased to sing.

The unwary two had been strolling along to rejoin Ellemara and Demon, Illamarra and Canada and other members of the gang awaiting them some twenty miles away. For Pigeon had sent them word to rejoin him at the Oscar and help raid Collins's station.

Captain had not thought a patrol was within a hundred miles of him. And now he was on the chain. He, Captain, who had helped put so many other men on the chain. And now he carried the cold links around his own neck. In chill rage he glared at the grim delight on the face of Constable Brice. What a capture!

Captain at last! The next man desired after Pigeon. Even though Ellemara was badly wanted he was not now such a prize a Captain. Little wonder the constable was thrilled.

As Captain turned to memorize the trackers the grins faded from their faces; hastily they turned away to fumble with gear or search for tracks. For they saw death in Captain's eyes should he escape and in time catch up with anyone or all of them.

It was the brother of a tribesman he had shot who had put Captain away. Others had tried but this man had successfully carried out the blood vendetta, using patience and perseverance and cunning. He had risked his life doing it, for he had travelled out of his own country, travelled by night, right through hostile tribal country to the white man's Lennard River police station. Here, despite his added fear of police he had grunted out his story to a tracker who translated to Constable Brice. The man explained where Captain and Bundermen were camped, adding that a stockboy called Danmarra had asked him to tell the policeman also that Ellemara was making for Mt Broome, only twenty miles farther away. Captain was expecting a "smoke" from Ellemara and Lillimarra. Then they would all join Pigeon again. The tribesman suggested that to kill or capture Captain the police must not rush his camp at dawn as was usual, for all approaches were closely watched and Captain would not be within miles of the place when the avengers arrived. But he knew well the gorge down which Captain would walk when the smoke went up to meet Ellemara. He suggested the police lie in wait in the gorge. They could get there some days before the signal smoke rose up. Captain would never dream the police would be "sitting down" waiting for him in that distant gorge. Simple native strategy. Yet so very often effective.

The tribesman was eager to guide them to the gorge. Brice led his patrol swiftly, but well away from Captain's hideout. Any native lookouts would never dream this patrol was going anywhere near that vicinity.

Buckland and Brice divided the patrol and separated, Buckland to double back towards Mt Broome and trap Ellemara; Brice to try to ambush Captain.

Brice travelled by night and made a wide circuit, then left the horses hidden under strong guard. He carried on again by night on foot and placed his ambush around the faint native path, prepared to wait for days and nights if necessary.

Thus Captain and Bundermen found themselves on the chain, with other sullen prisoners trudging behind and before the horses of the patrol. With each mile they were leaving the shelter of the Leopolds, the crags that had befriended them so well. With each long mile Captain's dumb rage was giving way to plans for escape. Frowning at the manacled neck of the tribesman in front, keeping step for step, his mind was swiftly revolving on the cunning methods of escape used by prisoners when he was a tracker, lordly riding his horse. "Yes," thought Captain, "what they could do I can surely do better! And then ... ! His eyes glared at the back of the tracker riding just ahead.

But Captain was not to escape Vengeance. He was to die in far-away

Rottnest Island. Thus the muttering of the first thunderstorms was the last that Captain was to hear of the Leopolds, the lightning flickering upon the crags the last he was to see of the fastnesses that had sheltered him so well.

For Ellemara too, a troublemaker all his life, the first storms heralding the rapid approach of a new wet season were the thunderous symphony of his "way out". For Danmarra the stockboy had never ceased planning and working night and day for the downfall of Ellemara who had robbed him of Wondaria, his young bride of the Laughing Waters. And at last Danmarra succeeded in his vengeance. For it was mainly through his information that Ellemara too found himself blinking into rifle muzzles, found himself on the chain. He was just about to climb big old Mt Broome, so far away from any patrol, yet he felt so strangely uneasy. The expression in his "snake's eyes" was troubled, yet he was not using them to see things for he knew he was safe. It was his "mind's eye" that would not see clearly, he could not make it out. Away up over Mt Broome big black clouds were piling up-more rain coming. There was a shadow over all the mountain, like the shadow on Ellemara's mind. As he began climbing a grassy spur men rose from under his very feet, his eyes were staring into the revolver muzzles of Constables Buckland and Anderson, he "felt" that rifle muzzles were pointing at his back too. He stood without movement, without sound as the cold chain was looped around his neck. There was a low muttering of thunder from the darkening mountain top far above and the first few drops of rain began to fall. All Nature seemed hushed. Then there was the tinkle of the chain as the trackers stepped aside.

Ellemara's breath came in a long, long sigh.

Ellemara's thoughts were bitter as he was marched away.

Strangely fearful, too, though uneasily he strove to brush them aside. A cynical grin curled the corners of his big mouth as he trudged the miles away. He had been on the chain before-he grinned as he thought of how many times. He had escaped, not only from the chain but even from the white men's jails - and from more than one of them! Of course he would escape again! If not from the chain, then certainly from the jail. There was no white man jail that could hold Ellemara, Ellemara the Killer, Ellemara the Cunning.

He almost laughed, his heart grew so light. He lifted up his eyes to the storm-blackened sky. He would see these crags again. Yes, again he would hear the murmur of water in a gorge, hear the lonesome call of the black cockatoo.

No Ellemara - never again!

Ellemara was to swing at the end of a rope in Derby jail.

38

VENDETTA DOGS PIGEON

THUS, swift disaster for the ringleaders of Pigeon's gang.

Lillimarra made back for the Barker Range, blissfully unaware that Fate was dogging his tracks. The patrols had been tracking him for two hundred miles, relentlessly following his every twist and turn. One early afternoon he strolled into the shelter of the Barker Range and met friends. They had just speared two fat beasts; already the stones in the cooking ovens were hot.

That starry night, Lillimarra gorged around the dull camp-fires, gossiping heartily with his friends. In the small hours, sleepily he scraped out a warm hole in the sand beside a dying fire. Gorged to repletion, feeling so safe he did not even think of safety, he fell into heavy sleep.

It took him quite a time to awaken, despite several kicks in the ribs. He lay there blinking, not even realizing it was daylight. Frowsy of face, eyes all screwed up, he lay there blinking.

Gradually, he did not like this dream. Grinning faces of trackers leering down at him. A white policeman standing a little aside, calmly lighting his pipe. Lillimarra bounded up, the jerk of steel upon his wrists echoed by hilarious laughter. He stood there trembling in every limb as they slipped the chain around his neck. One tracker was patting his back, crooning comfortingly: 'Whoa boy! Steady boy! Steady now!" but Lillimarra was too shocked to understand that he was the frightened "horse".

Thus another wet season came and went.

And Sandamara, he whom white men called Pigeon, when not hunting, spent this Wet deep within the Cave of the Bats, brooding and thinking.

He had Jinny his mother and Cangamvara his now fully trusted young wife for company, though they spoke only when spoken to. In the spells of dry weather they brought him vegetable foods which he ate morosely with his meat. At times they brought him news, for which he was hungry.

He had plenty to brood about, and think over. Captain and Ellemara and Lillimarra captured-his three best men. He brooded on rescue, but to leave his own country for distant Police Headquarters at Derby would be far too risky. He felt certain they would escape. Such a combination as Captain and Ellemara and Lillimarra the police could *never* hold. He must wait and work and plan quietly until they escaped and returned. So, for the time being, Captain and Ellemara were gone. And Lillimarra. Bundermen too. Carolan was shot, and Samba and Captain of Oobagooma. And Waggarrie and Langooradale and Goiro. Long Frankey too, and Big Paddy and Lucullia and Tumanurumberry. And others of less consequence. While more than a score had died by the spear in fights and vendettas.

Frowning deeply, Pigeon began thinking of the men who were left-Pyabarra and Tilbomer and Teebuck, Demon, Can¬ada, Boll, Putter, Byerbell, Fouringer, Muckerawarra, Mererimer, Warramarra, Mullenbuddin, Murramin, Bangarra, Bunnamurra.

He could think of another two score solid men apart from the numerous warrior tribesmen, if he could only get them all together and armed. Yes, he could still carry on.

Came the beginning of the dry season of 1896. In riotous life of vegetable, animal, bird, fish and man the Kimberleys came to life again.

Also the police patrols and with a vengeance. Sub-Inspector Ord was in charge of the strengthened and now well-mounted patrols, operating from Derby, the Lennard, and Fitzroy Crossing, with a police camp at Lillamaloora, occasionally at Oobagooma and Mt Abbott.

The police were patrolling from Oobagooma to the Lennard, from the Lennard to the Napier Range, the Richenda River into the Leopolds. Patrols were searching the Barrier Range and the Oscar to The Crossing, from The Crossing to the Geikie and well into the foothills of the Leopolds. With quick surprise visits along the Fitzroy and farther inland still along the Margaret and Louisa.

The alarmed tribesmen now never knew when they might run across a patrol, or a patrol run across them. The more notorious groups of cattle-spearers became quite resentful of the seeming fact that some patrol or other seemed to be personally chasing them, just them.

But not once did a patrol come across the track of Pigeon.

At agreed upon times, at a given rendezvous, generally midway among the Leopold foothills, Ord would meet all the patrols. Deep in the wild bush a camp conference would be held. Information from every patrol would be handed over and thoroughly discussed. A further concerted plan of action would then be agreed upon, a future rendezvous chosen. Then the patrols would mount and ride away again to each point of the compass. Little wonder that the cattle-spearers found scant chance of coming together again in a big way. Pigeon, occasionally marauding alone from the Cave of the Bats, grinned savagely at the news brought him by Mother Jinny and Cangamvara. He was not planning for a concentration yet, not until Captain and Ellemara and Lillimarra escaped and rejoined him. Meanwhile he was learning these new methods of the patrols, thinking deeply to familiarize himself with their ways. Soon, through questions sent out and spread by Mother Jinny and Cangamvara, he was to learn there were at times as many as eight different patrols seeking him and the more notorious cattle-spearers, He strove to learn a lot more-until the time should come for him to strike.

He was formulating a plan, a vast one. He would strike at Fitzroy Crossing, when he knew all the patrols were widely scattered. At one blow he would take enough arms, ammunition and stores to arm his men to fight it out with a patrol. He knew exactly where he could hurry his men to defy and fight a patrol, where if more than one patrol came he could still escape to fight again. Just for diversion, also, he would wipe out Collins's station. So Mother Jinny described his plan long afterwards.

Pigeon grinned mirthlessly. After the killing of Burke and Gibbs he had been beaten, but only just, and that only because of lack of time. Now he had plenty of time. This hide-and-seek that the remnant of his gang and the cattle-spearers were playing with the patrols would now play into his hands, give him a chance to plan and presently to organize. Then, if only he could arm his men and teach them how to shoot! Ah then, when the time came he could strike hard indeed.

Week after week as the plan grew he began to long for Captain, Ellemara, Lillimarra and Demon to join him in this safe sanctuary of the Cave of the Bats. Here they would finalize the plan, would grow enthusiastic and soon afterwards would act.

Then, after raiding The Crossing, when they had taken the arms from the telegraph station and the police station, he would put Captain, Ellemara, Lillimarra, and Demon in charge of four groups of men, make big "patrols" out of them, each much more numerous than a police patrol. Captain, Ellemara, Lillimarra and Demon well knew his ways now, they would become his able and enthusiastic lieutenants. With Captain second in charge of all, under him. Then, after raiding The Crossing he would easily overwhelm Collins's Oscar Range station, and with these added firearms form another "patrol" under Pyabarra perhaps. From then on he would fight the white man as the white man fights. The police patrols could have their horses, his "black patrols" would defy the horses in the more rugged of the ranges, let alone from the hideouts and cave systems.

Such was Sandamara, alias Pigeon's plan, bred in his mind within the Cave of the Bats, as, it was eventually told by his old Mother Jinny, though never a word passed her lips until that black day when the death wailing began for her son.

Midway through the year Pigeon heard the news that Captain was to be taken to far away Rottnest Island - which meant death. Ellemara and

Lillimarra were to swing in Derby.

Pigeon felt tragically alone.

It was in June 1896 that Captain, Ellemara and two others of the gang were sentenced to death in Derby. The sittings were conducted before Mr Wharton, Commissioner of the Supreme Court.

Far away to the south they took Captain to Rottnest Island, a sea-girt beauty spot about twelve miles off the coast opposite Fremantle. But the only beauty on the island then was of Nature. For on it were imprisoned the worst native offenders in the State. They built roads, mined salt and were penned in the old jail. The place and conditions, so the tale goes, would break a native's heart within twelve months. Many attempted to swim away, but few succeeded in surviving those twelve miles of turbulent waters.

Captain was destined never to see his tribal lands again. Perhaps Ellemara and Lillimarra, swinging on the end of the rope in Derby, met the better, at least the quicker fate.

A week after Pigeon heard of the death sentences he was hunting alone, morosely savage. A spear hissed by his neck, tearing away the flesh. He leaped aside on the second to bound away and hide, then to slither around and hide again, his heart thumping hammer blows, eyes a blaze of fury, rifle at the ready, thoughts of Captain and Ellemara now vanished from his mind as he glared and listened.

But there was nothing. Only the warm earth under him, the sweet smell of the grasses, the call of the birds.

Pigeon circled around to cut the tracks of the vanished spearman. Cautiously he followed the faint signs back a long way until a clear imprint stared up at him from soft ground.

With tigerish ferocity he studied the imprint.

Where had he seen this particular track before? He had seen it but once, it seemed a long, long time ago.

Ah! now he remembered. At Lillamaloora, the morning after the killing of Constable Richardson! This was the footstep of the hillman who had stood out to defy him after he had taken Cangamvara. Yes, this was the track of the *munjon* Marawon!

Marawon from Barellam Springs, who by tribal law was to have married Cangamvara, daughter of Cadwarry. Well, he, Pigeon, had taken Cangamvara against tribal law and the wishes of her father Cadwarry. And now Marawon sought his life by right of tribal vendetta.

Thoughtfully, with a new caution much more nerve-racking than caution against patrols, Pigeon made his way back to a hideout, greatly disturbed. He was hunted now not only by the patrols but by something even more implacable - native vendetta. Now truly he dare not lose caution any moment of the night or day. He *must* kill Marawon, before Marawon killed *him!*

Deeply he thought it out, well into the night. Marawon would be far away now, making back with all speed to his own adjoining tribal country. He could come again, any time he wished, travelling swiftly by night to lurk in wait near one of Pigeon's hideouts - obviously he now had found several. He could strike from ambush and swiftly be away again, return to his own country swifter than any could follow his tracks. Captain gone, Ellemara gone, Lillimarra gone. So many of the old gang gone. The patrols working ever closer. And now - this! A sullen, bitter savagery began burning in Pigeon's breast.

Time dreamed on.

Came a bright Kimberley day well into the dry season. Sub-Inspector Ord's patrol was riding the Lennard Range country. The trackers, breaking into a gallop, rounded up half a dozen frightened natives. In fear they yabbered that Pigeon, Demon, Pyabarra and Boll with a big mob of cattle-spearers were camped in the Wingina Gorge. Ord rode swiftly but, when nearing the gorge, with caution. Young Green, ambitious to become a settler, was riding with the patrol this day as he had for months past, without finding even tracks, much less catching sight of this elusive Pigeon, terror of the Kimberleys. And now...!

Excitement of whites and trackers alike transferred itself to the prick-eared horses as the patrol entered the gorge. Spaced wide apart, they were advancing swiftly but with extreme caution. But so far not a sign of a native, not even a track. They came to where the river boomerangs, apparently entering a sunlit cliff, the bare rock wall to either side. Ord was just about to declare he'd been led on yet another false scent when a rifle shot startled all as a horse reared and crashed with its rider, a bullet through its head. There was a wild scatter for cover as a solitary figure stepped out to the cliff edge above.

"Pigeon!", "Pigeon!", "Pigeon!" yelled the trackers as the figure stepped back and disappeared.

Another bullet came whistling from the cliff, answered now by the patrol. A hundred shots were fired before Pigeon quietly walked away. From the plentiful cover below they could see nothing above to aim at, could only fire at the spot from which the shots seemed to be coming.

Pigeon was quite alone that day - and Ord quite mad. After all those long months and ceaseless effort, Pigeon was up there on top of the cliff and there was no possible chance to get at him before he could get clear away. Which he did, in his own time, laughing derisively to himself, but grinding his teeth in futile anger, that though he could hit a sitting wallaby with ease at a hundred yards, he had not yet killed an alert white bushman at the same puny range.

It was not long afterwards that Constable McDermott's and Matthews's patrols met at Rose's newly formed Leopold Downs station. Only thirty miles nor'-west of Fitzroy Crossing was this rough-hewn homestead just north of the Oscar Range. Rose was only just forming this station and the homestead was merely a long bough shed with sides of bamboo, easy to build, besides being cool. It had rough bamboo table and bunks, big open fireplace and Boor of crushed ant-bed wetted and stamped hard.

To feed this "mob", this particularly large patrol (there were nine of them all told, Constable McDermott, specials Billy Matthews, Percy Rose, Felix Edgar, young Green and others besides the trackers camped out by the harness sheds) they had killed a beast that afternoon. In the evening all hands set to and cut the beef up in strips and salted it, yarning in great form as they hung it up in the cool on the shady side of the homestead. After the evening meal they smoked and yarned a while about folk and events along the river, particularly of Pigeon and his gang, but especially of Pigeon. Later they played cards until far into the night. In honour of the occasion two hurricane lamps were used and these threw their light out through the interstices of the homestead walls. Again and again someone brought up the ever-present subject of Pigeon, terror of the Kimberleys.

Years later, young Green laughed as he told me the yarn, though a good many wet seasons have come and gone since then. Several of the young bloods complained bitterly about Pigeon. He was only a "shadow abo", they said, he was hardly ever game to be seen and was too scared even to leave a track. Why didn't he give them a chance! If he was so game and wanted to clean up all the whites in the Kimberleys then why was he not game to show himself now and again! Bah! he was only a "shadow" outlaw! One of these days they'd catch up with this boasting nigger and fill him so full of lead his own mother wouldn't know him. And so on, right until the small hours when they spread their blankets upon the Boor and turned in.

It was just after dawn when the leading tracker stepped in through the open door and awoke the two constables. One glance at his face and McDermott said, "Why! what's the matter, Peter? What name?"

Voicelessly Tracker Peter beckoned. They followed him outside.

Out there was an open fireplace a few yards away from the homestead. From this fireplace had been carried fine white ashes which had been neatly smoothed in front of the homestead doorway. And there, deep and firmly impressed upon these ashes was the footprint of - Pigeon!

The two constables drew a deep, deep breath and gazed at one another. Every man of them had been certain that Pigeon had been at least a hundred miles away. And yet here he had been standing, watching and listening. Watching and listening through the open doorway, and the cracks between the bamboos. Listening to them talking, hearing the young fellows boasting ... !

Why had he not picked his mark, fired and vanished? McDermott stepped into the hut, woke them all and said quietly: "Come out here a moment. An uninvited guest has left his visiting card!"

Curiously they followed him outside, then stared down. It was Felix who first exclaimed: "My God! he could have shot anyone of us! He could have killed three of us and still got clear away!"

Then Rose exclaimed: "The beef! it's gone!"

Yes, it had. It was not that Pigeon was short of beef. But he did want salted beef so that he could stack a supply in his hide-out and thus have plenty should he deem it advisable to remain out of all sight for a goodly period.

The trackers soon told the story of other tracks. Pigeon had brought with him five strong young lubras, loaded them heavily with the freshly salted beef, left his "visiting card", and away.

"That salted beef saved someone's life last night," said McDermott grimly.

Needless to say, no man in the West Kimberley played cards at night within a lighted hut after that.

39

MARAWON SEEKS VENGEANCE

THE patrols, while constantly harrying scattered groups of the gang amongst the Leopold foothills, began paying increasing attention to the rugged little ranges to the south nearer the Fitzroy - the Napier, Lennard, Barker, Oscar, and Geikie. It was only here, in particular localities, that the tracks of Pigeon had ever been seen. That he should haunt this country fringing the scenes of his outrages and just back from the line of settlement, instead of seeking sanctuary with his fellows farther back in the mazes of the Leopolds, had seemed very highly improbable for a long time. But there it was.

The Fitzroy River Crossing patrols, stationed at the extreme eastern end of the Oscar Range, began to patrol keenly these westward ranges. Ever active, constantly in the saddle backwards and forwards in and out among the valleys and flats and gorges for many hundreds of miles. Ever searching for tracks, raiding hideouts, sternly questioning any natives they could run to earth. Investigating every camp or cooking fire, every hunting or signal smoke, every waterhole where natives might be fishing, or seeking lily roots and water bulbs, tortoise and river crocodile. Those tribesmen with guilty consciences were kept constantly on the run, to their outspoken indignation.

Pigeon found that no more could he freely roam these lands with a cynical grin at the overworked patrols seeking him away back in the Leopolds. He too must keep constantly on the alert, ever wary of who might be in a native camp before he visited it, daring to move only with extreme caution, ever careful to "lose" his tracks. He had developed that hunted feeling now, with "eyes in the back of his head".

One morning while on the prowl he stopped dead in his tracks, for again plain before him was the footprint of Marawon.

One snarling glance told Pigeon the track was two days old.

Marawon would be away back in his own country by now.

The lone avenger, lying in ambush, had been waiting by the entrance to one of Pigeon's favourite hideouts.

Pigeon knew he dare not use that hideout again.

A few weeks later he caught a distant glimpse of his enemy just disappearing around the base of a scrub-clad hill. Pigeon was running after him on the instant, a tigerish glee in his heart as he gripped his Winchester. He would maim his enemy with a bullet, then hack out his kidney fat and eat it slowly before his eyes. Or he would slowly chew it, then spit it in his face! Ah, that insult would hurt the worst!

He ran on with his senses dulled in such a feverish fury that he did not hear the galloping hooves until he had almost bounded out into the open. He threw himself behind a bush, the only cover. With pounding heart he heard the hooves pulling up, he crept forward and peered.

Only two hundred yards away his tall enemy stood motionless in his nakedness, left hand resting easily on his long, upright spears, right hand holding his wommera. Closing around him were the leading horses of a patrol. They had been following his tracks - Marawan's tracks.

Marawon made not the slightest attempt to escape. Why should he? Though he must have felt very uneasy.

Pigeon watched as Constable Anderson and Felix Edgar rode up to interrogate. Tracker Peter interpreted and they talked for quite a long time.

Pigeon recovered from the surprise. His trigger finger itching, he gazed behind him, frowning.

He was quite out in the open with no chance of a getaway should he fire. Those horses could gallop around him, they would open fire from all sides and it would soon be over.

His eyes blazing with thwarted hate he stared at the group. still questioning Marawon. They had cut Marawon's tracks and tracked him, just as Marawon had been tracking Pigeon. Pigeon's teeth gritted with rage. He could shoot Marawon dead, his next shot would bring Anderson from his saddle, and he might just possibly get big Felix Edgar too - hardly likely, though! But whether or not it must mean the end for him. And he did not wish to die now. His strongest instinct, stronger even than the almost irresistible urge to put a bullet into this cur Marawon, was to put up a fight from under cover in a hideout from which, if necessary, he could escape to fight yet another day.

He froze almost to the earth. Marawon had turned, was pointing his way. The men turned in their saddles and stared towards him.

Pigeon knew Marawon was pointing out this particular hide-out away behind him, the hideout by which Marawon had waited in vain.

A little bird fluttered to the bush just by Pigeon's head, and scolded down at him with might and main.

Pigeon grinned. What a surprise the trackers out in front would get if they knew Pigeon was behind this bush upon which a bird was chattering-idly, they would think it was striving to protect its fledgelings by scolding down at a snake.

Pigeon ground his teeth. "That snake in the grass Marawon!" The patrol wheeled around and rode away, Marawon guiding them. And Pigeon drew a deep breath as he saw they were riding away from his tracks.

Such a very narrow escape, when he was helplessly out in the open!

And now he knew that Marawon had explained that Pigeon was not in his hideout, for he, Marawon, had just come from spying there. Pigeon knew too that Marawon was leading them to yet another hideout that he had found.

And so he was. And he would give them a great deal of valuable information about Pigeon, his habits, favourite localities over which he roamed, and describe such hideouts as he had located. And would tell of certain tribesmen and women Pigeon trusted who did his spy and lookout work for him.

But that night Marawon noiselessly slipped away from the patrol camp, swiftly back through the night to his own country. Not only because his own life was in danger from the spears of the local tribesmen, but because he wished to seek his vengeance alone. With long, easy strides taking him with surprising speed over the country, he grinned into the night. He had now put the white men well and truly on the scent of his enemy

Sandamara, whom white men called Pigeon. They would chase him day and night, would surprise his hiding-places. They would harry him now as a dingo chases its game until it reels from fatigue and despair. While Marawon could rest, only to return.

Sooner or later he would bury a spear deep into Pigeon. Either that, or through his words vengeance would come with the white men's bullets. As he strode on he chewed his beard in a frenzy of hatred. Tribal law would be avenged. Bitterly Sandamara would rue the day he took Marawon's young girl Cangamvara.

When the patrol rode back into the bush Pigeon hurried to his own people. Those who were close by he took back with him and showed them Marawon's tracks. When they had memorized that hated imprint he turned on them with a bitter snarl, ordering them all, men, women and children, to scatter and run to every tribesman and woman within reach and bring them back to memorize Marawon's footprint.

Henceforth, when Marawon returned he too would soon be one of the hunted. For sooner or later some little group wandering over the country would cross his tracks. Immediately then a smoke signal would go up, the hue and cry would be on.

Came the breathless days of late summer. Muttering of a distant storm working up. Grass tinder dry, arising on the horizon was dense black smoke, frightening not only game from cover but a bullock or two also. Presently, a little mob of alarmed beasts would find themselves trapped, ringed by flame and smoke. When finally, in stampeding terror, blinded by smoke, they would come charging through the last little laneway apparently left open for them they would be plunging through to fiendish yells, leaping figures, iron-bladed spears ripping into their flanks.

But wild game and cattle were not the only things being hunted in the Kimberleys. Many men were hunting, and being hunted. And as the first storms came growling to tell of a new Wet soon coming Pigeon knew full well that he was one of these, now being relentlessly hunted. Much thinner now was Pigeon and with a haunted gleam in his eye, his lip curled in a snarl of mistrust.

Most of the patrols had now concentrated along the Lennard, the Barker, and the Oscar rivers and ranges. Over one hundred miles length of country. And taking a great deal more interest in caves wherever they came across them. Pigeon's women brought him news that the patrols were even examining some caves by candlelight. Presently, they were doing much more than this, almost systematically examining this strip of country by "foot-walking". Where the country was impossible for horses they would send the animals, always under strong guard, around the particular range, or along its northern or southern side as the case might be. Then on foot they would climb that range, spread out, and walk along its crest for ten, twenty, thirty miles and more, carefully combing it for hideouts, particularly for cave outlets and "dog-holes" away up there on top. And they had found a number, too.

In a sullen fury Pigeon listened to this increasingly ominous news. He knew there were some fantastically broken areas in that country containing hideouts that they would never find. But then, of the innumerable hideouts, there were only a very few of value to Pigeon, only those with a hidden outlet. And the police by now had found and examined three of them.

"Marawon!" hissed Pigeon and his hand clenched around his rifle.

Pigeon dare not use anyone of those three hideouts again.

Not only for fear of a police ambush, but because he knew that if the patrols could only chase or catch or coax him into anyone of the three then he would be doomed. For they would block the outlets. Once they knew he was in there they would block both inlet and outlet - he would be caught like a dingo hiding in a hollow log with both its ends closed.

Deep in his most secret hideout, the Cave of the Bats, the hunted man scowled at the slowly burning fire.

"Hunted!" "Hunted!" "Hunted!"

40

THE STOCKMAN SLEEPS SOUNDLY

IT was well into the wet season when a nasty shock sent Pigeon berserk.

A patrol captured Cangamvara!

Inspector Ord acted cannily with Cangamvara. He used her as a decoy. The little black vixen, slyly alert, morose, sulky, bubbling with laughter in turns, answered all questioning in the same way. Gave information when asked, and always that information proved misleading. So grimly Ord used her as a decoy, keeping her under charge of his best trackers night and day so that there could be no possibility of escape. Yet to a spy it would appear that she could easily be rescued, especially when the patrol slept at night. And this patrol seemed unusually sleepy, besides being lax in caution by day.

But Pigeon was much too cunning.

Ord well knew how highly Pigeon valued his favourite wife, his sharpest lookout and information bringer. And his old Mother Jinny, apparently nearly always with, or near him. But Cangamvara, with her friends, he used to send on service for him far and wide. As a "lookout" woman and bringer of information she must be invaluable to Pigeon. He would sorely miss her services. He would attempt a rescue - if it looked easy enough.

But Pigeon was too clever to walk into such a tempting trap.

Day by day Cangamvara walked freely along with this patrol dawdling over Pigeon's own country. She was always plainly to be seen of nights, chatting and laughing by a bright fire with other prisoners away from the trackers' fire. Any prowler out in the night could see her easily. Could even see her coiled up there when the camp slept.

And Pigeon did see her, both by day and night. But then, the eyes of Pigeon saw everything. Sneeringly he evaded the trap.

Yet he came within an inch of losing his life most simply and most unexpectedly.

It was at Mt Abbott police camp, merely a hut in the wilderness. A patrol would occasionally use it as a camp for a week or two. Then the hut would be shut up until needed again.

Pigeon made up his mind that the next time a patrol camped at Mt Abbott for any length of time, he would stroll along one night and shoot one of that patrol. He could do it so easily if they all camped in the hut. Just fire from the darkness, then disappear in the darkness.

And one day Mother Jinny brought him word from a tribesman that a patrol was again camped at the hut, apparently for some time.

Pigeon looked to his rifle. Then without a word he silently left the Cave of the Bats for the open bush.

It was Constable Buckland's patrol, with Constable Anderson and two specials, using the hut for the time being. Buckland's orders were that no lights were to be lit in the hut after dark. Also, if any man wished to smoke, he was only to do so under cover. And no man was to leave the hut without his express permission.

"We think Pigeon is at least a couple of days' ride from here," growled the experienced policeman. 'Well, he isn't! He's just where he is at the moment - and that might be not a mile away. Anyway, there's no man of this patrol going to get a bullet through the head if I can stop it. So see that every man obeys orders."

By night, the horses were guarded some little distance away by a constable and the trackers.

Now, one of the specials was an ambitious young fellow very anxious to distinguish himself. And he had heard one of the trackers mention to Anderson that Pigeon was known to have prowled up to the hut in the night once or twice, walking along the track leading from the waterhole.

"Why shouldn't he come tonight?" thought the young fellow.

The patrol leader had said he might be only a mile away (Buckland did not believe Pigeon was within a hundred miles of the place, if that). Presently, the young fellow picked up his rifle and groped for the door.

"Where are you going?" demanded Buckland.

"Oh, just outside," muttered the young special and Buckland nodded in the darkness.

The young fellow stepped outside, quietly closed the hut door.

It was a dark night. His heart already beginning to beat fast, his eyes straining to pierce the darkness, he took off his boots, then stealthily stepped out along the path.

Pigeon, as it happened, was coming up along that path, coming with phantom quietness, but taking it easy. Already he could see that there were no lights in the hut - obviously the men within were wary. However, Pigeon felt he had plenty of time, it would only mean patience and he would get a man. He came on, not keyed up to his usual caution.

The young special had now crept a couple of hundred yards down the path from the hut. Very lonely it was now, very dark, very dark, very silent. He stood there listening, trying to hear something, trying to see ahead. He was just about to step forward again when a black shadow loomed up right before him ....

The special with a gasping cry whipped up his rifle and fired.

An amazed black face vanished in the flame of the rifle.

What Constable Buckland said when the patrol came tumbling out of the hut - when in the morning the excited, grinning trackers pointed down to the tracks of Pigeon ...

What Buckland said! Oh well! well! well!

More and yet more the patrols began to hem Pigeon in, patrolling more and yet more across his favourite haunts, ever searching, ever searching both by foot and horse. Finally, they appeared to be closing in. So much so, and in such dread was he also of the prowling tactics of his lone enemy Marawon that he decided to "lose" himself for quite a long time. So he vanished - deep into the Cave of the Bats, with only old Mother Jinny to bring him food, and news, and company. And here again he planned and scowled deep into the fire throughout most of another wet season .

Thus, no longer could the patrols find any trace, nor sign, nor track of Pigeon, nor hear whisper of him except in misleading information. Yet again he had completely vanished. In exasperation, yet with dogged perseverance, they kept searching for him "on the blind" throughout the constant hardships of the Wet.

Well before the end of the Wet Pigeon had finalized a plan.

And old Mother Jinny slipped quietly away to get in touch with Demon, Pyabarra, Murrumin, Canada, Yarramarra and all the best men possibly to be found. When all were ready, Pigeon would meet them, and they would carry out the plan.

It was a vast plan, but now, because of the loss of his best men, and most of the firearms, and loss of prestige, a desperate plan, yet it had quite a chance of success if timed and carried out well. The plan was to attack Collins's Oscar Range station, kill the three white men there, take the arms and ammunition with which the oft-threatened station was now plentifully supplied, then double back swiftly and attack the Fitzroy Crossing police station, choosing a time when the patrols would be widely scattered.

At the Oscar Range station were Jack Collins, Fred Edgar and at the time Alf Mynall, on a visit buying stock. Also there had recently arrived the stockman Tom Jasper, the same stockman who had been working at' Oobagooma when that station away on the coast had been threatened some time before. As Jasper was about to ride from The Crossing to Collins's station, Pilmer had warned him to be wary of Pigeon.

But Jasper laughed.

"He's got you blokes bluffed," he said, "but I'm not scared of him-nor of a dozen like him."

"Other men have said that before," replied Pilmer grimly, "Burke and Gibbs for instance."

"Bah!" replied Jasper, "those two asked for it, they wouldn't even carry a revolver. I've got enough guns to fight all Pigeon's mob. If he bails me up I'll give him a go for it on my own."

"Take no chances with Pigeon," warned Pilmer, "or I may have to turn my patrol into a burial party."

But Tom Jasper rode away unconcerned. And now he was working for Collins.

Cleverly Pigeon had planned. It was not until the last moment that even Demon and the picked men knew exactly what that plan was. Their preparatory job was to whisper to the tribesmen to travel in all secrecy to the precipitous range directly behind Collins's homestead. Even their hideout camps were allotted - nine camps, scattered along the range but quite close to the homestead. One particular camp was to be left for Pigeon and his men.

Under shadow of night the tribesmen congregated. That area of the Oscar Range had been bare of natives for weeks past. Now even the station stockboys were unaware that they had come. They were under cover, in quiet excitement waiting for Pigeon.

He was coming through the night. With Demon behind him, and Yarramarra and Boll, Mullenbuddin and Warramarra and Pyabarra, Murramin and Woinmarra and Canada and a score of others. Black bodies lost in the night, striding silently along, carrying war spears, their leader's rifle and revolver, coming with eyes a-gleam.

It was not until the small hours, not until within sight of the black shadow of the homestead that Pigeon stopped his little bodyguard and whispered his detailed plan. Just before daylight they, with the tribesmen, would silently encircle the homestead. Then, at the thrice repeated hoot of the night owl, they would hurl themselves upon it from all sides. Their weight of numbers would break straight in. They would kill the three white men and any visitors that might be camped there, and every station native fool enough to oppose them, loot the homestead of arms, then make straight back towards The Crossing and attack the new police station and telegraph station simultaneously in the following dawn.

Their eyes gleamed, fingers twitched on revolver and spear hafts as they stared towards the easy prey.

Pigeon was about to lead them around the homestead to the tribesmen awaiting them in the dense blackness of the range when Demon hissed warningly. In a moment they were peering beside him.

And there, just around the homestead by the stockyard, stood out the whiteness of a tent.

It was Tom Jasper the stockman's tent. For the last week he had been at work repairing the stockyard. He camped beside it, in his tent. Despite Collins's protests he had stubbornly refused to sleep within the homestead. It was only eighty yards away, anyway; if anything happened he could run there within a few strides. He swore he could not be taken by surprise. "No nigger can surprise me," he declared. "I sleep with 'one ear open'. And my bedmates are a Winchester, a double-barrelled gun and a revolver. I've got other mates too, plenty of them. There's the station native camp and the natives' dogs within a stone's throw. And there's the homestead dogs too. Even if he did come, Pigeon would have no more chance of surprising me than he would the man in the moon."

And of all of them, white men, station boys and their women and children, it was only Tom Jasper the stockman who slept soundly.

And now - Demon had spied the tent!

In phantom silence they began to edge right out around the - homestead towards the tent. Stealthy as black panthers, the panther lust for the kill surging up within them.

Even when they came right to the tent Pigeon did not mean to attack. Even though there be a man asleep within the tent he would not attack until all the tribesmen were with them. What luck it would be, though, if one of the white men was actually at their mercy out here. That would mean only two of them to be killed within the homestead. But he would not attack all the same, not until all the warriors had joined them and were ready to rush.

And then they were peering within the tent. Plainly their tigerish eyes could see him, a white man sound asleep, fully dressed, revolver within his belt, rifle lying beside him. Sound asleep!

They all crowded at the doorway. Faint sound as of one deep, indrawn breath, rifle, revolver, spears slowly raised!

The reports and savage grunts woke the startled night. There was a long-drawn instant of utter silence.

Tom Jasper had moved but once convulsively, two bullets in his head, two long spears buried deep in his body, another quivering in the packsaddle by his head.

Sudden furious barking of station dogs, frantic yapping of native dogs, a shout and sounds of hurried awakening in the homestead. Then spurt of flame and a rifle shot, followed swiftly by another and another. and another.

"Quick!" snapped Pigeon, "grab the guns and all the ammunition!"

There was a large supply in the tent.

Shouts came from the homestead, answering shouts from the stockboys' camp. And now a bullet came hissing through the tent, then another; the white men had guessed what had happened.

A bullet twanged through an iron-bladed spearhead and hurled it from Mullenbuddin's hand. The shaggy Mullenbuddin glared down open-mouthed at his prized spear - the spear he had hurled through the white man Burke!

Pigeon cursed, then sprawled out flat and began firing at the spurts of flame from the homestead walls. Demon, with a growl of sheer joy, pulled a double-barrelled shotgun from under the dead man's blankets and aimed at flaming green eyes. To the thunderous report came shrieking howls from dogs caught in the spray of shot. Demon threw back his head and laughed at the hideous howls, a laugh blood-curdling as his name. Then Boll suddenly sprawled with a startled grunt, a bullet through his thigh. Retribution had come fast for Boll because he had put a bullet into the sleeping stockman. A curse from Pigeon and they were up and running for the black shadow of the range. Pigeon had made a bad mistake. As he ran he cursed that primitive urge to kill on sight that had given the homestead the alarm.

Pigeon was uneasy also at the unexpected volume of fire which had come from the homestead. He did not know of the presence of Maynall.

They joined the eager tribesmen at the foot of the range, staring back towards the homestead from which rifles were still firing into the night. Came a burst of rapid fire, Same stabbing rapidly into the night from the homestead walls.

Pigeon well knew that rapid fire. Three or four men with repeating Winchesters could keep up a fire that would seem to be coming from a dozen or more men.

But Pigeon and Demon and his crowd as they glared out towards the thoroughly awakened homestead could not tell for sure. There might be visitors at the homestead, certainly there were more men than two. Perhaps trusted stockboys from the station camp had run to join them. And all would be well-armed.

Collins's homestead by the Oscar Range had been often threatened. Collins had prepared for attack. Now that there could be no surprise it would prove a tough nut to crack.

Pigeon ground his teeth in a tigerish rage. If only he had stopped them from killing Jasper until the mob were ready placed to rush the sleeping homestead!

And now they heard another sound - galloping hooves clearly ringing in the night, a horseman galloping from the homestead to warn Fitzroy Crossing and bring the Fitzroy police patrol.

41

THE FIGHT AT THE HOMESTEAD

COLD dawn came. The range crest emerged in black outline of sombre rock. Pink grew the sky. Gradually the blanket of night lifted from the plain. The rough little homestead took shape, then the stockyard. And a white blob that was the trampled-down tent of a dead stockman.

The plain emerged under dawnlight. There came trumpet calls from a line of brolgas dancing in the dawn-a wonder dance those tall grey joysters pirouette to the new-born day. Birds whistled among the trees clinging to the rocky escarpments of the range. Away across at the homestead the door opened, a stockboy strolled out. Pigeon aimed, fired. The stockboy leapt high and bounded back into the homestead to a yell of hilarious laughter from the range.

A shot came from the homestead. Both Pigeon and Pyabarra answered it. In reply, bullets came whining up towards the rocks. But the range was too distant. Pigeon's advance men could hit. the homestead, but it would take a good rifle and a good shot to hit a man at that distance. Alf Collins, Fred Edgar, Maynall and the stockboys could not yet locate where the shots were coming from, while the black figures they could now see all along the range crest would be too far away.

The sun shone warmly down. Now and then there was the "crack!" of a rifle, answered from the homestead.

Ever so far up in the sky, a dot like a fly fleeting within palest blue, an eagle came circling. A crow slowly Hying over the homestead alighted upon the stockyard rail; the sun shone glossy upon his black plumage. The sun shone whitely upon the collapsed tent.

The crow, lazily, said "Kark!"

When Collins's blackboy came galloping to The Crossing only thirteen miles away, Senior Constable Pilmer wired Ord at Derby: "To Sub-Inspector Ord. Thomas Jasper shot dead by natives at Collins's station night 15th. Large mob in range near station fired on Collins and Maynall. Leaving at once in pursuit. R. H. Pilmer."

Ord started movement by wire and horse which warned all stations and in the course of days started every patrol in the West Kimberley hurriedly converging towards the Barker and Oscar ranges.

Meanwhile it was 10 o'clock in bright sunlight when Pilmer's patrol came swiftly riding up to the Oscar Range homestead. As Collins shouted a warning from the door a bullet came whining, followed by another and another. The patrol wheeled around until out of range, dismounted, and returned to the homestead on foot.

Collins pointed to the tent. Ten black crows were sitting on the stockyard rail.

"I warned him he might turn my patrol into a burial party," frowned Pilmer. "Over-confidence killed him. He was an experienced man and should have known better."

They buried Torn Jasper right there, by the stockyard. The boys with the pick and shovel sweated until their black hides shone glossy as the disappointed crows perched along the stockyard rail. For every now and then would come a distant rifle shot, a "ping-ing-ing!" as a bullet hit the gravel and whined away.

Pilmer scattered his men towards the foot of the range, trying to locate where the shots were coming from. It was not from those black figures yelling defiance high up that the danger was coming but from sharpshooters hidden between the homestead and the range. Or, as it seemed now, from some shrewdly concealed position down near the range base. Presently, Pilmer's trackers began to pin the sound. From cover they began to fire, gradually locating the hidden position.

Demon began firing with savage abandon, scowling as Pigeon snarled at him to save ammunition. Thereafter, they fired only now and again.

Only Pigeon and Demon, Bunnamurra, Canada, and Murramin had rifles. Pyabarra had Jasper's double-barrelled gun, two others had shotguns, Boll, Woinmarra and half a dozen others had revolvers. The remainder had only spears. Guns, revolvers and spears were useless at this range.

Pigeon's tactics were playing right into Pilmer's hands. His patrol consisted only of himself, Constable Nicholson and four trackers, only six men all told. There was no chance of cornering Pigeon's gang, let alone that big mob yelling from their sheltering hills. But every hour he could hold them there a noose was drawing closer around Pigeon for Chisholm's patrol was only twenty miles from The Crossing and Pilmer had sent him word at the gallop. Within a couple of hours Chisholm would be riding fast across country. Buckland's patrol was but thirty miles away; in a few hours he also would receive word. If Pilmer could only hold Pigeon until other patrols could arrive and surround him!

"Wishful thinking!" said Pilmer grimly to Nicholson. "The black devil always has a getaway."

The afternoon drew slowly on. An occasional rifle shot told that

Pigeon was still there.

Under fair cover, each man of the patrol had gradually crept closer towards the approximate spot where the shooting was coming from. Pilmer ordered each man to aim only there.

The little gang, safe under excellent cover, had long since grown contemptuous of the desultory fire. The whine of a passing bullet, the "smack!" as another flattened against a rock without anyone being harmed throughout the day, were now despised sounds. Both Demon and Murramin were now taking risks, eagerly peering for sight of a good target to shouted directions from the spearmen behind and up above them. It was towards sundown when to the sound of a "thud!" and a groan Murramin fell back with a bullet through the body. Demon jerked up and glanced aside at the sound, then "smack!" and Demon sprawled down with a bullet clean through the shoulder. With a startled expression on his face he glared at Pigeon who cursed savagely at the blood welling between Demon's fingers where he was clenching his shoulder.

It was a clean wound, no bones were broken, Demon could still fight. But he had received a nasty shock.

"Smack!" and Pyabarra yelled as the bullet broke his arm. To violent curses from Pigeon they all slid back amongst the boulders.

All day long and not a man hurt. And now, within two minutes, three of his best men hit!

Murramin was dying, plain to see that, Pyabarra's shattered arm hung uselessly beside him. Demon would be a sick man for some time, while Boll's leg was now stiff from the wound received after Jasper had been killed.

Pigeon had so very, very few men left, men who knew the white man's ways, men who could use guns. There were others but they were far away, scattered amongst different tribes. Now that he had failed to loot the station he could not give even the men with him guns. This might have been his last chance to gather good men together again.

He glanced out towards the setting sun. Then at the shadows settling upon the range. He gazed long, in a strange silence, as if he felt the shadows settling upon him too.

Long afterwards, survivors among his friends whispered about how in silence they had gazed upon his face, reading what they saw there. "His face looked as if it had lost all hope," they whispered, "like the look on the face of the dying Murramin."

Constable Pilmer was gazing around too. The natives were spreading out, a group of them here and there upon the little hills surrounding the homestead. It looked very much as if Pigeon was getting ready for an all-out attack upon the homestead tonight.

Pilmer, quite unaware of the casualties to Pigeon's gang, retired to the homestead to make ready for the expected attack, anxious to make as sure as possible that the precious horses would be safely guarded.

"It looks like an all-out attack tonight right enough," said young Constable Nicholson.

"If only they *will!*" replied Pilmer eagerly, "then we've got them! We have Collins, Maynall and Edgar in the homestead, and the four trackers and Collins's armed boys to place where we will. We'll wipe out the whole gang or we'll deserve to be wiped out ourselves."

"Every man will be looking for a shot at Pigeon anyway," said Nicholson. "Whether or no, you'll get what you want."

"How's that?" demanded Pilmer.

"Well, even if we don't get Pigeon and smash up his gang then you'll be holding him long enough for some of the nearer patrols to come up."

"Yes," agreed Pilmer hopefully. "Chisholm should be here about midday tomorrow, Buckland's patrol a couple of hours later. If we can only hold Pigeon until then!"

"How many do you estimate are in the complete mob?" asked Nicholson curiously.

"Something over a hundred," answered Pilmer, "from the glimpses of little mobs I've noticed drifting around us in late afternoon. But they're only *munjons.* It's only Pigeon's armed men we've got to watch."

"Well," smiled Nicholson as they approached the homestead, "*munjons* or no *munjons* it is going to be a dark night. If Pigeon, and you know he is a surprisingly good man, if Pigeon can convince those hundred spear- and club-men to make one concerted rush upon the homestead then they'll break straight into this flimsy hut in a score of places. It will be a lively few moments!"

"All the more reason for us to shoot quickly and straight," replied Pilmer confidently as they entered the hut, "and make sure you impress the fact upon the others too!"

Pilmer did not then know that but a dozen of Pigeon's particular gang carried a medley of firearms. Nor did he know that three of his best men had been hit.

Throughout the silent night eyes, ears, and rifles waited tensely for the coming of Pigeon.

42

DEMON FIRES HIS LAST SHOT

PIGEON was not silly enough for that, though he would have risked his life for the chance to kill but one more white man. Silently and alone he prowled all around the homestead. So silently that not even a dog barked.

But every waiting man inside was well under cover. No chink of light showed between the walls by which a prowler might get a shot inside. It was pitch dark inside there and the quietness spoke of tensely waiting men.

At last Pigeon gave it up, turned back to the hills, his heart full of bitter fury blacker than the night.

He felt now that the last blow had come, almost the very last.

For with the coming of night word had been brought him that a patrol had captured old Jinny, his mother.

It was Ord's hurrying patrol. It was Ord too who had captured Cangamvara. And now Mother Jinny was a captive. Now there would be no Mother Jinny to keep him company, no Mother Jinny to steal out and bring him food and news. When he was starving, he must now risk creeping out and hunting for himself, like a hunted dingo hard pressed. And soon - eager trackers would be seeking him everywhere.

Pigeon was a deathly danger to friend and foe alike when sullenly he rejoined his men.

Murramin was dead.

Pyabarra was moaning with his shattered arm. Demon crouched sullenly, his shoulder now stiff and sore. Boll's swollen leg was hurting him. Mullenbuddin squatted there glowering, his dark thoughts all about the bullet that had smashed through his shovel-bladed spearhead after the stockman had been killed that morning, that prized spear blade that he had driven right through the white man Burke's body. An ill omen this to the shaggy Mullenbuddin - the bullet through his spear blade might have gone through his head, the only head he had ... Mullenbuddin's head! The next bullet... !

Canada looked scared, Warramarra very sulky and Woinmarra queerly troubled, glowering at his revolver, the revolver with which he had so eagerly fired at the sleeping stockman Tom Jasper.

When no attack came by 3 a.m. Constable Pilmer's increasing uneasiness urged him to action. Leaving Collins, Maynall and Edgar within the homestead, his patrol stealthily crept outside, then cautiously began edging towards Pigeon's position. Nicholson and two trackers were to creep around Pigeon then, bare-footed, up a pinnacle directly behind him. Meanwhile Pilmer and two trackers would steal as near to Pigeon as they could with safety. Then under cover they would wait for daylight, which should find Pigeon under fire from the pinnacle above.

This plan would put Pigeon's men in a nasty position, providing Pigeon had not moved camp farther back into the hills.

Which he had.

The Oscar Range by the homestead rises sheer in cliffs, with one break in it just there, a precipitous gully with water gurgling over its tangled bed of rocks and undergrowth. It runs six miles inland between the cliffs to end in a grassy plateau of horseshoe shape where the Napier Range joins the Oscar. Pilmer feared that Pigeon might have retired back to this ideal camping place, with its cave "getaways".

They made for the black mouth of the gully. There was no dull glow of campfire coals, no slightest sound of natives - they must have moved off up the gully. Cautiously the patrol moved forward. It was black down there between the cliff walls but up above the sky-lit rim loomed queer shadows with outline of dwarf trees. They crept on, finding it difficult to move quietly amongst this tangle of brushwood and rocks. No sound came but the gurgling of barely seen water.

Again and again the trackers paused, an occasional gleam in their eyes as they held their faces up towards the starlight above.

They were sniff, sniff, sniffing. Sniffing for smell of smoke or hidden campfire, sniffing for odour of wild men. On again they crept.

Before dawn came a sudden downpour. Which did not cheer Pilmer, not because of the discomfort, but because such heavy rain would wash out all tracks before daylight came. Just before dawn they emerged on to the open plateau, still in shadow land. A warning hiss came from the trackers.

A faint tang of smoke at last had come to their questing nostrils. They whispered that they smelt a still smouldering camp-fire deep within the pitch-black mouth of a cave. Certain that there would be an outlet to the cave, Pilmer decided to climb this hill and drop down, the other side, if possible to find the getaway and block it. He posted Nicholson with Trackers Hector and Billy in hiding by the cave mouth while he set off with Trackers Big Ned and Bob to try to find the cave outlet, devoutly hoping that Pigeon would awake to find himself trapped.

At dawn they were stealthily climbing down into a steep, rock-walled gully right behind the cave hill. Just as Pilmer lightly dropped to the gully bottom a bullet whizzed down and flattened viciously. Pilmer wheeled around with upflung rifle and saw Pigeon upon a rock high up on the bank above. Pilmer dropped to his knee in the spinifex, fired with shaking hand. Pigeon fired again and Pilmer instantly fired back. Both men then fired simultaneously as Pilmer leapt to the shelter of the gully bank with a stinging pain in his thigh. Flattened against the gully wall, anxiously he felt his leg, stretching it with a sigh of relief as he felt no bone broken. He saw then that his cartridge belt, revolver holster and thick, heavy moleskins were well plastered by shot pellets. Eagerly Bangarra had begged Pyabarra's gun and taken a pot shot at the policeman, but the leather holster and heavy cartridge belt had taken most of the charge. Gingerly he began climbing back up the bank to where he could now see Trackers Ned and Bob crouched behind rocks, firing down into a camp.

To wild yells, fresh shots now broke out from Nicholson and his trackers who came hurrying over the hill. It had been Pigeon in the cave all right, but alarmed, he and his men had simply walked through the cave which opened out into a dozen getaways behind the hill.

"Quick feller! Look out!" suddenly yelled Tracker Ned.

"Pigeon him down there! Pyabarra! Demon! Plenty feller down there longa gully!" and Pilmer got a glimpse of Pigeon flying to the shelter of a rock, his men now under two fires. Even so, and after their losses of the evening before, they fought back gamely for a lively half-hour. Then, from down amongst the spinifex Demon saw Pilmer's head as he fired. With an animal-like eagerness Demon wriggled to get his shoulder into a comfortable position, to make dead sure. His wounded shoulder was stiff and very sore, it hurt when he bent his arm. At last he got the rifle firm, his eye still as cut glass as he sighted along the barrel. His finger slowly bent around the trigger, and then ... !

Demon's eyes flashed urgently, he sank down with a bullet through the brain.

43

PIGEON'S "MOB" FIGHTS AGAIN

PILMER and his trackers found themselves overlooking Pigeon's main camp. Fire at first was lively but Pigeon's excited men aimed wildly and were no match for the cool shooting of the patrol. Canada snatched Pigeon's rille and put a bullet through the hat of Tracker Billy firing from a ledge high above, but almost immediately he slid back with a flesh wound through the leg which dampened his ardour considerably. All the tribesmen with the exception of Pigeon's little crowd now darted Into caves and with goggle-eyed excitement watched the fight from there. Bangarra was firing wildly from Jasper's double-barrelled gun and the heavy reports in the little glen reverberated far along the range. Bunnamurra, safely wedged between two towering rocks, also got a glimpse of Pilmer's head as he fired from a height above. Bunnamurra excitedly awaited his opportunity, unaware that Big Ned, Pilmer's favourite tracker, was working his way along the ridge crest directly behind and above him. Big Ned spied the black body wedged down there between the two boulders. He whipped up his rifle, aimed steadily, and fired. Bunnamurra collapsed with a bullet through the body. And so did Bangarra, almost at the same instant.

Pigeon, seeking a target with a hopeless, savage fury, deliberately raised his head. He drew fire all right-two bullets whining to flatten upon the rocks beside him. Pigeon disappeared. In a frenzy at sudden blindness he dashed his hand across his eyes. Blinking through the blood, he could see again. It was only a forehead graze from a flying splinter of rock, one of his many narrow escapes.

But it was the end of the fight. Pigeon with his few remaining men made an immediate dash for the caves.

Pilmer and Nicholson warily made their way down to the abandoned camp. Demon lay there, very silent. Never again for Demon the click of kylies, the Dream Time song at eventime. Nor for Murramin. Nor Bunnamurra. Nor Bangarra.

Very soon, too, the trackers found the blood tracks of three wounded men. But, to the bitter disappointment of Pilmer and Nicholson, no sign of Pigeon. All hands had disappeared into a honeycomb of caves. Pilmer was certain there must be an outlet. Pigeon would flee to some favourite hideout now and do his "vanishing act". Pilmer recovered three revolvers, two rifles and a shotgun with ammunition, burned fifty-odd spears. Then he sent for the horses. The patrol would scatter and ride the valleys and flats, poke into gorges and ravines for sign of tracks coming from the range. Pigeon must be found, must be brought to bay.

Next day they found the blood tracks of several wounded tribesmen. And presently Tracker Ned pointed to a little footstep.

"Little feller boy," he grinned towards Pilmer, "hit longa leg. Him plenty feller tired now. Soon we find him."

And they did, wedged like a terrified lizard deep within a cleft in the rocks, squeezed in and clinging so tightly that the grinning trackers had to lever him out with a sapling. He clung to it as a terrified monkey would to the branch of a tree. In speechless terror he stared up at Pilmer, his eyes "big as saucers".

He had been accidentally hit in the stampede when the patrol first fired down at the camp. Pilmer bandaged the wound and sent the lad back to Collins's homestead for treatment.

This wild little child of the hills was christened "Larry". His mother never claimed him. The police took him to Derby where he soon recovered. He became very fond of the whites and, when quite recovered, definitely refused to leave the police station. Thereafter, to this day, his life has been at the service of the whites. Except for periodical walkabouts, he generally worked for the police. He was our Tracker Larry, in *Over the Range.*

But though Pilmer's patrol searched by horse and foot until sundown they found no track of Pigeon that day.

Pigeon had decided to fly alone and to hide within the Cave of the Bats until the patrols lost the scent and scattered away back to the Leopolds, as they had done so often before. The final remnants of his gang were again broken up, while the tribesmen were discouraged by the failure of the attack on the homestead and the trouncing the patrol. had given Pigeon's men. Quickly they split up into groups, and family groups. Through caves, then ravines, they slipped away from the vicinity of the patrol, intent on scattering far and wide. Pigeon's few remaining men Bed too, though they clung together for a time.

Pigeon, his savage face caked with blood and dust, scowled his farewell as he fled alone. Climbing sure-footed as a mountain goat up a narrow ledge to the sunlit summit above, he stepped out into the sweet bush air right on top of the range. With long, tireless strides he made towards the west.

The range just here was flat-topped. It was only three miles across but ran for twenty miles from east to west without a break, with precipitous sides, a valley to right and left. Stunted trees grew on this range crest, scraggy bushes and coarse grasses upon the scanty soil. Ever and anon were harsh areas of bare, hot rock. But always came the call of the birds.

A huge carpet snake, a glistening mass of brown, black and gold coiled upon a grey rock bathed in sunlight, caused Pigeon to lick hungry lips. But he dare not tarry. He must slip along this range crest and cross over to another as swiftly as possible, leaving that accursed patrol ever farther behind as by foot they slowly, arduously searched the range.

By mid-afternoon he had come to the end of the crest, climbed down and was "halfway across a valley, making for another range, when he wheeled around with upflung rifle. Sound of hoof beats! Yes, a patrol, riding around a low hill!

Pigeon's eyes blazed. This patrol was riding down the valley, must cut his tracks. Would the trackers see them?

They did. An excited shout, a beckoning arm, then swiftly they gathered around these most discussed, most notorious tracks in all the Kimberleys, in all the great State of Western Australia.

The tracks of Pigeon.

44

THE PATROLS ARE CLOSING IN

TWO mounted men trotted up to the trackers. Pigeon recognized Constable Chisholm and Joe Blythe. As the trackers pointed out the tracks they began following them with a frightening swiftness. Bent almost double, Pigeon raced for the range. No time now to "lose his tracks", it would be a race for life should they see him. They did not for quite a while. But eventually he heard a shout from far behind. He leapt to it then, racing for life towards the beckoning boulders of the range. And it took a good horse almost to run him down. At the growing sound of galloping hooves his feet barely seemed to touch the ground as the big grey rocks drew nearer. So too did those galloping hooves. Then the crack of a revolver, the whine of a spent bullet falling just behind. Very soon, a bullet clipped the ground beside him, followed by another droning overhead. With long-drawn gasps Pigeon raced, glaring towards an enormous grey boulder as if the very urgency of his longing would draw it to him. He cared not one whit for those bullets now whistling viciously, it was only that boulder he wanted. He just made it, bounded past its huge grey side and disappeared among a maze of its fellows.

Pigeon, who so contemptuously believed he could lose Pilmer's patrol and leave it twenty-four hours behind was really twenty-four hours late himself. The stresses of the last day and night were to continue. He had lost Pilmer's patrol, yes, but had run into Chisholm's. They were right on his tracks, they would cling like grim death. While he after last night's fight and this long walk and now famishing must carry on all through the night again.

That night he doubled straight back across the valley and at daylight was walking. south upon the crest of the Oscar Range. All that day, never stopping to hunt for food, he carried on, then veered southward towards the Fitzroy, his hope being that the patrols would seek him northward. Of course he could not know of Sub-Inspector Ord's wire from Derby to the Commissioner of Police in Perth:

March 18th 1897. Am leaving for Fitzroy via Lennard as I hear murder was committed by Pigeon and blacks. From the Lennard Constables Chisholm and Buckland will ride to and patrol the north end of the Oscar Range. Anderson the northern end of the Barrier Range. Pilmer and Nicholson the southern end of the Oscar. Spong and myself will ride straight up the Fitzroy along the telegraph line. Fear there will be some more shooting as the natives have arms. Corporal Pearson will remain in charge of Derby. Ord.

Pigeon, running away from patrols, was running right into an approaching pack of them. By dawn he was near the southern limit of the Oscar Range. He turned south, clambering down the headwaters channel of Mt Wynne Creek. The creek flows straight down the side of the range out on to the plain and the Fitzroy. Pigeon was tired now and famished. By the creek near the foot of the range was a native camp, a favourite rendezvous of Canada and Boll and Woinmarra. Pigeon believed they would have made straight for there after the brush with Pilmer's patrol. By this time they would have raided the plain and speared a bullock or two. Pigeon's jaws worked in hungry anticipation.

"Roast beef! Juicy roast beef!!"

He would eat there and learn the news. Eat and rest and get the sleep he so badly needed now. Then eat again. Then, refreshed, travel around the range back towards the north-east, cross the flat country in the night and reach the sanctuary of his beloved Barker Range.

And right then he stopped dead in his tracks, like a statue poised upon a spur of the range, gazing out over the plain. Away out there, by the white man's telegraph line, was coming a fast riding patrol. Even as he watched he saw the leading horsemen turning sharply south.

He knew instantly. They were going to raid the native camp.

Hiding movement by riding up beside the long, dark line of timber that was Mt Wynne Creek, they would suddenly break out at the gallop and surround the camp at the foot of the range.

In but another ten minutes Pigeon would have been down in that camp. Bitterly he cursed the patrols, cursed all white men. Then wearily began climbing back up the range.

At the crest, he walked directly north across it, only a couple of miles for the range end petered out here. He would cross the flat on the opposite side then climb the next range, then turn again west towards the Barker, while that accursed patrol after raiding the camp would ride east, every mile both he and they travelled taking them farther and farther apart. He hoped they would not catch Canada and Yarramarra and any of the gang who might be there. That this camp would be taken by surprise he felt certain. Savagely he remembered how often he had tried to train all of them never to lose caution an instant day or night. And to constantly use the keenest sighted women as lookouts. Morosely he thought of all those tribal women he had harshly trained as his own lookouts, how good they were, and now they were all gone. Even Cangamvara and old Mother Jinny. Not one of them left to him now, he was completely alone. His hand twitched on his rifle, his teeth gritted with an animal-like ferocity as tensely he wished for a chance to put a bullet through the brain of Sub-Inspector Ord.

In a white fury he came to the northern edge of the range and stared down unbelievingly. Just emerging from the trees down there on the flat, coming from the west, were the leading trackers of another patrol. And now appeared behind them a mounted constable, then another, then two more trackers, followed by a dozen packhorses and a police boy.

So! they were going to ride *both* sides of the range! One patrol would ride the south side, riding along it from west to east. So that if anywhere along its length Pigeon and his men had come down onto the plains of the Fitzroy then their tracks must be cut. At the same time this other patrol would ride the northern side, so that if Pigeon and his men had broken away to reach the Leopolds to the north, then their tracks must be cut.

Grimly Pigeon squatted down to watch. An expert tracker, he saw in a flash how efficient was the work of these patrols. Many a time he had been boss tracker of a patrol and he was still proud of the reputation acquired in those long distant days. When the white police met they used to boast of the prowess of their trackers. How often he had glowed as Constable Richardson boasted, "Ah yes, your boy is good. But Pigeon has brains. And with the scent of a bloodhound, the eyes of a hawk. Once he finds a track, nothing can shake him off!"

Ah! those days seemed a long, long time ago. And now Pigeon was the hunted man. It was his tracks now that the trackers were tracking. And from what he had already seen this morning, and from his position now he realized at a glance the co-ordinated work of three patrols hunting him over hundreds of miles of country. The patrol that by now had raided the camp was combing the southern side of the Oscar right away east to Fitzroy Crossing, while this patrol riding below was combing the northern side to The Crossing. Riding down towards them was Pilmer's patrol, maybe now thirty miles behind him. Difficult indeed for any man to continue to escape such co-ordinated work.

Ah! but it was Pigeon they were hunting. He sneered, squatting there waiting for the patrol to draw level and pass by away down below. He had come along the crest of the range. They would not find his tracks down there either along the northern side or the southern, since he had luckily seen the first patrol in time. He would wait for them to ride by. Then he must hunt and sleep. He dare not risk a shot. He must find a rock python to eat, or possums. And sleep until nightfall. He would cross the flat country by night now, he daren't by day. There was some twenty miles of it and if a patrol cut his tracks by day while he was out there they would run him to earth like a hunted dingo. Sullenly he realized how implacably these patrols were closing in upon him. Feeling as a hard-pressed panther might feel he glared down upon his enemies. And kindly was the sunlight upon the harsh grey rocks, the grey trees, the lean, dark body of her primitive son.

The patrol was directly below now. Clearly Pigeon recognized the two constables Chisholm and Buckland, both talking to Tracker Mick. Pigeon frowned. He would much like to shoot Tracker Mick, for Mick was a good tracker. The patrol halted. Tracker Mick and a comrade dismounted, handed over their horses, then walking towards the range edge, began to climb.

Pigeon stiffened. The two trackers would climb the range side, then foot-walk along the crest. While the patrol rode east down there beside the range, the two trackers would walk parallel, a goodly distance apart, away up on top. Sooner or later they must find his tracks up here.

Ah yes! maybe. But these two trackers would never track again! Pigeon settled himself comfortably among the rocks, his hands fondling his rifle. Mirthlessly he grinned towards the two dark figures toiling upward. He would wait until they got so close that he could not possibly miss. He chuckled at the thought of the amazed expression that would be on Tracker Mick's face as presently he would look up to stare into Pigeon's rifle muzzle. Yes, Pigeon would get them both, he could not miss. And there would be two less trackers to dog him, two more rifles for him now when he had no men to use them. But he could hide the weapons and he would welcome their ammunition for he was very short. And then - the patrol down below could do what they liked about it.

There were only the two police and the two other trackers.

The police boy must stay there and watch the horses. Let the white police climb and get him - if they could.

Feeling happier than for a long time past Pigeon eagerly waited for Tracker Mick to climb up and look into his rifle muzzle. Then Pigeon glanced over his shoulder and his face looked as Tracker Mick's would have - only Pigeon was not looking into a rifle muzzle, except in his mind's eye.

That other patrol! They would foot-walk too! Long ago they would have raided the camp, two or more of their trackers would have climbed the range and been walking towards him, might have picked up his tracks, might be almost upon him!

Pigeon slipped back amongst the rocks and, jumping up with every sense alert, was hastening back towards the extreme end of the range.

Of course! those two trackers were working *together*. They would not move until their foot-walking trackers had met up on top of the range. Then the horsemen would ride along both sides of the range while the footmen walked along the crest! If Pigeon was anywhere within that range, or if he tried to break away in any direction then they must cut his tracks, even if they did not corner and shoot him! If they cut his tracks then both patrols would be in hot pursuit behind him, sending a horseman to hurry along Pilmer's patrol also.

And now - they must cut his tracks. Very soon three patrols would be at his heels.

At the run, Pigeon sped down the range end and vanished amongst the timber on the flat. And fear snapped at his heels. The Cave of the Bats was far away and Mother Jinny was not there.

The Cave of the Bats, Tunnel Creek, Dimalurra.

45

THEY FIND HIS CAVE OF THE BATS

PIGEON lived his last few weeks in a hunted nightmare. Utterly weary and near exhaustion he did at last elude the patrols and reach his longed-for Cave of the Bats - to find Inspector Ord's patrol camped by the entrance. He lay there a long time, making strange, whimpering little sounds in the grass. Then he tried to creep around them in the night. But his fevered imagination pictured lurking trackers "everywhere".

As a matter of fact Ord had recruited for each patrol twice the number of trackers they would otherwise have used. Besides this, prisoners were now being used as trackers also, willing too, even though on the chain themselves. In addition, various tribesmen over a wide area, apart from Pigeon's tribe, eagerly offered information, for Pigeon's native enemies now came into the open, eager to help track him down. Those men who claimed his life in tribal vendetta as vengeance for the fathers and brothers and sons he had shot or speared, now combined against him. But the most implacable of all was Marwon, to whom Cangamvara, daughter of old Cadwarry, should have been wife by tribal law. So Pigeon now was reaping the whirlwind of vengeance. Useless now for him to waste time hiding his tracks. By day, if they were not found by the police patrol trackers, they would be found by his native enemies. And now they had even blocked him from vanishing into his Cave of the Bats.

Desperately he wished for that sanctuary. In spite of the frightening darkness, the loneliness, now both Mother Jinny and Cangamvara were gone, he would rest in security. No food now in his time of dire need, but desperately needed rest. Nervously he peered from amongst the bushes, the grasses, the rocks, sniffing the cool night air. But dim shapes of men, or guarded horses, or smell of trackers or smoke of sheltered cooking fire seemed everywhere.

A stone, dislodged by some incautious foot, came tinkling down from the cliff face above. And Pigeon knew that trackers were on guard up there too, though there was but a wallaby pad leading from ledge to ledge to the cliff rim.

But it was the only possible way that a monkey-like human could climb the cliff and thus walk straight across the ridge summit and drop down to the outlet of the cave. To go around the ridge meant a twenty-five-mile walk through the night.

Pigeon ground his teeth, the whites of his eyes rolling hate as his hand twitched around his trigger guard. He could smell, occasionally hear a muttered growl, from two trackers hidden in the long grass but twelve feet before him. He could crawl to within feet of them, could shoot them both. But the whole camp would be upon him, he would be surrounded in a tight little circle, then shot to pieces in the dawn.

No, he would get some of the white police first. He would live just to take a few more white men with him.

Grinding his teeth in tired fury he crawled back, back. Then rose stealthily and commenced the long walk through the night to get around the range. Doggedly he pressed on. He must reach the outlet to the cave before dawn, for at dawn they would discover his tracks around the camp, and mounted men would be following him within moments.

And they were.

But Pigeon reached the outlet and found it unguarded. They had not located it yet. He crept far into the sheltering blackness, sprawled down in exhausted sleep. He slept for twenty-four hours. Gradually he awoke, heard his heart slowly beating within that deathly silence. Presently he realized how stiff and sore he was. And weak! He must have food, if he was to live and fight.

He groped for his rifle. Then, one hand against the cold, guiding wall, he began the silent walk back to the outlet. From the scrub-shrouded entrance way he peered out into daylight. No sign of Man.

Cautiously he crept out and down into the ravine that led into the gorge, then out into the open bush. An area of lightly timbered, eat country. ringed by hills spread invitingly before him.

He had gone only a few hundred yards when a bullet whistled past, followed by another. He ducked and ran.

He had been fired upon from some height above. Then he stopped dead in his tracks, fiendish hate in his eyes as he glared down upon the tracks of Marawon.

Pigeon knew instantly what had happened. Marawon must have become suspicious that somewhere near here was an outlet to the Cave of the Bats and had guided two trackers here to hide and watch. Now they would search until they found the outlet. Pigeon stumbled on in a raging fury. If only Marawon would follow him now! He ground his teeth until he frothed with rage, imagining himself gouging the life out of his implacable enemy. Marawon did follow on but at his leisure, in grim enjoyment of the certainty that he was dodging the tracks of an enemy whose time must surely be drawing near. Marawon now was in no hurry. He lit a signal smoke.

Pigeon saw the thin blue column slowly, gracefully rising. He raved, shaking clenched fists at the sky as he hurried on, hurrying away from his beloved Cave of the Bats. From a hollow in a stunted tree he hauled out a small range possum. He broke its neck and ripped it open with his teeth, wolfing it raw as he strode on.

Gone now was the confident, well-conditioned, smartly efficient Pigeon of time gone by. This wild-eyed native had slipped right back to the primitive, the hunted primitive. Skinny his flanks, hollow his stomach, deep lined now his face. His once shining skin was caked with mud and ashes, his once well-proportioned body now drooping and scarred with wounds. A stubble on his deeply lined cheeks, hair grown long and lank. He paused a moment and scraped clay from a creek bank, clawed back the long hair and fastened it at the back of his head with a ball of clay.

He must keep that hair from falling across his eyes because at any moment he might have to whip up his rifle to fire. He glanced back, hoping that Marawon was following. But only the familiar bush stretched away behind him. On a distant flat a mob of 'roos were quietly feeding, around him was the happy bird life of the Kimberleys.

No sign of Marawon. With a snarl Pigeon hurried on, making back for the Oscar, scowling as he tried to think out the most likely move of each patrol-finding it difficult to think. He would try to contact some of his demoralized band so they could hunt and sleep and watch in mutual protection. Then, if they could not break away to a safe hideout, they would follow on behind a patrol. Play the same game as Ellemara had played with Constable Richardson's patrol so long ago.

Yes, so long ago.

Ellemara - who had swung from a gallows in Derby. Lillimarra had swung too. His long legs must have kicked!

Captain was gone. And Carolan. And Langooradale. And Waggarrie and Long Frankey. And Big Paddy. And Demon and Tumanurumberry, Oobagooma Captain and Sambo. Murramin, Lucullia, Bunnamurra, Bangarra, Goiro - all gone!

Suddenly, Pigeon felt weak and alone.

That evening, to his delight, he cut the tracks of Canada and these presently led him to the tracks of Woinmarra, the ex-police boy Dicky, so proud of emptying his revolver into the white stockman Tom Jasper. These were joined at evening by a few other stragglers of the gang as they came together after the day's hunting.

Pigeon found them at eventide, by faint tang of smoke in the deathly still air. Away down in a dark gully, they were invisible. But Pigeon glared down at the frightened whites of their eyes as they glared up, nervous hands gripping rifle and spear.

Quietly, he climbed down: Deep were their grunts of relief and pleasure. Crouching there, in low gutturals they told him how, since the attack on the station, they had tried again and again to break through to the Leopolds. In vain. Always they had been driven back to the Oscar, the Geikie, the Napier, the Lennard, the Barker. They had not thought that all the white men in the land could muster so many patrols. But it was not the patrols so much, they could have slipped between them at night and made a break for it. It was the tribesmen. Every man's hand seemed now against them.

Pigeon grunted. With distorted features, clenched fists, he growled that Marawon was even now dogging his tracks night and day. "We'll set a trap for the dog right now!" he snarled, "and cut him to pieces when he comes with the dawn."

They glared meaningly, licking famished lips. The wallaby now roasting in the ashes was their only meal during the last two hunted days. And there were ten of them!

But Marawon did not come walking into the dawn trap. In late afternoon, leisurely following in Pigeon's direction, easily he had read the meeting of the tracks. He knew they would huddle together that night, awaiting the coming of the dawn and the fears it would bring. So, grinning, he had turned aside, began hunting for his evening meal. He would camp where he cooked it, and chew over his rapidly approaching vengeance. Then just after dawn he would send up a signal smoke.

And it was soon after dawn, while waiting for the coming of Marawon, that Canada pointed in guttural alarm. And their fierce eyes saw, away behind them, rising in the still, clear air, the lean blue column of a signal smoke.

Smoke that would bring the trackers of the nearest patrol. With guttural cries of outraged despair they seized their weapons and made off.

46

DEATH JOKES WITH JOE BLYTHE

THEY travelled steadily until midday, then spread out a little, hunting as is their manner when travelling. Pigeon was wading through a patch of long grass, alert to stun any startled wallaby with his throwing stick or drive it towards the spears of the others. The pounding of galloping hooves caused him to wheel around ....

Racing out from the scrub was Pilmer, a hundred yards to his right appeared Constable Nicholson, then half a dozen trackers galloping away out to the left. A yell as they caught sight of Canada, caught out in the open.

Canada ran frenziedly, twisted and turned. But he was too far from cover. They cut him off, galloped him down. As bullets whistled around him he threw down his rifle in despair, surrendered. A yell as a tracker saw figures disappearing into the scrub, pounding of hooves as four men spurred trained horses in the attempt to cut them off.

Then Marawon appeared, nonchalantly carrying his spears, just following on after the horsemen had sighted the quarry. Pigeon, his eyes peering from the long grass, whipped up his rifle. But just then Pilmer shouted something to Nicholson.

Slowly, in bitter despair, Pigeon lowered the rifle.

Again he had had his most hated enemy between his rifle sights. But to fire meant his own inevitable death.

Pigeon and all the others, swiftly scattering, got away in the long grass. At the crouching run, hiding, running, hiding, running, like hunted animals, knowing it meant only time before the trackers would be on their tracks again.

They came together again at sundown at a quiet pool in the ranges, which they had been making for when they started out that morning. Straightaway they waded into one end of it, working up the pool in line to drive anything in the water before them, hungrily feeling about with their feet to disturb tortoises, fish, or river crocodile. They were ravenous and they had no fish spears, only war and hunting spears. But their hunting craft had gone to the wind for now they were hunted, were all eyes and ears and nerves for sign of the pursuers they knew must be on their tracks. For long past now, their sleep had been broken by dreams of galloping hooves, just as Ellemara's had been.

By nightfall they had secured only three tortoise and a baby crocodile. Not a feed for one really hungry man, let alone nine famished man-animals. They felt sure the pursuing patrol would surround this camp by dawn so they travelled on through the night. Pigeon convinced them that they should abandon the idea of the Leopolds for the time, and seek a hideout with him in the Barker Range, the heart of his own country, and of Woinmarra's also. They would be safe there until they could break away to the Leopolds,

"If you still want to," he added grimly.

They answered but by despairing looks; lonely in their depleted numbers, knowing that now avenging spears would be awaiting them in the Leopolds.

They carried on doggedly. By dawn, even their iron endurance was feeling the strain.

In early morning, a hazy smoke signal from a distant crag ahead alarmed them. Unceasing pursuit, danger turning them back or aside in unexpected directions, hunger and privation were playing havoc with their judgment. That smoke was but a hunting smoke. In growing dread they turned aside, now making towards Mt Hardman Creek.

Came bright midday, bathing distant mountain peaks and nearby hills, the tangled pindan of the southern plains, bathing timbered flats and rock-walled water pool and scrubby gully.

Mounted Constable Chisholm's patrol, with Joe Blythe as special constable, were riding along Mt Hardman Creek. Every man was alert. A tracker caught sight of a native on the hunt; the man wheeled around at tinkle of horse's hoof upon rock. That tribesman was Woinmarra. As the tracker yelled and spurred his horse, Woinmarra ran.

Pigeon, hunting a few hundred yards away, wheeled around to see Woinmarra racing across a strip of flat country, four horsemen galloping to cut him off. Just as Canada had tried so Woinmarra tried desperately to escape. But he was too far from cover. As they closed upon him he whipped out his revolver, the revolver that had helped kill stockman Jasper. But his nerve failed. Limply his arm dropped. Sinking to his knees, he surrendered. Pigeon watched them snap the handcuffs upon his limp wrists. To the dull ache in Pigeon's mind seemed to come a memory of long ago - how he had often done the very same thing, grinned as he slipped the cuffs upon a wanted man.

With a shock he remembered now, the last man he had slipped the cuffs upon was - Ellemara!

Woinmarra was now tragically sorry that he had emptied his revolver into the sleeping stockman Tom Jasper.

Another tracker wheeled his horse at sight of tracks, followed them at the canter towards a patch of scrub. At his shout Chisholm and Blythe with blackboy Wisego raced their horses to get around the scrub.

Soon Pigeon watched them emerging. They had four of his late, bedraggled comrades with them. From his hiding place Pigeon watched them put on the chain with Woinmarra.

Eagerly the trackers again scouted around. One suddenly reined up, leaned over his horse's neck. Pigeon knew him well, he was Tracker Mick. He slipped from the saddle and knelt to the ground to shout exultantly "Pigeon!"

As at an irresistible signal each man, white and black, came galloping and running to that shout: "Pigeon!"

They had found the tracks of Pigeon.

With a bitter curse, Pigeon slunk away. He was beginning to care less now; all he wanted was to eat and eat and eat, then sleep and sleep and sleep.

And now, once again, he trudged on alone, his face towards the Barker Range. Hardly knowing it, he was making back again towards his Cave of the Bats.

That day, Chisholm's patrol tracked Pigeon for thirty miles.

Tracker Mick with a grim grunt pointed out now and then the evidence of a hunted man pushing doggedly on against growing weakness and fatigue. Thirty miles in a day after all he had recently gone through is amazing evidence of the dogged tenacity of the bush aboriginal.

Chisholm's patrol camped on the tracks that night. As soon after dawn as it was light enough to see, they were on his tracks again.

Within several hours, Tracker Mick grunted as he nodded down towards the plain tracks before his horse's hooves.

"Him slowing down. Fresh tracks. Pigeon he no more far ahead now!"

They came upon him at noon. They were riding up along the bank of a wooded creek and heard lubras' excited voices just ahead. They broke into a gallop and there were the lubras grouped around Pigeon in a natural clearing among the trees. Tracker Mick raced straight for him. Pigeon ran up along the creek bank then wheeled around and fired.

He missed and ran on again as Tracker Mick reined in his horse, took steady aim and fired from the saddle.

Pigeon fell, a bullet in the fleshy part of his thigh. As Charlie Blythe came galloping up Pigeon staggered upright and faced him. Blythe whipped out his revolver shouting: "Drop that rifle, Pigeon! Surrender quick feller!"

With the horseman almost upon him Pigeon raised his rifle and fired point blank. Blythe's revolver hand was flung violently back as Pigeon's bullet chopped through his trigger finger and smashed the revolver away into the air. Pigeon vanished backward down into the creek as Blythe's horse plunged aside.

The others galloped to the bank and peered over at the pool while Wisego ran to help Blythe.

There was no sign of Pigeon. He had disappeared into the pool or the long grass fringing the creek bank. They must start tracking all over again. But first, they must find where he had emerged from the pool - if he were not still in it. With a creepy feeling at the back of their necks, anticipating a bullet any moment, tensely they scouted around. A tracker picked up a fully loaded Colt revolver, dropped by Pigeon when Tracker Mick's bullet had hit him. Constable Richardson's revolver, returned to the police at long last. They picked up, too, seventeen rifle cartridges carefully Wrapped in a dirty piece of rag.

"At least that is a revolver less, and seventeen bullets that he cannot use against us," said Chisholm with satisfaction.

But no sign of Pigeon.

Meanwhile, Blythe already was suffering severe pain from his shattered hand. It was a "miracle chance" that had saved his life that day. With the revolver outstretched in the very act of firing, Pigeon's bullet had smashed fingers and trigger guard. Otherwise the bullet would have gone straight through Blythe's chest.

Reluctantly, Chisholm saw Blythe must receive medical aid as soon as possible, otherwise he would probably lose his arm. And Derby was a long, long way away to a wounded man.

Chisholm headed his patrol back towards the Derby road.

Pigeon must wait for the time being, or the chase be taken up by some other patrol. Anyway he was exhausted and wounded again; he must soon be caught now.

The patrol rode back towards the head of Mt North Creek and followed it down until late that night when they camped in a natural clearing, the only space amongst timber for miles, with tall grasses all around them.

All the rest of that night Wisego sat up beside Blythe, constantly bathing his wounded hand with hot water. Blythe couldn't sleep for the pain of his shattered fingers. In the small hours he awoke Chisholm.

"I hear something!" declared Blythe.

"It is only a wallaby hopping through the grass," replied Chisholm.

"No," insisted Blythe, "it is Pigeon crawling through the grass."

Neither the two trackers on watch, nor Wisego had heard anything alarming. Chisholm put it down to nerves and imagination of a man in pain who had received a severe shock. He kept a sharp camp watch throughout the night, though he believed the wounded Pigeon would be thirty miles away by now. He felt sure that Blythe had only heard a wallaby, or bush rat, or a snake crawling through the grass.

Starlight shone softly down upon the silent camp, there in its lonely little clearing amongst the sleeping trees, with Wisego the blackboy bathing his boss's hand.

Members of the Ngaluma tribe on the Upper Sherlock station, thirty miles east of Roebourne, Western Australia, 1895.

47

DEATH CLAIMS POOR WISEGO

AT the first streak of dawn the billies were put on to boil while two trackers walked away to bring in the hobbled police horses. Wisego, two bridles over his arm, went also to bring in his own horse and Blythe's.

The billies were boiled before noise of approaching hooves told of the police horses being driven towards camp. Just then the "crack!" of a rifle shot startled them. They snatched weapons and crouched down into cover. The bush listened awhile, the horses prick-eared.

"Wisego's gone!" declared Blythe agitatedly. The scared eyes of the trackers confirmed it.

Then birds ventured to whistle, their friends answered; they finally ushered in daybreak with reassured song. Constable Chisholm left Mick with two trackers to guard camp. With the other three he scouted out to search for Wisego. They found him lying face down in the dewy grass. Pigeon had shot him dead from behind an anthill as he bent down to unhobble Blythe's horse. Beside the body Pigeon had firmly implanted his tracks - his warning of death to the trackers.

Chisholm saddled up and the patrol rode on down Mt North Creek. By midday they were nearing the Lennard when to Chisholm's great relief they saw the approaching horses of the Lennard River patrol, in charge of Constable Buckland, with Constable Anderson.

Two Lennard River boys were detailed to ride with Blythe to Lukin's Lennard River station. From there, Lukin would get him into Derby as quickly as possible. Upset by the death of Wisego, and moaning with the pain in his arm, he could barely sit his horse now.

After the wounding of Blythe, Pigeon had acted with consummate skill and cunning. Particularly considering the long strain and continuous pursuit since the attack on Collins's station.

As Blythe's horse had reared away from him Pigeon had slid back into the stream and, underwater but for the tip of his nose amongst the water-grass, had defied detection. Later, he had doggedly followed the tracks of the patrol all the way back towards the Lennard - the very last thing Chisholm and Blythe and the trackers expected him to do. Why he had not shot Chisholm, or finished off Blythe while prowling about the camp in the night, will never be known. Why he had dragged out the long, hateful hours glaring at his enemies from the night, then shot poor Wisego in the dawn as he kneeled helplessly before him, is a secret of his own.

Long afterwards, his old mother Jinny explained that Pigeon liked to do "just that". A "lot of times by night", she declared, and sometimes by day he had watched a camping patrol from a few yards' range, gloating on each white of the party one by one, and how he held each life in the touch of his trigger finger. Was it that his own gloating overcame him? Did he gloat too long, until finally doubt assailed him as to his own escape and he vanished with the dawn, leaving only his tracks as witness?

That at different times Pigeon actually did this in a number of well authenticated instances was for long afterwards discussed by members of the different patrols.

Having seen Blythe safely away riding towards the Lennard the two patrols combined and rode back to where Wisego had been shot, camping there that night. Wisego, very stiff, still lay there.

Next morning they buried him. Then the combined two patrols, Buckland with Anderson, and Chisholm's patrol were again on Pigeon's tracks. The chase was on again - the last grim phase of the long, long chase.

Twenty miles ahead, Pigeon that morning was squatting down, rifle across his knees, grimly watching half a dozen frightened lubras cooking him the first real meal for days past. He had come upon them returning to their camp with their dilly-bags filled with vegetable foods and small game. He made them scoop out the sand, make a cooking fire and cook the lot for him. This meant precious time but he cast that dread to the winds. He enjoyed squatting there, grinning deep down at their fear though he knew they were thrilled by it. He made them squat before him while the food was cooking, made them wait and watch goggle-eyed as ravenously he devoured the lot - all the food they had collected that day for their husbands and families. Finally, full-bellied at last he stood up, tapped his rifle. "Hungry husbands await you," he grinned. "Tell them I have enjoyed their meal, it now lies warm in my belly. If they follow to take it from me 1 will repay them with another feed - the bullets in this!" And again he tapped the rifle. Then with a sneer on his lips he limped away.

An emaciated Pigeon this, fresh mud plastered on his new wound. Later, it was found he had been wounded nine times altogether since the fight in Wingina Gorge. Lumps in his hide were flattened bullets which out of curiosity were nicked out with a penknife. But Pigeon now still had plenty of fight in him; to the very last gasp he wanted to kill "one more white man"!

Near sundown the two patrols were close upon Pigeon. Queerly enough his tracks had been veering around toward Lillamaloora, where almost three years ago he had shot young Constable Richardson. Right at sundown an excited tracker waved and pointed at the ground. There had been lit a very small fire, the ashes were still warm. Beside it was the half-roasted tail of a lizard that Pigeon had dropped in alarm.

Chisholm and Anderson immediately spurred their horses into the long grass when Buckland shouted warningly:

"Hey! come back here quick! I think I caught a glimpse of him!" And he had too; they found his track where he had stood watching them.

That night, Pigeon's hate blinded his judgment. He overestimated his strength, forgot distance and time. But only by a bare two minutes. That vital two minutes.

He knew that he could slip away from this big, active patrol by the tunnel of Mt North Creek, that black tunnel that would take him under the range to the other side. But first, he must kill another man.

He failed. Though he moved quietly as death itself, they lay hidden in the night, intently alert, both at the camp and around the horses. A fool each man would have been to do otherwise, when he well knew that at any moment death might. creep beside him. Gripping rifle or revolver each waited tensely alert for the coming of Pigeon, or the coming of dawn.

48

PIGEON'S LAST FIGHT

WHEN Pigeon realized that there was no chance of a surprise kill and a getaway, he stole away through the night, heading for the creek tunnel. And only the eyes of the owl and the everlasting stars noted his passing through the night.

They were following his tracks with the dawn. And they moved much faster, there was hardly need of tracking for very soon Tracker Mick guessed the quarry was heading direct for the creek tunnel.

Came four o'clock in the drowsy afternoon. The limping Pigeon, dead tired, famished again, was taking it easy now, almost at the tunnel mouth. Within minutes he would be in there-in there with his rifle, and safety.

Galloping hooves caused him to wheel around in startled amazement. They were almost upon him. At the full gallop two horsemen were racing to cut him off, others appeared galloping behind them. For priceless moments Pigeon gaped, then leapt forward with astounding speed. Given but a bare two minutes more he might just have made it. Afterwards they estimated he was only a hundred yards from the tunnel mouth, though it was rough going. But they cut him off. And now the others were almost upon him.

He raced up along the creek bank, dodging amongst boulders and timber that immediately checked the horsemen. Then he was bounding up a steep, grassy hill-slope. The nearest tracker reined in, whipped up a shotgun and fired. Pigeon leapt in the air but bounded on and up. He had been hit in the back by shot pellets, though at long range. He appeared to be racing for a vividly green tree that grew out from the bottom of a small, ledgy cliff. He snatched at the tree, began climbing up the cliff from ledge to ledge with amazing speed. As each horseman came galloping as close as possible the rider dismounted, aimed and fired; bullets began smacking the cliff face around the frenziedly climbing figure. Just as he reached the cliff top a bullet struck him in the thigh. Something dropped down from his belt - his last reserve of spare cartridges! Seventeen of them neatly parcelled in paper bark.

"You hit him, Buckland!" called Chisholm as the figure hauled itself over the rim of the cliff.

The party could not scale the cliff but three of the trackers attempted it and succeeded. They had commenced the climb when a bullet came from above but fire from the ground party covered the climbing trackers and

Pigeon fired only twice again.

With his heart in his mouth Tracker Mick worked his way up over the cliff rim, followed in trepidation by the two others. Mick immediately saw splashes of blood upon the rocks. With the utmost caution he followed though very soon the signs told him that Pigeon was badly wounded and was striving only for shelter. Presently the bloodstains led them to it - a dog-hole in the surface, leading down to a cave.

A tracker ran back to the cliff edge and shouted the news.

Chisholm yelled back for one man to stand by the hole while the other two scouted around to find and block any outlet. Leaving but two trackers to guard the horses the whole party scrambled down along the creek to where they could climb up on to the range. It was near sundown before they stood around the hole.

"I reckon he's dead in here," said Buckland as they stared at the bloodstained entrance.

"Perhaps not," cautioned Anderson. "He has lived through a good many wounds, and escaped. No man can swear Pigeon is dead until he sees him lying dead. This hole may be only a dog-hole. If so, we've got him. But again, there may be a regular catacomb of caves down there."

"Stay by this hole two of you," ordered Buckland. "The rest scatter out quickly and find any outlet or cave or hole before sunset. Get busy now."

They found several, sat around them to watch out the night. Lying away down there in the darkness, Pigeon must have refused to believe his race was run. Otherwise he could at least have died there alone. Or did he believe he still had a chance? Or was it that he wished to die out under the open sky? No one will ever know.

I have wondered whether it was when he started firing at the trackers climbing the cliff that he first discovered he had lost his last few cartridges and that all the bullets he had left now were the three in the half-emptied rifle magazine. Or was it down here, in the cave? Or did he only discover the loss when weakly he sank down to put up his last fight?

Badly weakened now from loss of blood he must have lain there a long time, to recover what strength he could. Evidently he knew this dog-hole. Knew it had no other outlet but that it led to another, really a small underground cave, that had three or four. But only dog-holes, each one leading up to the surface.

Presently he began to crawl into the blackness. How long it took him to crawl to the cave and feel his way to the outlet he sought, no one will know. It must have been hours. And presently he began to climb up the sloping hole. There must have been many a painful pause. He saw the stars through the mouth of the hole, just before dawn. No trackers barred this tiny

tiny outlet. They had found three others, but not this one.

Pigeon crawled out into the open air. Bloodstains showed where he lay there listening. Then, leaning on his rifle for support, he began to hobble away. Presently he found a stout stick and, with this as aid, he began to limp along just a little faster.

Dawn broke. All through the night, to the watching patrol had come neither sight nor sound of Pigeon.

"We will watch these holes," said Chisholm anxiously to the trackers. "Scout right out all around, all of you, and see whether there are any more dog-holes."

As the glorious sun came up over far distant mountains quickly the trackers picked up blood tracks. Eagerly they followed in the fast growing light. Within twenty minutes they came up with Pigeon, saw him hobbling ahead along the crest of the range. They began to run to get within close range. Pigeon gazed limply around. The trackers shouted to him to drop his rifle. Instead, he sank down, raised his rifle. The trackers scattered for cover, opened fire. Pigeon fired back, slowly, three times.

And the third time was his last cartridge. He sank back, mortally wounded.

He was lying there on a flat rock. As the trackers came running up he struggled to rise to a near sitting position.

In bitter gasps he cursed the trackers. Then gasped: "Give-me-cartridges! And I'll-fight-you-you ...!"

Slowly the life light faded from Pigeon's eyes.

NATIVE TROUBLES.

THE NOTORIOUS "PIGEON" SHOT.

Derby, April 7.

News received from the Lennard River, states that the head police constable, Chisholm and a party consisting of Anderson and Buckland, after following "Pigeon" for some days, came upon him on the morning of the 1st, and after a severe contest shot him. This ends the career of the most desperate native that the colony has known. It is hoped that the police will now turn their attention to capturing his associates. The public here are jubilant over the event.

The following telegram has been received by the Commissioner of Police from Corporal Pearson, of Derby :—"Derby, 7th April.—"Pigeon, was shot dead by Lennard River police on the 1st inst. Full particulars on arrival of Lennard party."

EXPLANATORY NOTES

IN view of the increasing interest taken in the Australian aboriginal, in the vanished and fast-vanishing life of this last of the world's Stone Age men, perhaps a few explanatory notes on this particular true story may prove of interest to the reader.

ELLEMARA

Maybe the reader interested in historical and ethnological fact will think I have overdrawn the character of Ellemara and his sinister influence upon even hostile natives. Well, here is an extract from a report on Ellemara by Sub-Inspector Drewry.

> To the Commissioner of Police, Perth.
>
> Constable William Richardson was shot on or about November 3rd.
>
> For some short time previous to his death he had been ill with fever, but had managed to arrest Muckerawarra, Tilbomer, Teebuck, Talburner, Tumanurumberry, Luter, Meremimer, Byerbell, Fouringer, Putter, Tye¬mering, Laweraway, Lillimarra, Wongamarra, Bundermen for either cattle killing or absconding from jail; some for both; some of these natives were the worst characters in that part of the district. I think Richardson wished to crown his efforts by recapturing Ellemara. Receiving information that he was at a Pindan Soak, about 20 miles from Lillamaloora, he sent Native Assistant Pigeon and Captain to arrest Ellemara. This Pigeon did. And it was while Pigeon and Captain were walking back their prisoner the 20 miles to Lillamaloora that Ellemara managed to talk them into killing Richardson. The extraordinary power this native has over other natives can be gauged by the fact that Pigeon is a Lillamaloora boy while Captain is a native of the Euela district (2000 miles to the south).
>
> (Thus, to both the police trackers Ellemara, besides being a badly wanted law-breaker, was a "foreign" and hostile native to both trackers personally.)
>
> When the Barker Range natives tried to kill Richardson several months before his death, Pigeon stuck to him in a way that would have made any man confident of his native. Captain also thought a great deal of Richardson.
>
> Derby, W.A. 23/1/95.
>
> I think it my duty to state that at the time when Ellemara was sentenced at Derby Court last, I wrote officially to the gaoler bringing to his notice the fact of five previous convictions for felony against this native,

Ellemara. Also the fact that he had already broken out of both Derby and Roeboume gaols, requesting him, as this native had already attempted to spear the Police before, to see that he got no chance to escape or he would immediately avail himself of it. He did escape, and these murders were the outcome of his escape.

Drewry ends his report: On Jan 16th I arrived in Derby for orders, as to try to go to the Leopolds this time of the year would mean that you would be continually camped on account of flood and boggy country. All the natives would become aware of your presence and clear out elsewhere.
As regards the racehorses Connie and Max O'Pell at 10/- per day.

This charge is not excessive as I had no agreement as to compensation if killed or hurt. 10/- a day is the usual rate of hire for a horse in Derby. The Stores carried include Government stores and rations. There is rather over a ton of stores left for use of the camp. Many horses were loaned at various times for which no charge was made.

I forward an approximate statement of the expenditure. Some of the dates cannot be filled in up to this date. It will also take some time to get all the accounts in. I trust that my actions in this matter will meet with your approval. I must apologize for the dirty state of this report but it is due to the large flying ants which come after rain and crawl over the paper while one is writing.

> I have the honour to be, Sir,
> Your obedient servant, Overend Drewry.
> Sub. Insp. 26.1.'95.

The following is an extract from a letter about Ellemara from Lukin, J.P., to the Premier of Western Australia:

Ellemara has a bad record for 10 years. Eventually arrested, sent to Cossack for 12 months. Absconded. Caught by Allen killing sheep in Dezring's paddock. He was brought here (as stockboy) with cattle. He ran away and at once commenced killing sheep.

Warrants were taken out by stations but he continued killing sheep wholesale for years. I could prove 1,000 cases of sheep and cattle killing during this period. He was eventually arrested, sentenced to 12 months in Derby jail. Then sent down to Cossack as an absconder. Sentenced to one month then returned here, commenced sheep and cattle spearing again, he caused immense trouble before again being arrested. Sentenced to three years, but escaped. Rearrested, escaped again. And yet again. The Chinaman speared at Lillamaloora accused this man. He also speared Young at the same station, and twice attempted to spear Police. He has a charmed life and I shall never believe him dead until I see his dead body.

Constable Richardson was delayed at Lillamaloora Police Outpost a few days because of sickness, a delay which proved fatal as it gave Ellemara time to use his influence, an influence over the native mind which has always surprised me. He at last induced the trackers to murder Richardson, they wouldn't have thought of it otherwise. They meant to collect the hill natives, to march down river and attack the avenging party, then, attack all whites later. They were not given time for the entire programme. Lukin.

The Belief of Aboriginals of Many Tribes as to Ellemara

To the aboriginals far and wide he was known as Ellemara the Killer, Ellemara the Cunning. He was greatly admired, and even more dreaded. Their description of him was "Ellemara the Killer, he who 'carries evil spirits in his eyes' ". The aboriginals believed it was the "whisperings" of these evil spirits that gave him such great cunning, enabled him to travel long distances with safety among hostile tribes, and gave him the power to influence any whom he met.

TRACKERS AND "QUEENSLAND BOYS"

Sub-Inspector Drewry's references to his "Queensland boys" might cause some confusion in the minds of readers who realize that North Queensland is far away on the Australian east coast, while the West Kimberley lies within the extreme north-west coast of Western Australia. Possibly these trackers came not from Queensland, but from our present-day Northern Territory, the boundary of which adjoins the East Kimberley, and which, in early days, was often alluded to in the west as "Queensland".

Today, many Australians vaguely think of all Northern Australia as "The Territory", whereas Northern Australia from east to west comprises northern Queensland, the Northern Territory, and the Kimberleys of Western Australia. So great is the area of our country, and so little do many of us know about our North that - well, we simply do not "know about it".

A prime objective of the isolated Kimberleys police force, as with all "bush" police forces in all States, was that their trackers should have been born as far away as possible from the district in which they were to work as trackers. This made them much more dependable. For they would thus be hostile "foreigners", with every local aboriginal's hand against them by tribal law. While the trackers would have no compunction in hunting down their quarry, for the local aboriginals, in turn, were "foreign" and hostile to them. The local aboriginal and the "imported" tracker were more "foreigners" to one another than members of the most far apart white races. Also, the tracker would be far less likely to fail in his duty than a "local boy", let alone desert. For he knew full well that should he desert he would have to run the gauntlet of death through the country of every tribe before he should reach his own country.

Which helps to explain Sub-Inspector Drewry's surprise that Ellemara should safely travel through the country of hostile tribes and his certainty that Captain would be speared when he ventured into the Leopolds: "It will be against all tribal customs if they do not kill Captain."

Captain's country was far to the south. But Pigeon was a "local boy", that is, he was born in the Lillamaloora country. But Pigeon never took a chance, he never left his own country. Why Captain and others of the gang were not speared when in "hostile" country, I hope I have explained sufficiently clearly in the story. Much that happened, and reasons for it, let alone problems of aboriginal custom and ways of life, have necessarily had to be omitted in these times of conservation of space, of paper and other shortages.

PHYSIQUE

My own experience of the Kimberley natives is that their physique excels that of most other aboriginals in southern areas. However, let Sergeant (then Senior Constable) Pilmer's journal state his opinions: "In the Kimberleys the aborigines, having abundance of food both vegetable and game, are of a magnificent type, intelligent, and not lacking in bravery. They would attack and fight at the least provocation. Many of these natives were from 5 ft. 10 ins. to 6 ft. 6 ins. in height, very muscular, and with a wonderful torso. The lubras were all tall, well-built and athletic, and prolific in children. It was a common thing to meet a mother of seven."

The question of the physique of members of "Pigeon's gang" once drew an exasperated reply from Inspector Ord to an inquiry from the Commissioner of Police, Perth. Ord wrote: "The photos of 'Pigeon' in the newspaper --- of date --- are a rank fraud. He and Lillimarra were strapping athletes. The shortest of them all was Pyron, and he was 5 ft. 9 inches in height. Long-haired and bearded, they were in tip-top condition, covered with heavy scars (cicatrices of warriorhood) across chest and shoulders. They were armed with repeating rifles, guns and revolvers, not with South Australian weapons as the newspaper account states."

RELICS OF PIGEON

Those disturbing three years in the Kimberleys, the days when "Pigeon's mob" were out, excited great interest throughout the State, by far the greater proportion of the scanty population being far to the south. Quite possibly more than one alleged "Photo" of "Pigeon" was printed and sold. Any "abo" would do as "subject", for no one south of Derby would ever have seen Pigeon. (In this regard, I have been offered photos of "Pigeon", taken years after Pigeon was shot.) Not only photos but Pigeon's alleged "skull" was exhibited down south, at a charge of so much per person to view it.

Old-timers in the Kimberleys laugh at the idea that Pigeon's photo was ever taken, let alone that his skull was dug up from its faraway, wild resting-place and taken south to Perth.

Pigeon's body was soon "put in a tree" by his tribesmen as is the immemorial burial custom. Then the skeleton was carried in all tribal reverence to rest among the tribal forefathers, within the Cave of the Bats.

A lone Aboriginal chained to a tree, Western Australia 1895.
A sad reminder of the Frontier Wars.

ION IDRIESS

ETT IMPRINT has the following Ion Idriess books in print in 2023:

Flynn of the Inland
The Desert Column
The Red Chief
Nemarluk
Horrie the Wog Dog
Prospecting for Gold
Drums of Mer
Madman's Island
The Yellow Joss
Forty Fathoms Deep
Lasseter's Last Ride
Sniping
Shoot to Kill
Guerrilla Tactics
Trapping the Jap
Lurking Death
The Scout
The Wild White Man of Badu
Gold Dust and Ashes
Headhunters of the Coral Sea
Gouger of the Bulletin
Back O' Cairns
Men of the Jungle
Coral Sea Calling
Man Tracks
Lightning Ridge
Over the Range

www.ingramcontent.com/pod-product-compliance
Lightning Source LLC
Chambersburg PA
CBHW030232170426
43201CB00006B/195